AUTODESK® SMOKE®

ESSENTIALS

AUTODESK® SMOKE®

ESSENTIALS

Alexis Van Hurkman

Acquisitions Editor: Mariann Barsolo
Development Editor: Pete Gaughan
Production Editor: Christine O'Connor
Editorial Manager: Pete Gaughan
Vice President and Executive Group Publisher: Richard Swadley
Associate Publisher: Chris Webb
Book Designer: Happenstance Type-O-Rama
Proofreader: Louise Watson, Word One New York
Indexer: Robert Swanson
Project Coordinator, Cover: Todd Klemme
Cover Designer: Ryan Sneed
Cover Image: Alexis Van Hurkman

For general information on our other products and services or to obtain technical support, please contact our Customer Care Department within the U.S. at (877) 762-2974, outside the U.S. at (317) 572-3993 or fax (317) 572-4002.

Wiley publishes in a variety of print and electronic formats and by print-on-demand. Some material included with standard print versions of this book may not be included in e-books or in print-on-demand. If this book refers to media such as a CD or DVD that is not included in the version you purchased, you may download this material at http://booksupport.wiley.com. For more information about Wiley products, visit www.wiley.com.

Library of Congress Control Number: 2013923612

10 9 8 7 6 5 4 3 2 1

Dear Reader,

Thank you for choosing *Autodesk Smoke Essentials*. This book is part of a family of premium-quality Sybex books, all of which are written by outstanding authors who combine practical experience with a gift for teaching.

Sybex was founded in 1976. More than 30 years later, we're still committed to producing consistently exceptional books. With each of our titles, we're working hard to set a new standard for the industry. From the paper we print on to the authors we work with, our goal is to bring you the best books available.

I hope you see all that reflected in these pages. I'd be very interested to hear your comments and get your feedback on how we're doing. Feel free to let me know what you think about this or any other Sybex book by sending me an email at contactus@wiley.com. If you think you've found a technical error in this book, please visit http://sybex.custhelp.com. Customer feedback is critical to our efforts at Sybex.

Best regards,

CHRIS WEBB
Associate Publisher, Sybex

ACKNOWLEDGMENTS

There are always so many people to thank with projects like these. First and foremost, I want to thank Marc Hamaker and Steve Vasko at Autodesk, who were impressed enough with my idea of creating a how-to book that was integrated with the making of an original movie that they greenlit this, the first third-party book about the Autodesk Smoke platform. As I was writing and revisiting all that I had learned from working on the movie in the course of creating these lessons, Marc-Andre Ferguson, Ken LaRue, and Brian Mulligan were instrumental in explaining and deciphering many of Smoke's less-obvious capabilities. I also need to thank Aaron Vasquez, Brian Mulligan (again), Joel Osis, and Christopher Benitah, the compositing artists who used Smoke for the effects in my science fiction short, *The Place Where You Live*, some of which functioned in simplified form as exercises in this book. I also must thank the staff at Wiley who helped produce this book; it's a long road from an author's scribblings to a bound volume on a shelf. Lastly, I want to thank my friend and colleague Michael Sandness for the Smoke tips and tricks he volunteered and my wife, Kaylynn Raschke, for her support and patience as I labored dutifully in the world mine.

ABOUT THE AUTHOR

Based in Saint Paul, Minnesota, Alexis Van Hurkman worked previously as a freelance editor and composing artist, but he currently divides his time working as a writer, director, and colorist. He has grated features and shorts that have played at the Telluride and Sundance Film Festivals; programs that have aired on The History Channel, The Learning Channel, and BBC Four; and video art pieces that have been exhibited at the NYC Museum of Modern Art, the Whitney Museum of American Art, and San Francisco's Yerba Buena Center for the Arts.

He has written and taught widely on the subject of video post-production in columns and blogs, authored books that include *The Color Correction Handbook* (Peachpit Press, 2013) and *The Color Correction Look Book* (Peachpit Press, 2013), created video courses for Ripple Training, and written for the DaVinci Resolve, Apple Color, Apple Shake, and Final Cut Pro user manuals.

When not otherwise occupied, he writes and directs works of fiction, most recently the short *The Place Where You Live*. His feature *Four Weeks, Four Hours* was screened at festivals internationally in 2006.

Website: www.alexisvanhurkman.com
Twitter: @hurkman

About the Technical Editor

Brian Mulligan is a multi-award-winning editor and has a strong commitment to his craft and to broadcast television. Local broadcast television reflects and influences the ideals of a community and, for the past 20 years, Brian has helped shape the on-air television culture at WTHR-TV in Indianapolis, where his work is seen by 1.2 million households every day. Being a broadcast editor often means you are an editor, producer, writer, and graphic designer. Brian has been an Autodesk Smoke editor since 2006. He is active in the Autodesk community, with his Autodesk "Expert Elite" position on the forums and as a beta-tester for Smoke. Brian also blogs about Smoke for Premiumbeat.com.

Twitter: @bkmeditor

Contents at a Glance

Contents

CHAPTER 10   ## Working with Audio   **217**

CHAPTER 11   ## Color Correction   **233**

CHAPTER 12   Adding Titles   277

CHAPTER 13   Exporting from Smoke   289

APPENDIX   Answers to Additional Exercises   299

Introduction

When I started pre-production on the movie that served as the inspiration for this book, I was, like you, vaguely familiar with Autodesk® Smoke® and curious about what its integrated capabilities could bring to my workflow. And like you, I was new to its ways — just a raw recruit. Over the course of editing my film and participating in its compositing (alongside vastly more experienced Smoke artists than myself), and within the span of four versions of the software, I was in a position to know which aspects of Smoke were easy to pick up and which would require more in-depth explanation. In essence, I was the very first student of this book.

Autodesk has been making huge strides in making Smoke a friendlier application than previous versions. It's no secret that Smoke has a unique interface; reworking it for wider accessibility is a challenge in that the very power that Smoke brings to the post-production experience is what makes it more complex to learn. Fortunately, Autodesk has done a great job of moving the user interface forward in a way that enhances usability without sacrificing functionality.

This book distills my experiences editing and compositing my movie using Smoke, providing you with a fun series of real-world lessons that teach you this application's many layers as an editor, a compositing environment, and a finishing tool that let you incorporate sophisticated effects at the very earliest stages of your edit. It also extends your workflow by adding high-quality greenscreen keying, 3D compositing, color correction, and text effects to help you complete even the most sophisticated of projects in one integrated application.

It's often said, but truly I hope this book is as fun to read as it was to write.

Who Should Read This Book

If you're an editor, a compositing artist, or a filmmaker who's looking to mix the chocolate of editing with the peanut butter of compositing — all within one environment — then this book is for you. More to the point, if you're new to Autodesk Smoke and want to learn it in a practical, hands-on fashion, this book is designed to walk you through the various tools available in Smoke while working through real-world examples from an effects-intensive short film.

As you begin to learn about Smoke, you'll have the best experience if you already have some familiarity with other editing and compositing applications.

This book is designed to give you a quick start by familiarizing you with Smoke basics, but it's not meant as a primer on post-production fundamentals. However, Smoke's more advanced editing and compositing tools may be new even to experienced users, so these operations are explained in detail.

What You Will Learn

Autodesk® Smoke® Essentials walks you through a beginning-to-end workflow using Smoke. Beginning with a lesson on setting up Smoke for the first time, you move on to the basics of learning the Smoke interface and importing media. Then a series of lessons covers basic through advanced editing and trimming techniques, culminating in the various timeline effects that you can add, including transitions, timewarps, and Action effects. Next, the powerful ConnectFX compositing environment is covered, as you walk through the creation of some pretty sophisticated effects. Lastly, finishing tasks are covered, including audio basics, color-correction techniques, and the process of adding titles, culminating in a lesson on how to export from Smoke.

What You Need

This book was written for Autodesk® Smoke® 2015. If you don't already own Smoke, you can download a fully functional trial version at www.autodesk .com/products/smoke/free-trial.

▶ Autodesk Smoke is currently available only for the Mac.

Autodesk Smoke 2015 has the following system requirements:

- ▶ Apple® Mac OS® X version 10.7.5 or later, 10.8.x and 10.9.x
- ▶ 64-bit Intel® multicore processor
- ▶ 4 GB of RAM (8 GB or more recommended)
- ▶ 3 GB free disk space for download and installation
- ▶ Minimum 1440 x 900 display (1920 x 1200 or higher recommended)
- ▶ U.S. keyboard (required to map hotkeys properly)
- ▶ Wacom® Intuos Tablet (Intuos2, Intuos3, Intuos4, and Intuos5 USB models are supported.)

A detailed list of recommended systems and graphics cards for Smoke can be found at www.autodesk.com/graphics-hardware.

For playback performance, it's recommended to install Smoke on a system with a separate storage volume/partition for the media storage location (such as on an external Thunderbolt drive or array).

FREE AUTODESK SOFTWARE FOR STUDENTS AND EDUCATORS

The Autodesk Education Community is an online resource with more than 5 million members that enables educators and students to download — for free (see the website for terms and conditions) — the same software used by professionals worldwide. You can also access additional tools and materials to help you design, visualize, and simulate ideas. Connect with other learners to stay current with the latest industry trends and get the most out of your designs. Get started today at www.autodesk.com/joinedu.

What Is Covered in This Book

Autodesk® Smoke® Essentials is organized to give you a grand tour of the capabilities of this integrated editing, compositing, and finishing tool. Since Smoke can appear to be somewhat unorthodox to the new user, the lessons are organized to make it easy for you to get started, even if you have no prior experience using Smoke.

Chapter 1: Before You Begin   Walks you through the very first things you need to do to configure Smoke after you've installed it but before you've actually started working on your first project.

Chapter 2: The Smoke Interface   Guides you through the different parts of the Smoke user interface, touring the dedicated controls for media management, editing, and compositing and showing you the basics of getting around and controlling program playback.

Chapter 3: Importing Your Project's Media   Covers how you import media using the MediaHub and how you organize it in the Media Library.

Chapter 4: Editing a Rough Assembly   Shows you how to create a new sequence and edit together your first simple scene of shots using the thumbnail viewer, drag and drop editing, cue marks, and simple trimming.

Chapter 5: Editing Dialog and Advanced Trimming Takes you through the process of editing a more complicated dialog scene using three-point editing and advanced trimming techniques in order to maintain continuity, create split edits, and add cutaway shots.

Chapter 6: Adding Transitions and Timewarp Effects Teaches you how to add and edit dissolves between two clips, how to create dissolve-to-color effects, and how to add and customize wipes, and ends with a lesson on creating timewarp effects for fast-forward or slow-motion effects.

Chapter 7: Using Timeline Effects Walks you through the numerous timeline effects, including picture-in-picture compositing, motion tracking, and greenscreen keying.

Chapter 8: Introduction to ConnectFX Gives you your first look at using ConnectFX to create powerful compositing effects in Smoke, starting with how to apply ConnectFX to a clip and how the CFX editor is organized, then moves on to how to loop clips and deal with log-encoded media, match moving, rotoscoping, and simple compositing using blend modes.

Chapter 9: Using the ConnectFX Action Node Shows you how to use the Action node inside of ConnectFX to create even more sophisticated composites, including multilayered keying and multilayered compositing.

Chapter 10: Working with Audio Teaches you how to refine your production audio in Smoke using audio effects, editing in music and sound effects with precision, and how to mix audio using timeline controls and the mixing desk.

Chapter 11: Color Correction Covers color-correction techniques in Smoke, including how to use the Colour Corrector and Colour Warper effects to make primary and secondary adjustments, how to add color corrections as gap effects to a scene of clips all at once, and how to limit color-correction effects using a mask.

Chapter 12: Adding Titles Teaches you how to add text effects on the timeline as well as how to create styled pages of text and how to save and reuse text styles.

Chapter 13: Exporting from Smoke Discusses how to prepare a sequence for export and the different options that are available for exporting projects and media from Smoke.

Companion Files

Solutions are provided, online, for all of the "Additional Exercises" found at the end of each chapter. Also, I've built sample movie files for you to use as you follow along with the book's tutorial exercises. All these supporting files can be downloaded from the book's companion web page at www.sybex.com/go/smokeessentials.

The *Essentials* Series

The *Essentials* series from Sybex provides outstanding instruction for readers who are just beginning to develop their professional skills. Every *Essentials* book includes these features:

▶ Skill-based instruction, with chapters organized around projects rather than abstract concepts or subjects.

▶ Suggestions for additional exercises at the end of each chapter, where you can practice and extend your skills.

▶ Digital files (available via download) so that you can work through the project tutorials yourself. Please check the book's web page at www.sybex.com/go/smokeessentials for these companion downloads.

AUTODESK® SMOKE®

ESSENTIALS

Before You Begin

This chapter discusses the very first things you need to do to configure Autodesk® Smoke® software after you've installed it, prior to working on your first project. In the process, you'll learn how to set up your working environment and how to create and organize your projects.

Topics in this chapter include the following:

▶ **Opening Autodesk Smoke**

▶ **Choosing your storage volume**

▶ **Creating and managing users**

▶ **Creating and managing projects**

▶ **Smoke preferences for audio playback and broadcast monitoring**

▶ **Other important preferences**

Before You Open Smoke

In this first chapter, you'll be guided through the process of opening Autodesk Smoke for the first time. You should already have Smoke installed on your system, along with any drivers that are required for the external video interfaces you're using; if not, please refer to the installation instructions that accompanied your disk image or installation disc.

Because of its underlying architecture, there are certain aspects of your Smoke application environment that you need to configure using a separate application, Smoke Setup, as shown in Figure 1.1, located in the Utilities folder of the Smoke 2015 folder.

Most crucially, Smoke Setup lets you configure the video and audio devices that you'll be using while you work, as well as the media storage devices you want to use with Smoke.

If you've updated from previous versions of Autodesk Smoke, you will have multiple folders in the Applications/Autodesk folder, one for each version you've installed. For example, you might have four folders, one each for Smoke 2013, Smoke 2013 SP2, Smoke 2013 Ext1, and Smoke 2015. This is normal, but you want to be sure to open the Smoke Setup application for the version you're using.

FIGURE 1.1
The Smoke Setup
application

The following procedure will walk you through the process of setting these things up:

1. Open Smoke Setup. The Smoke Setup application window appears, with seven panels of configuration options to choose from, as shown in Figure 1.2. At the moment, there are two you care about, starting with the General panel.

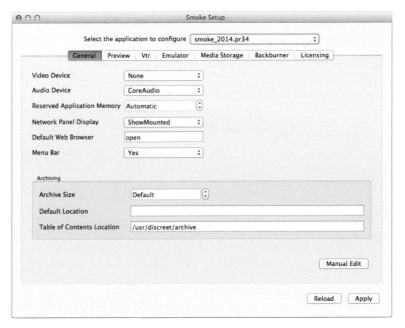

FIGURE 1.2　The Smoke Setup window

2. If you have an AJA or Blackmagic Design (BMD) video interface connected to or installed on your computer, you can choose it from the Video Device pop-up menu. Make sure that you have the correct drivers installed for the Blackmagic Design or AJA interface you have. If you don't have a third-party video interface, you should choose None.

3. If you choose an AJA or BMD video device, you may also want to make the same selection from the Audio Device pop-up menu. If Video Device is set to None, then you should choose CoreAudio in order to play audio out of your computer's audio interface or from any third-party audio interface that you're using.

4. Open the Media Storage panel, as shown in Figure 1.3.

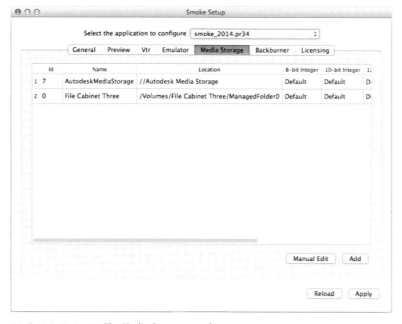

FIGURE 1.3 The Media Storage panel

The Media Storage panel is a list where you can add all of the storage volumes that you want to use with Smoke. You were prompted to choose a disk location to add a Media Storage folder upon installing Smoke, but you can add as many volumes as you like and switch among them as you please. Be aware, however, that when you create a project that's linked to media that was imported or transcoded to a particular storage location, the media needs to stay where it is.

5. To add an additional disk location, click Add. The Media Storage Folder dialog appears, as shown in Figure 1.4.

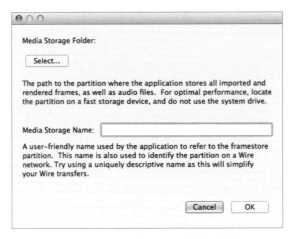

FIGURE 1.4 The Media Storage Folder dialog

6. Click Select, pick a fast volume connected to your computer, and click Choose. You can choose any volume you like—an internal hard drive or SSD, an external RAID, or a removable disk. Keep in mind that the performance of Smoke depends highly on the performance of the storage volume on which your project and media are stored, so you want to use a fast volume whenever possible.

7. Type a plain English name into the Media Storage Name field, which is how you'll refer to that volume in the list, and then click OK. Your new volume appears in the Smoke Setup list, and a directory is created that corresponds to the path in the Location column.

8. When you're finished adding directories, click Apply, and then click Quit.

Smoke is now configured and ready for use. Whenever you need to change AV interfaces or volumes, quit Smoke, open Smoke Setup, and make the necessary changes.

It helps to choose a Media Storage Name that corresponds to the physical drive (for example, OWC Drive or Promise Array) to make it easier to keep track of which Media Storage folder is on which hard drive.

Smoke directories contain all project data and media created by Smoke, and they *must never be deleted or manually altered*. This cannot be stressed enough—deleting or altering a Smoke directory may result in a catastrophic loss of project data. In all cases, you want to interact with project data and media from within Smoke. These directories are, for all intents and purposes, a black box that you should not open.

Opening Autodesk Smoke

Once you've configured your environment using Smoke Setup, you're ready to open Smoke and start working. However, Smoke is a database-managed application, so there is a little more setup required when you first open Smoke to make sure that your projects and media end up where you want them.

Smoke is a one-window application that always takes up the whole screen. You can always hide it using ~CM+H, or use application switching or Mission Control commands to jump to different applications. Generally speaking, however, once you open Smoke, you'll be working within the Smoke environment, which has dedicated controls for media import, export, and file management.

The Startup Screen

When you first open Smoke, the Project panel appears, which presents you with the name of the host computer and a set of three pop-up menus for setting up a project in Smoke. The Project panel is shown at the bottom of Figure 1.5.

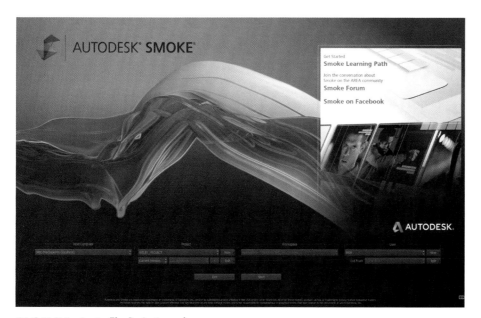

FIGURE 1.5 The Project panel

These pop up menus let you choose, create, and edit projects. You can select the Workspace, which is used for multiple system workflows. Finally, it's where you define and choose a user. You'll also notice a series of four links at the upper right of the Project panel that take you to some invaluable resources for learning more about Smoke:

Smoke Learning Channel   This is a constantly updated and expanded set of video tutorials covering all manner of Smoke functionality.

Smoke Forum   This is a user-driven forum focused on issues related to Smoke.

Smoke on Facebook   This page provides a way to get updates on what's happening with Smoke over time.

Creating and Managing Projects

The group of controls on the Project panel is for choosing, creating, editing, and deleting Smoke projects, as shown in Figure 1.6.

FIGURE 1.6 Project management controls

If this is your first time using Smoke, there won't be any projects available in the list. You'll need to create one.

1. Click New (in the Project group). The Create New Project dialog appears, as shown in Figure 1.7.

2. Type **Introductory Project** into the Name field (Smoke automatically adds underscores to replace any spaces you type).

3. Click anywhere outside the Name field to force the Setup Directory pop-up menu to update with the project name, which will be used to create that project's directory inside the automatically managed Smoke directory at /usr/discreet/project/, as shown in Figure 1.8.

   You'll ignore the Setup Mode button for now. Later, however, when you have multiple projects using different settings, this pop-up menu will let you copy the saved setup used by another project to use as the starting point for a new project that you're creating.

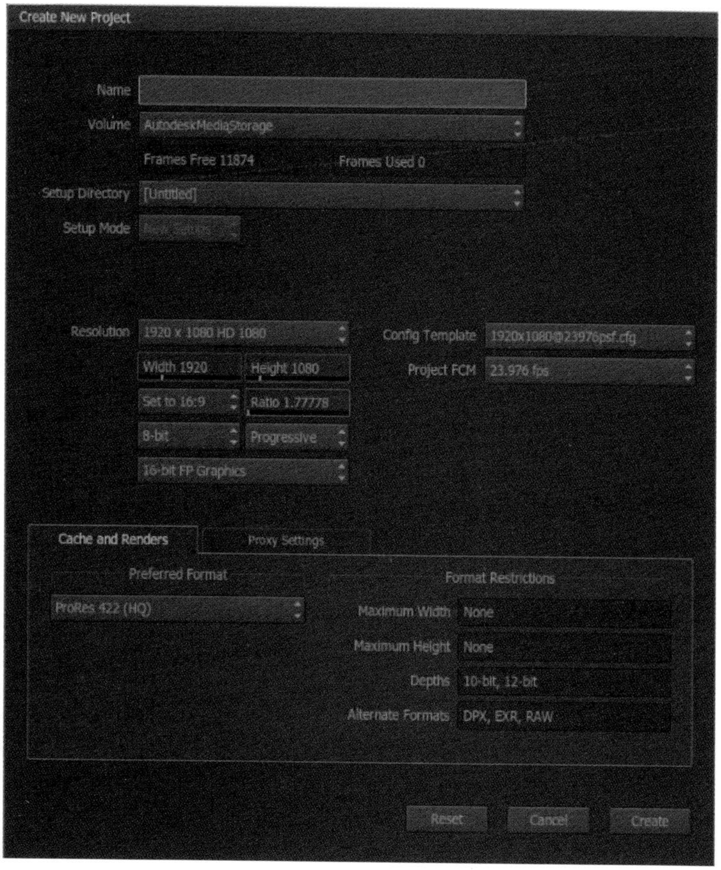

FIGURE 1.7 The Create New Project dialog

FIGURE 1.8 The updated Setup Directory pop-up menu

Choosing Your Storage Volume

When you open the Storage Volume pop-up menu, every storage volume that you added using the Smoke Setup application appears within.

1. Choose another volume from the Storage Volume pop-up menu. For maximum performance, this should be the fastest and largest volume attached to your computer.

2. Click Open.

   As mentioned previously, each storage volume contains its own media files, all of which are referenced by the project data contained within the Smoke database, which is located in /usr/discreet/project/.

3. Choose 1920 × 1080 HD 1080 from the Resolution pop-up menu to configure most of the Resolution controls, as illustrated in Figure 1.9.

FIGURE 1.9 The Resolution controls

   This is the default resolution for new sequences you create within this project. If necessary, you can override this setting when you create new projects and use the setting you choose there. Choosing a new resolution automatically updates the width, height, and aspect ratio controls.

4. Choose 10-bit from the unlabeled default project bit depth pop-up menu (options here are 16-bit fp, 12-bit, 12-bit u, 10-bit, and 8-bit). This setting dictates the default bit depth with which new sequences are created. You can always select a different bit depth later on, and you can have as many sequences using as many different bit depths as you like.

   In general, the media you're using within your project should determine the resolution and bit depth you use.

5. The Config Template Pop-up should have changed to 1920x1080@23976psf.cfg to configure the Resolution controls and set the master frame rate of the project to match the media used in this tutorial. This is based on the resolution set earlier.

   It's very important that you verify or select the correct frame rate in the Config Template, because once you set it, you cannot change it. If you choose the wrong frame rate, you'll need to create a new project with the correct one and use that instead.

6. Check the currently selected unlabeled Graphics Rendering pop-up menu. In general, you should choose 16-bit FP Graphics. However, significantly slower machines can be set to 8-bit Graphics for improved performance—but the quality will be lower.

7. Choose ProRes 422 (LT) from the Preferred Format pop-up menu of the Cache and Renders tab, as shown in Figure 1.10.

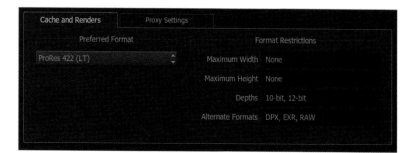

FIGURE 1.10 The Cache and Renders tab

Smoke uses this codec when rendering effects to be cached for real-time playback. Since the media in most of the examples in this book are in the ProRes 422 (LT) format, choosing this same codec will save you some disk space as you work. Be aware, however, that choosing a codec with lower quality than the source media with which you're working will result in a loss of quality when rendering. You can always change this setting later on.

8. Click Create to create this project file. The new project now appears in the Project pop-up menu, as shown in Figure 1.11.

FIGURE 1.11 The Project pop-up menu

If you changed the Graphics Rendering bit depth pop-up menu to 8-bit, you'll get a Project Depth And Visual Depth Mismatch warning dialog.

All media in this book use the Apple ProRes family of codecs. In particular, most media are in the Apple ProRes 422 (LT) codec, which is a 10-bit codec. Media used by some of the compositing exercises use the Apple ProRes 4444 codec, which in Smoke is identified as having a bit depth of 12-bit u.

9. Click Confirm to move on. This won't cause any problems.

Aside from the project's frame rate, which is now unalterable, you can always change a project's other settings by clicking the Edit button, as shown in Figure 1.12.

FIGURE 1:12
The project's Edit
button

10. The Modify Project pop-up menu at the bottom left of the Edit Project dialog lets you choose different operations including deleting the project, deleting the setups, and deleting that project's clips. Choose an operation from this pop-up. Then choose any other options you might want to change if you're modifying the project, and click Done to make the change.

You can also change a project's settings while that project is open by choosing File ➤ Project and User Settings and then clicking Edit in the Project and User Settings dialog.

Here's one final reminder to reiterate a very important point: Smoke does not expose an easily identifiable project file in the OS X Finder. All project and media files *must* be managed from within Smoke. Any attempt to manually manage the files located within directories created by Smoke could cause insoluble problems.

Creating and Managing Users

The last pop-up menu in the Project panel is for choosing a user, as shown in Figure 1.13.

FIGURE 1.13 The User pop-up menu

User settings contain Smoke preferences data specific to that user, as well as which keyboard shortcuts are used. This allows multiple Smoke artists to use the same workstation while keeping things configured to their personal preferences. Users and projects can be mixed and matched at will. At first, there are no users, and you'll need to create your own as follows:

1. Click New (in the User group). The Create New User Profile dialog appears, as shown in Figure 1.14.

FIGURE 1.14 The Create New User Profile dialog

2. Type **Student** into the Name field. You can enter your own name, but you must use alphanumeric characters with no spaces and no special characters.

3. Make sure that the Keyboard Shortcuts pop-up menu is set to Smoke (FCP 7). This is the default keyboard shortcut set for Smoke on the Mac, and these are the shortcuts that are referenced in this book.

You'll want to leave the Directory path alone, and leave the button underneath it set to New Preferences, because you'll be creating a completely new set of preferences for this user.

Opening a New Project

Now that you've defined a storage volume and created a new project and user, click Start at the bottom right of the Project panel to open that project and begin. The Smoke user interface appears with your empty, new Introductory_ Project ready for you to get started. Smoke only opens one project at a time.

At this point, you're ready to work. However, now that you're inside Smoke, there are one or two remaining setup tasks left to do.

Important Preferences

While you've already performed some configuration using the Smoke Setup application, this only defined the broad strokes of how Smoke uses hardware and disks. Now that Smoke is open, there are many other ways that you can customize Smoke to reflect your preferred methods of working. First, however, you need to choose Autodesk Smoke ➤ Preferences to open the Preferences window, as shown in Figure 1.15.

FIGURE 1.15 The Smoke Preferences window

The Preferences window has 11 tabs containing a multitude of customization options. The settings you choose here are saved within the user profile you used to open Smoke. The following sections explore some of the most important of these options.

Audio Playback

The very first tab contains the controls for audio playback in Smoke. There are numerous options for choosing sync delays, audio metering display, the tone standard and reference level for bars and tone generation, as well as a listing of the audio-mixing performance characteristics of your workstation. However, the most important setting for you to verify as you set up Smoke for the first time is the Outputs menu at the end, which is shown in Figure 1.16.

FIGURE 1.16
The Outputs pop-up
menu

The audio outputs you selected should be reflected here. This will depend on if you are using internal Core Audio or external audio from AJA or BlackMagicDesign. If you don't configure the audio output, you'll be wondering why you can't hear anything.

Broadcast Monitor

The third tab, Broadcast Monitor, as shown in Figure 1.17, is where you configure video output. As stated previously, Smoke is a single-monitor application, but you can choose to output the video signal that you're working on either to a broadcast video interface (either internal or externally connected) or to a second computer display.

FIGURE 1.17 The Broadcast Monitor panel

If you only have a single computer monitor and no broadcast video out, then leave the top pop-up menu of the Broadcast Monitor group set to Off. Otherwise, choose Dual-Display Preview if you have a second computer display, or choose the name of your AJA or BMD broadcast video interface if you want to output to an external video display of some kind.

When you choose an option other than Off, the Broadcast Selection menu below updates to show you what options are available. These menus are illustrated in Figure 1.18.

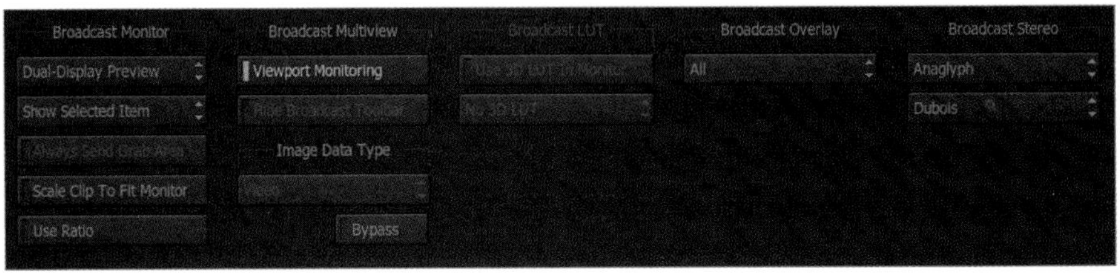

FIGURE 1.18 Available Broadcast Monitor controls

The Broadcast Selection pop-up menu, below the Broadcast Monitor menu, provides two options:

Screen Grab   Mirrors the entirety of the primary Smoke display to a second display. This can be useful in presentation or educational situations.

Show Selected Item   Outputs the currently selected viewer to video out so that only the video stream is being viewed on your external display. This is the preferred mode for getting a full-screen preview of what you're working on.

Once you've configured these first two pop-up menus, a variety of other controls become available to let you set up how clips are scaled to fit mismatched displays—whether to output based on the viewer settings in Smoke or whether to independently apply a LUT or look up table, how to apply overlays, and how to handle stereoscopic 3D media.

Input Devices

The fifth tab, as shown in Figure 1.19, provides controls for customizing your preferred input device, whether it's using a mouse or a pen and tablet.

While Smoke was originally designed with pen and tablet users in mind, it's perfectly fine to use Smoke with a mouse. However, if you are using a pen and tablet, Smoke inherits the settings chosen from the Wacom Tablet panel of the System Preferences. This behavior is different from previous versions of Smoke, which overrode all system settings for tablets and mapped the primary Smoke display to the entire tablet surface. Now, however, your tablet will be mapped in System Preferences.

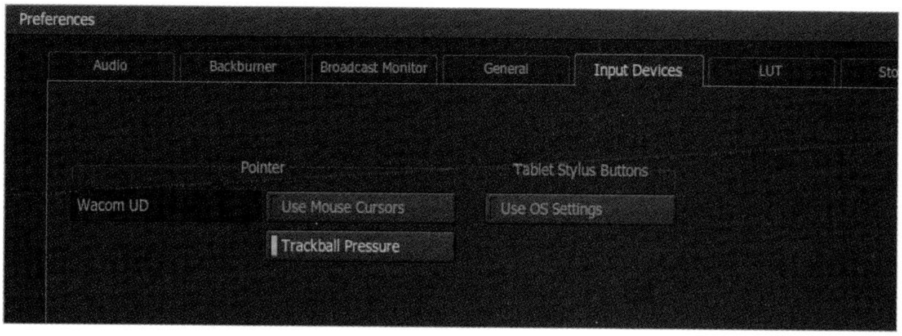

FIGURE 1.19 The Input Devices tab

User Interface

Lastly, the User Interface tab, all the way on the right, as shown in Figure 1.20, provides a number of controls for customizing the color of the interface to make it brighter or darker, changing the location of the onscreen calculator that lets you click to enter values into number fields, toggling snapping of thumbnails, and so forth.

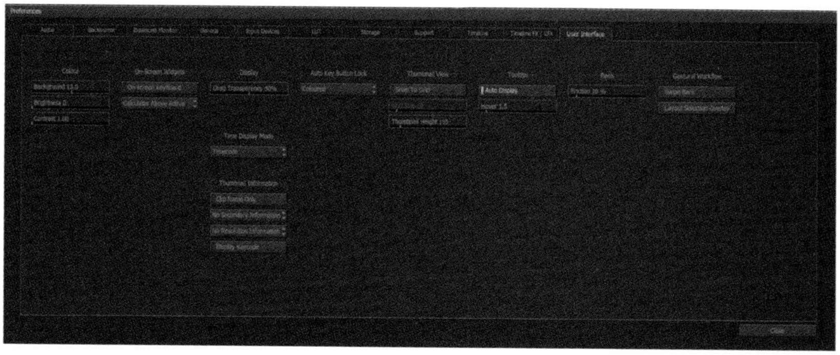

FIGURE 1.20 The User Interface tab

The Tooltips options are of particular note as you go through the process of learning Smoke. Just about every control in Smoke has a verbose tooltip that explains its function, and these controls let you determine whether they appear, adjust how long (in seconds) you have to hover the pointer to make a tooltip appear, and the duration in seconds that tooltips remain before disappearing.

By using these controls, you can have tooltips appear quickly and remain for a long time when you're just getting started. Once you have the hang of things and don't want tooltips getting in the way, you can set them to appear after a longer delay. Then when you've mastered Smoke, you can turn off Auto Display altogether so that they don't end up obscuring the UI during contemplative moments of your workday.

THE ESSENTIALS AND BEYOND

Now that you've seen how to configure Smoke to get started, it's time to explore some of the additional educational and reference options that are available from the Project panel and Help menu.

ADDITIONAL EXERCISES

▶ Choose the Smoke Learning Channel from the Help menu to open this YouTube channel in your media browser, and bookmark it.

▶ Go back to Smoke, and then choose Smoke AREA Discussion Forums and bookmark it.

▶ Return to Smoke, choose Smoke Help from the Help menu, and choose 2014 ➤ Help ➤ User Guide ➤ Preferences ➤ Broadcast Monitor Preferences to read more about the different Broadcast Monitor settings.

CHAPTER 2

The Smoke Interface

This chapter guides you through the different parts of the Autodesk® Smoke® user interface. Because Smoke is an integrated environment spanning the editorial, compositing, and finishing stages of postproduction, the interface is similarly organized into discrete areas where you can focus on each task as it arises.

Topics in this chapter include the following:

▶ **Understanding the MediaHub and Media Library**

▶ **Importing projects using Conform**

▶ **Using the viewer**

▶ **Working in the Timeline panel**

▶ **Applying timeline effects**

▶ **Getting into ConnectFX**

▶ **Finding more functions in Tools**

The Four Tabs

Smoke has four functionality panels within which you perform different tasks. These panels are accessible via tabs that run along the bottom of the Smoke interface, as shown in Figure 2.1.

FIGURE 2.1 The four panels of functionality

These four functionality panels are as follows:

MediaHub This panel is a browser that lets you import file-based media that you want to use within a project. It's also where you import media and sequences from other projects and where you create and manage archives for long-term storage or project exchange. Media that you import using the MediaHub is stored in the Media Library.

Conform   This panel provides an interface for importing XML, AAF, or EDL project files from other applications and for relinking the resulting sequence to its corresponding media.

Timeline   This panel is where you'll spend most of your time in Smoke. It's where you edit and where you find all of the tools and controls needed for accessing the advanced compositing features in Smoke.

Tools   This panel contains a variety of features that you can use for processing clips and sequences in different ways. For example, the Clip Tools tab contains filters for *denoising* to remove noise from an image, transform tools for stabilizing or flipping, and fields tools for dealing with interlacing. The Utilities tab has tools for letterboxing, adding timecode window burns, altering timecode and frame rate, and managing stereo 3D media.

Each panel facilitates a specific stage of postproduction workflow. To get started, first you'll use the Conform panel.

Importing Projects Using Conform

In order to tour the interface, you'll need to load a project. This is a perfect excuse for using the Conform panel. Smoke is frequently used as a *finishing* application, where you import edited sequences from other NLEs (non-linear editors) in order to add effects, titles, color correction, and any last-minute editing changes in preparation for exporting the final polished program.

Smoke is capable of importing EDL, AAF, and Final Cut Pro 7– or Final Cut Pro X–formatted XML project files from a variety of applications. In the following exercise, you'll import an EDL file and relink its accompanying media to it. The procedure works the same for AAF and XML files.

When exporting an XML or AAF file to import into Smoke, it's best to place the XML or AAF project file within the same directory as the accompanying media to guarantee the easiest import.

1. Open Smoke, choose the Introductory_Project project and Student user you created in the previous chapter, and click Start.

2. Click the Conform tab.

3. Right-click anywhere within the Conform list, and choose Load FCP XML/AAF/EDL from the context menu. The Media Import dialog appears.

   Smoke uses its own file browser to help you find what you need (as opposed to using the OS X file browser). A "Local Devices" list shows you all of the volumes currently connected to your computer, and controls above (shown in Figure 2.2) let you navigate "Home," choose from a bookmarked file directory, and view the current file path.

FIGURE 2.2 Browser navigation controls

4. Double-click any volume to view its contents, and the left sidebar will update with a list of that volume's subdirectories, while the contents pane at the right shows any compatible media and project files. Double-click any directory in the list to view its contents, "drilling down" farther into the current file path. If you accidentally open the wrong folder, click the up-arrow button to move back up in the directory hierarchy. The path field shows you where you are as you navigate.

5. When you find the directory with the downloaded book media, click the Bookmarks pop-up menu and choose Add Bookmark to add it to the Bookmarks pop-up menu. This will make it easy to get back to this directory whenever you need to find it.

6. Now, find the Living_Room_Scene EDL file in the "Scene EDLs" directory and click it to select it in the list.

7. You return to the Conform panel, but now the timeline contains a series of red-outlined clips, and the list above it contains a series of clips with a red warning icon in the Status column, as shown in Figure 2.3. At this point, the project information has been imported, but you need to relink the clips in this sequence to their accompanying media. At the bottom of the Media Import dialog, a set of tabs let you choose settings for the imported project. Click the EDL Import Options tab, and then click the "Resolution From Project"

button to change it to "Select Resolution," and check to make sure the settings are correct. The resolution should be set to 1920x1080, with Set to 16:9, 10-bit, and Progressive selected. When you're done, click Import.

Living_Room_Scene					
Status	Matches	Record In ▾	Name	Media ▾	Source Timeco
✗	N/A	12:30:00+00	A009_C007_12105S	A1	11:39:58+00 /
✗	N/A	12:30:00+00	A009_C007_12105S	A2	11:39:58+00 /
✗	N/A	12:30:00+00	A009_C007_12105S	V	11:39:58+00 /
✗	N/A	12:30:04+07	A009_C012_1210D3	A1	12:18:49+12 /
✗	N/A	12:30:04+07	A009_C012_1210D3	A2	12:18:49+12 /
✗	N/A	12:30:04+07	A009_C012_1210D3	V	12:18:49+12 /

FIGURE 2.3 Offline clips in the conform list

8. Click Set Search Location to open the Set Directory browser, and use the Local Devices list at the left to navigate to your media, double-clicking each volume and directory until you open the main folder, to which you saved your downloaded media files. As you navigate, the Current Path Field at the top updates to show you the current directory hierarchy; you can click any button in this field to navigate back up the hierarchy.

9. Once you've opened the directory containing all of the downloaded QuickTime media, click Set. The media should appear at the top of the Media Library in a separate Conform Media list at the top, as shown in Figure 2.4. However, there's a problem; none of the clips in the conform list appear to be relinked, and there's a new yellow warning icon in the Status column. This icon lets you know that, while a match has almost been made, there's some sort of conflict preventing an easy solution.

FIGURE 2.4 The Conform Media list

10. To fix this, open the Match Criteria pop-up menu and choose Source Timecode. The Match Criteria pop-up menu contains all of the possible media attributes that can be used for linking the clips in a sequence with media files on disk. These attributes are dynamically assignable so that changing which attributes are checked automatically updates the conform list. As you can see, setting Smoke to use Source Timecode to find a match immediately fixed the problem. Now that you've found a match, as indicated by a green check mark, there's one more step to link the media you've matched to the clips in the sequence.

11. Click the arrow at the right of the Link Selected button, and choose Link Matched Sources from the pop-up menu, as shown in Figure 2.5. Simply clicking Link Selected only links the currently selected clip, but choosing Link Matched Sources automatically relinks all of the clips in the conform list that have green check marks. The clips in the timeline should now appear without red outlines.

FIGURE 2.5 The Link Matched Sources command

12. Click Preview to open a viewer, move the pointer to the timeline ruler at the bottom of the timeline, and then click and drag within the timeline ruler to move the positioner back and forth along the timeline. You should see the newly relinked timeline clips appear within the viewer.

Now that you've imported a project file, it's time to examine the rest of the Smoke user interface.

The positioner is what other applications refer to as the playhead. It's a yellow line in the timeline that indicates the currently visible frame as well as the likely frame where the next editorial function will happen.

Understanding the MediaHub and Media Library

The second step on our tour will be the MediaHub panel, used for importing media, importing sequences from other projects, and creating and restoring archives.

1. Click the MediaHub tab at the bottom of the Smoke window. Three Browse For buttons appear at the top of the MediaHub panel, as shown in Figure 2.6. Click Files if it's not already selected.

FIGURE 2.6 The Browse options

Files mode of the MediaHub lets you manually browse your filesystem in order to locate media that you want to import into your Smoke project. Right now, it should be set to the same directory you selected when you conformed the EDL in the previous exercise. Only now, you can see all of the clips in thumbnail view. Two controls, a Thumbnail Size slider and a Display Type pop-up menu, let you modify how the contents of the browser are displayed.

2. Drag the Thumbnail Size slider to change the value to 25. The thumbnails shrink so that more clips can be seen.

3. Click the pop-up menu to the right of the Thumbnail Size slider, and choose List, as shown in Figure 2.7.

FIGURE 2.7 MediaHub display options

The browser changes to List view, with a series of columns showing different media attributes for each clip. Drag the horizontal scrollbar to the left to see the other columns that are visible. There's a lot of information available, but you can reveal even more.

4. Right-click the header of any column to display a list of all available media attribute columns that can be exposed, and choose File Size to make that attribute visible as a column as well.

5. Drag the File Size attribute to the left to position it to the right of the File Location column, and then click the File Size header once to sort the browser in ascending order by size. Click it again to browse in descending order. When you're finished, right-click any column's header and uncheck File Size.

You'll learn more about importing media from the MediaHub into the Media Library in Chapter 3, "Importing Your Project's Media."

6. Click Projects at the top of the MediaHub. In Projects mode, the MediaHub displays a list of all of the projects on the current computer within the Local Projects list at the right of the MediaHub browser. If this is a brand-new installation of Smoke, the Local Projects list will be empty; but if you had other projects on your computer, such as those shown in Figure 2.8, you could double-click any project to access its workspace, then double-click the workspace item to access its Media Library, and double-click the Media Library to access its sequences.

FIGURE 2.8 The Local Projects list with a variety of other projects

In this way, you can import sequences from one project to another. The Autodesk Network section of the Projects Browser lets you access other projects on other Smoke workstations connected to the current network, which is useful for a shared environment.

7. Click Archives at the top of the MediaHub. In Archive mode, you're set up to create and access archives, which are consolidated collections of Smoke project data and media that you can use to back up a project for long-term storage, or to which you can export selected sequences and media for moving to another Smoke workstation.

   Whenever you choose a MediaHub mode, the tab underneath the browser updates to show the different options and controls that are available within each mode. For example, in Archives mode, this tab is labeled Archive Options and shows the various options that are available for customizing the creation of new archives.

Now that you've seen the three modes of the MediaHub, it's time to move on to the timeline, which is where you'll be doing the majority of your work in Smoke.

Working in the Timeline Panel

The Timeline panel is where you'll do most of your work in Smoke. When you first open the timeline, the viewer is set to Thumbnail mode, and the FX Ribbon is hidden.

1. Click the Timeline tab at the bottom of the Smoke window, and then click the View Mode pop-up menu and choose Player.

2. Click the FX tab underneath the viewer and to the left of the timeline tabs.

   At this point, you can see that the Timeline panel is divided into three sections (excluding the Media Library, which is available from all of the panels), as shown in Figure 2.9.

3. Click the FX button to close the FX Ribbon.

Using the Viewer

The viewer can be put into several modes. These modes are available from the View Mode pop-up menu, as shown in Figure 2.10.

FIGURE 2.9 The three sections of the Timeline panel: the viewer, the FX Ribbon, and the timeline

FIGURE 2.10 Available viewer modes

1. Click the View Mode pop-up menu and choose Thumbnails. The viewer and controls disappear, replaced by an empty workspace containing two thumbnails. In Thumbnail mode, each clip and sequence in your project is visible as an icon. Since the current project only has two sequences, that's all you see here.

2. Click the Gear pop-up menu, and choose Arrange ➤ Clean Up All to arrange the thumbnails so that they don't overlap. Alternately, you can click the Gear pop-up menu and choose Arrange ➤ Fit All, both to arrange the thumbnails and to resize them to fit into the available width of the viewer space, as shown in Figure 2.11.

FIGURE 2.11   The result of using Fit All to arrange the available thumbnails automatically

3. The first thumbnail is black, since it's an empty sequence, so shrink it to get it out of the way by clicking it and then pressing Option-Minus repeatedly until it's shrunken down. You can resize individual thumbnails to different sizes in this manner.

4. Move the playhead over the bottom of the second thumbnail so that the pointer crosshairs appear with left and right arrows, and then click and drag to the left or right to scrub through the timeline. Dragging above the thin strip at the bottom that displays a tiny playhead moves you slowly through the clip, while dragging right on top of the bottom strip moves you much more quickly (see Figure 2.12).

   Using each thumbnail's navigation controls, you can identify specific frames in each clip and even set in and out points by pressing the I and O keys.

5. Double-click the large thumbnail to change the viewer to Player mode. (This is the same as choosing Player from the View Mode pop-up menu.) Player mode is useful for seeing the frame at the position of the playhead as large as possible, which is good for watching your edited sequence play through.

FIGURE 2.12 Dragging the bottom of an icon to scrub through the video

6. To make the image in the viewer even larger, move the pointer to the dividing line between the transport controls and the FX Ribbon, and when the pointer changes to the resize cursor (see Figure 2.13), drag this border down to shrink the available vertical area of the timeline and enlarge the viewer.

The User Interface tab of the Preferences has two buttons for turning on Swipe Bars and Layout Selection Overlay. When both are enabled, you can tap the upper-right corner of the screen to open an overlay for clicking the layout that you want to use.

FIGURE 2.13 Resizing the viewer

7. Click the full-screen button (the button with two diagonal arrows), or press Ctrl+Esc. This blows up the image to take over the full space of the primary display, with transport controls available if you move the pointer to the bottom of the screen. To get out of Full-Screen mode, press the Esc key, or move the pointer to the bottom of the screen and click the full-screen button again.

8. Drag the border between the viewer and timeline back up so that all three tracks of the timeline are fully visible. It's time to examine the available transport controls.

   Each viewport appears with a set of transport controls, a scrubber bar that lets you quickly drag through the entire clip, a set of transport control buttons with obvious controls (see Figure 2.14), and a timecode display.

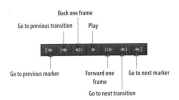

FIGURE 2.14 Transport controls in the Smoke viewer

9. Click and drag within the gray scrubber bar that appears underneath the image in the viewer to move the playhead. This is a good way to scrub quickly through an entire sequence. Next, click and drag within the red-outlined timecode field, and you'll see that you can scrub this way as well, although scrubbing with the timecode field is much more precise.

10. There's a third way to play using the pointer, and that is to move the pointer to the bottom third of the image itself. This lets you shuttle forward at various speeds by dragging to the right and shuttle backward at various speeds by dragging to the left (see Figure 2.15).

FIGURE 2.15 Shuttling with the pointer in the viewer

11. Click the timecode display, use the mouse to enter 1231.. (periods are a shortcut for entering pairs of zeroes), using the onscreen keypad that appears, and then click Enter. The playhead jumps to 12:31:00:00.

    While the transport control buttons are fairly obvious, you might have noticed that three of these buttons have black dots at the bottom-right corner. These black dots mean that those buttons are also pop-up menus that you can use to alter their behavior.

12. Click and hold the Play button down until a pop-up menu appears (see Figure 2.16), and then choose Backward. The sequence starts playing backward until you stop. There are other options within this pop-up menu to alter the behavior of the button as well as to change the playback looping behavior.

FIGURE 2.16 Opening
the Play button's option menu

By now you must have noticed that the clips being linked to are pretty low-contrast and washed out. In fact, this is log-encoded media converted from the camera-original raw format. Workflows using log-encoded media are increasingly common, because they're a good way to retain detail and data fidelity in your clips for compositing and grading. However, they don't look very nice while you're editing. Fortunately, Smoke has an easy way to monitor log-encoded media.

13. Click the word *Video* at the lower-left corner of the viewer, and choose Log from the pop-up menu that appears (see Figure 2.17). Log applies a temporary linearizing gamma curve to the image shown in the viewer, which has the effect of showing you a good approximation of how the image is supposed to look based on a Cineon to Rec.709 conversion of the image. This is only for display; this image adjustment is not rendered when outputting your final program.

FIGURE 2.17   The Viewer Gamma pop-up menu

There are also overlays you can enable in the viewer to help you as you work. These are found in the Options pop-up menu at the bottom right of the viewer.

14. Click the Options pop-up menu, and choose Show Overlays. A set of overlay controls appears in the viewer, to the right of the image (see Figure 2.18). These let you turn on various reference overlays like title and action safe, a grid, a center point, a custom working area, free guides, and letterboxing.

15. Click the Safe pop-up menu, choose Action & Title, and then click the Letterbox pop-up menu and choose 2.35:1. Notice how the safe guides automatically resize themselves to the letterboxing you've added. These overlays can be turned on or off at will, and they are never rendered as part of the image.

16. Set the Safe and Letterbox pop-up menus back to None, and then turn off Show Overlays in the Options pop-up menu.

17. Press Option+2 to set the viewer to Source-Sequence mode. This is the source-record mode available for editing, where the left-hand viewer is used for opening clips from the Media Library for setting in and out points in preparation for editing, and the right-hand viewer shows the frame at the current position of the positioner in the timeline.

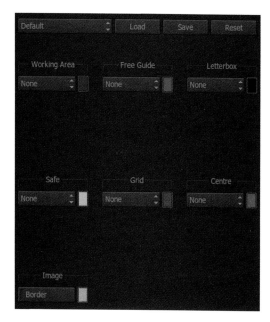

FIGURE 2.18 The viewer overlay controls

There are two other viewer modes: Triptych player (for comparing three clips in a row) and Trim mode (for viewing edit points while making trim edits), which will be shown in later chapters.

Using the Timeline

Now that you've learned how to work with the viewer and how to control playback, it's time to take a look at the timeline itself. If you're familiar with other editing applications, there will be no surprises here. Nevertheless, the Smoke timeline does have some unique features worth exploring.

Multiple sequences can be opened into multiple tabs running along the top-left of the timeline area (see Figure 2.19). Click a tab to switch to that sequence. Additionally, whichever clip or sequence is currently open in the source viewer, when in Source-Sequence viewing mode, appears within a green tab at the left. As you can see now, it's perfectly possible to open a sequence into the source viewer, in which case that sequence can be treated as any other clip and edited into another sequence, either whole or in part.

View mode key shortcuts are memorable because they correspond to the number of displays you get: Option+1 is for the single player, Option+2 is for the dual Source-Sequence, and Option+3 is for the three-image Triptych.

FIGURE 2.19 Multiple timeline tabs

A series of tool and mode controls to aid you while you're editing appears at the upper right of the timeline. These will be covered in greater detail in Chapters 4 through 6.

The timeline itself is split in half: video tracks appear above and are numbered in ascending order, while audio tracks appear below and are numbered in descending order. The Patch Panel area appears at the left, and it contains a variety of controls for controlling track content while editing, as explained in Figure 2.20.

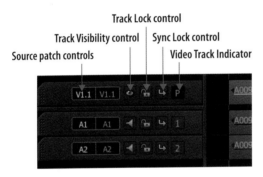

FIGURE 2.20 The Patch Panel controls in the timeline

Keep this orientation in mind as you use the following exercise to walk through the various methods that are available for navigating and resizing the timeline:

1. Drag anywhere within the timeline ruler located underneath the timeline to scrub the positioner back and forth along the edited sequence. If you're used to other applications, it'll take a bit of time to get used to the ruler being at the bottom rather than at the top, but otherwise it works the same.

2. Drag within the timecode display at the right of the bottom scrollbar to scrub at a much slower rate, for precision positioning using your mouse or pen. Similarly, you can click the timecode display and use the onscreen calculator to enter a timecode value to which you want to jump.

3. While we're investigating playback methods, press the spacebar to play forward through the sequence, and then press the spacebar again to stop. Press Shift+spacebar to play in reverse, and then press the spacebar again to stop. The spacebar is a common and easily remembered playback mechanism, but there's an even more flexible set of keyboard shortcuts that are compatible with many other NLEs you may have experienced.

4. Press the L key to play forward at full speed, and then press L repeatedly to increase the playback speed. Each press of the L key increases the playback speed even more, such that pressing L 10 times will send the positioner rocketing through your sequence. Press K to stop playback. Pressing J plays in reverse at full speed, and pressing J repeatedly also increases the reverse playback speed.

5. Press and hold the K key and tap the L or J key to move the positioner forward or back one frame at a time. Hold the K key down along with the L or J key to move the positioner forward or backward in slow motion.

   So far, you've been working with the timeline showing the entire sequence. However, if you want to do more detailed work, you'll need to zoom in.

6. Press ⌘+= to zoom into the timeline, and then press ⌘+– to zoom out again. To zoom using your mouse, click the bottom scrollbar so that the pointer displays a four-arrow cursor (see Figure 2.21), and then drag up to zoom into the timeline or drag down to zoom out of the timeline. In fact, while zooming with the scrollbar, you can zoom and scroll at the same time, which can make navigating the timeline really fast.

You'll notice that the positioner in the timeline is locked to the one in the scrubber bar of the Sequence viewer. Playback and transport controls in one work identically to playback and transport controls in the other.

FIGURE 2.21 Zooming with the scrollbar

You can also resize the tracks displayed within the timeline, which can make it easier to see different track-based controls.

7. In the Patch Panel area, move the pointer to the bottom border of any timeline track so that the pointer turns into the resize cursor, and then drag up or down to resize just that track. If you increase the height of an audio track enough, you'll see dB markers appear to indicate the volume of the waveform being displayed (see Figure 2.22).

FIGURE 2.22 Changing individual track height

Pressing Shift+Z fits the entire sequence into the available width of the timeline. Pressing Shift+Z a second time returns the timeline to its previously zoomed state, so you can toggle back and forth.

8. Move the pointer to the vertical scrollbar on the right, and then click and drag to the left to increase the size of all the tracks relative to their individual sizes. Then drag to the right to decrease the size of all the tracks.

9. Now that your timeline looks thoroughly chaotic, click the Timeline Layout button to return all timeline tracks to their default sizes, and fit the entire sequence into the available width of the timeline. Clicking the arrow at the right of the Timeline Layout button opens

a pop-up menu that presents several different options for resizing specific aspects of the timeline, as shown in Figure 2.23.

FIGURE 2.23 The timeline layout options

At the very bottom left of the timeline is an additional pop-up menu for configuring other aspects of the timeline.

10. Open the Options menu, and choose Hide Waveforms. There are additional options for controlling whether audio is scrubbed or not, how snapping behaves, and other intersections of editorial functionality with timeline behaviors.

With the basics of timeline navigation in hand, it's time to look at one other aspect of the Smoke UI that affects the Timeline panel widths.

Resizing the Media Library

The *Media Library* is where all of the clips that you import and the sequences that you create are organized. You've probably noticed that, as you open each of the panels in Smoke, the Media Library is always available so that you can choose clips and sequences to work with.

You'll work more intensively with the Media Library in the next chapter. For now, it's useful to know that there's a View Mode pop-up menu at the bottom of the Media Library (see Figure 2.24) that lets you choose different layouts or even hide the Media Library altogether if it's not necessary.

By default, the Tall option is checked, giving you the maximum height for navigating a full Media Library. However, if you turn Tall off, the timeline will expand to the full width of your computer display, giving you more room to work. You also can turn on the Right Side option to display the Media Library to the right of the viewer.

FIGURE 2.24 The View Mode pop-up menu lets you choose different ways of displaying the Media Library.

Furthermore, if you choose Hidden, the Media Library disappears altogether, giving you the maximum amount of space for the viewer and the timeline. You can always show the Media Library again by opening the View Mode pop-up menu and turning off Hidden.

Lastly, you've no doubt noticed that the Media Library is too narrow to display more than one or two columns of information. Turning on the Details option of the View Mode pop-up menu replaces the viewer (as well as the timeline if Tall is turned on) with a full-monitor-width Media Library panel with the same options for displaying and rearranging metadata columns that you saw in the MediaHub (see Figure 2.25). If necessary, you can use this view to sort the Media Library by any column you want before turning off the Details option to return to the Media Library's Normal view.

FIGURE 2.25 The Media Library in Details mode

Throughout this book, the Media Library will be shown in its default Tall view, at the left of the screen.

A Quick Look at Timeline Effects

Smoke is known for its tight integration of visual effects and editing, and in this section we'll take an overall look at how effects are accessed. All of this will be covered in much more detail in later chapters; for now, it's enough to see where everything is located.

About the FX Ribbon

Clicking the FX tab, as shown in Figure 2.26, above the timeline and to the left of the timeline tabs, opens the FX Ribbon.

FIGURE 2.26 The FX tab that opens the FX Ribbon

   When open, the FX Ribbon appears between the viewer area and the timeline. Many effects can be applied right within the timeline, and the FX Ribbon provides the controls for both adding effects to clips in the timeline and editing them. The following exercise provides a quick tour of adding and editing effects.

1. Move the playhead to the first clip in the timeline. By default, effects accessed from the ribbon controls are applied either to the current clip at the position of the playhead or to the selected clips.

2. Click the FX button (different from the FX tab that opened the ribbon) to reveal a pop-out menu of all of the effects that are available (see Figure 2.27). These include 2D Transform, Action, Blur, Colour Correct, Colour Warper, Flip, GMask, Resize, Spark, Stereo Toolbox, Text, and Time Warp.

FIGURE 2.27 The Video Effects pop-out menu

3. Click the 2D Transform button. Immediately, the FX Ribbon becomes populated with a series of controls associated with the 2D Transform effect. These controls let you make fast, simple changes to the timeline clip.

4. Click the Scale parameter, and drag it to the right to increase the size of the clip, zooming in to the women at the door. The 2D Transform effect can be used for adding camera shake, stabilization, and transforms to the clip to which it's applied.

5. Click the blue "On" light of the 2D Transform button, which appears at the top of the ribbon, to disable this effect (see Figure 2.28). Each ribbon effect you add to a clip adds a button at the top of this ribbon. Click this light again to turn the effect back on.

FIGURE 2.28   The 2D Transform effect's "On" light

As you can see, it's actually pretty simple to add effects as you're working in the timeline.

Accessing Custom Editors

Most of the ribbon effects have parameters that you can edit right within the Timeline panel. However, most effects have a more detailed set of controls, referred to as an *editor*, which can be accessed to create even more impressive effects.

1. Click the Editor button at the left of the FX Ribbon. The 2D Transform editor replaces the Timeline panel, with the viewer showing the image you're working on above and the 2D Transform controls appearing below.

2. Click the Zoom button's arrow control, and choose Fit from the pop-up menu in order to see the entire clip within the available size of the viewer (see Figure 2.29).

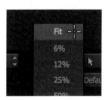

FIGURE 2.29
The Zoom menu

3. Now that all of the 2D Transform controls are visible, click the Position Y control and drag it to the left, moving the image down to give the women more headroom in the shot.

There are many, many more controls found in the 2D Transform editor, but that's all we have time for right now.

4. Click the EXIT button to return to the Timeline panel. At this point, perhaps you've changed your mind and decided that you don't want to reposition this clip after all.

5. Either right-click the 2D Transform box at the top of the FX Ribbon and choose Delete from the contextual menu, or drag the 2D Transform button from the FX Ribbon to the bottom of the screen until the trashcan icon appears (see Figure 2.30), and then drop it to delete the effect. Don't worry; Smoke has multiple levels of undo, so you can always restore the effect if you didn't mean to make this change.

FIGURE 2.30 Deleting an effect at the bottom of the screen

Each effect in the FX Ribbon has a dedicated editor that provides a more extensive set of controls. As you've seen, it's really easy to get into and out of these editors to create the adjustments you need.

Getting a Glimpse of ConnectFX

No tour would be complete without at least a quick look at *ConnectFX*, which is Smoke's node-based compositing environment. ConnectFX is an incredibly powerful tool that lets you create nearly any effect you can imagine. It has been used in blockbuster movies and commercial spots the world over. In this exercise, you'll learn how to create a simple ConnectFX (CFX) effect, in the process seeing how to access and exit the CFX editor.

1. With the first clip in the timeline selected, click the FX button and then click the Create ConnectFX button that appears in the pop-out menu. The Timeline panel is replaced by the CFX editor (see Figure 2.31), consisting of the ConnectFX Schematic, a viewer, and the ConnectFX editor along the bottom, which is displaying the nodes that you can use to apply effects to the current clip.

FIGURE 2.31 The initial three parts of the CFX editor

2. Drag the Damage node from the Node Bin at the bottom so that it appears over the red line that connects the two nodes in the schematic. When the red line is highlighted in yellow (see Figure 2.32), drop the node and it will be connected in between the two nodes. At this point, nothing has happened yet — you need to edit this node's parameters to actually create an effect.

FIGURE 2.32 Connecting a node to create an effect

3. Double-click the Damage node in the schematic to open the node editor along the bottom of the screen. A series of buttons and fields appear corresponding to the effect that node is capable of creating.

4. Click the little "On" light at the left of the Dust, Scratches, Defocus, and Hairs buttons to turn them on (see Figure 2.33). As each of these buttons is enabled, the image in the viewer updates to show the effect being applied to the clip. If you like, scrub through the clip using the transport controls, or play it back to see how it looks.

FIGURE 2.33 Turning on options in the Damage node

5. With this simple effect completed, click the EXIT CFX button to go back to the Timeline panel. You should now see that a CFX button appears in the FX Ribbon for this clip.

   Now that you see the rest of the scene, however, you decide that you don't really want to use this effect.

6. Click the Remove CFX button. The CFX effect is removed, and the clip goes back to the way it was before.

As powerful as ConnectFX is, the fundamentals are actually fairly simple to use. Even if you decide to focus on the editorial aspects of Smoke, keep in mind that there are a lot of simple creative effects that you can add using CFX without the need to dig into the deepest parts of the application.

Using the Tools Panel

The last area of Smoke that we have yet to explore is the Tools panel. As described earlier, the Tools panel contains a variety of utilities that you can use to process clips as well as sequences for the purposes of creating alternate media with effects or format conversion permanently applied.

The following exercise shows one example of how to apply one of the functions in the Utilities tab to a sequence:

1. Click the Tools tab at the bottom of the Smoke window, and then click the Utilities tab and click the Burn-In Timecode button. The pointer now appears with the text "Pick Clip," which is your cue to click the clip in the Media Library you want to add a timecode window to (see Figure 2.34). Click the Living_Room_Scene sequence.

FIGURE 2.34 The Pick Clip cursor

2. Next, the pointer appears with the text "Render Here," which is your cue to click a library or bin icon in the Media Library to which you want to save the resulting processed clip (see Figure 2.35). The Tools functions all work by creating a duplicate of a piece of media that contains the processing that you're applying.

FIGURE 2.35 The Render Here cursor

3. Click the Default Library icon. The Burn-In Timecode editor appears with controls for customizing the window burn effect by changing the text color, the background color, the font, and so forth. To go ahead and create the new, processed clip, click the Render button at the left. To cancel the procedure, click the EXIT button.

Most of the functions of the Clip Tools and Utilities tabs work this way, and once you've created your duplicate effected media, you'll use those clips as you would any other that you imported into Smoke.

THE ESSENTIALS AND BEYOND

Hopefully, this tour has served as a good orientation for you in terms of where everything in Smoke is located, and has provided you with a solid foundation for adjusting the viewer, playing and navigating your projects, and working within the timeline. With this in mind, subsequent chapters will focus on specific features, exploring each aspect of the Smoke workflow more deeply.

ADDITIONAL EXERCISES

▶ Create a new, empty project file.

▶ Try importing the Lab Scene and Opening Scene EDLs using the Conform tab to get the hang of using it to import different projects.

CHAPTER 3

Importing Your Project's Media

Before you can begin assembling your masterwork, you must first import the media that you require and organize it in a way that makes it easy to find what you need. The Autodesk® Smoke® platform provides a media-browsing interface in the MediaHub that lets you navigate and browse media files on various volumes connected to your computer. The Media Library then provides the organizational structure where all of the clips imported into your project reside.

Topics in this chapter include the following:

▶ **Importing media with the MediaHub**

▶ **Organizing media within the Media Library**

▶ **Using folders with thumbnails**

▶ **Closing libraries and locking clips**

Importing Media into a New Project

The first thing you'll do is to create a new project that you'll use to work through all of the remaining exercises in this book. You'll then learn how to import and organize all of the media that you'll need in order to access it quickly as you work your way through:

> Ordinarily, you'll want to set the Cache and Renders tab to a high-quality codec, such as ProRes 422 (HQ) or ProRes 4444, but choosing ProRes 422 (LT) saves space on classroom computers.

1. Open Smoke. Click New to create a new project. Type **Smoke Essentials Tutorial**. Next, choose 1920×1080 and select 10-bit from the group of Resolution pop-up menus, and select ProRes 422 (LT) from the Cache and Renders tab. Make sure the config template shows 1920×1080@23977psf.cfg and the frame rate is 23.97. When you're finished, click Create.

2. Select a user (choose Student, which you created in Chapter 1), and then click the Start button (see Figure 3.1).

FIGURE 3.1 New project settings

Now that you have a new, empty project file, you'll add the media you need to work on.

Importing Media with the MediaHub

The first step in any project is to gather and organize the media you'll need to use. In Smoke, this is done using the MediaHub in conjunction with the Media Library:

1. Open the MediaHub, and then open the volume on your computer in the Local Devices list where you stored and organized the downloadable media that accompany this book.

   When you downloaded the media following the instructions in the Introduction of this book, you ended up with a single folder of clips containing five subfolders named Audio, Opening Graphics Elements, Opening Scene Effects Clips, Portal Graphics Elements, and Scene EDLs. You'll be using all of this media throughout the various chapters of this book, so you'll need to import all of it.

2. Right-click the Media Library, and choose New ➤ Library from the context menu.

3. A new library appears in the Media Library with its name highlighted. Type **Unsorted Media**, and press the Return key. The resulting library is similar to a folder into which you can place clips (see Figure 3.2).

FIGURE 3.2 Creating a new library

4. With the new Unsorted Media library selected, select one of the clip icons in the file browser and then press ⌘-A to select all of them.

5. Now look at the General tab underneath the file browser, and make sure that the Cache Source Media button is turned *off* (see Figure 3.3). Turning this button on results in the imported media being transcoded to the selected media drive. Turning this button off leaves the media where it is and places a reference of the media inside the Smoke directory of the selected media drive.

All media are transcoded as file sequences using the format specified by the Preferred Format setting of the Project Settings — either as DPX image sequences or as Apple ProRes files created as a sequence of one-frame ProRes files.

FIGURE 3.3 Turn Cache Source Media off.

6. Click the Alpha Channel Processing pop-up menu, and choose Ignore Alpha Channel. None of the clips you're importing have alpha channels to define transparency for compositing operations, so setting this option to Ignore prevents unwanted alpha clips from being created for the ProRes 4444 media that you're importing.

7. Click the Import button to add all of the selected clips in the Media Browser to the selected Unsorted Media library. If you click the

disclosure triangle at the left of the Unsorted Media library, you can see a hierarchical list of every clip you've imported.

8. Next, click the Opening Graphics Elements folder in the sidebar, and then Shift+click each of the downloaded folders that appear underneath it except for the Scene EDLs folder, and click Import. This imports each selected folder and whatever media it contains into the selected location of the Media Library.

Keeping Your Media Organized on Disk

Because Smoke relies on its database to keep track of all media and project correspondences, you must not move, delete, or rename media after you've imported it into a Smoke project. Doing so may cause considerable problems. Because of this, make sure that the media you want to use in Smoke is where it's supposed to be *prior* to importing it. If there are clips that you need to eliminate, remove them from your Smoke project first by selecting them in the Media Library, right-clicking them, and choosing Delete. Afterward, you can remove those clips in the Finder.

Organizing Media within the Media Library

Now that you've imported all of the media you're going to use, you need to organize it to make it useful. First, you'll log each clip's scene, shot, and take number. Then you'll use that information to quickly organize each set of media into folders.

1. Open the Timeline panel, and set the View mode to Player (press Option+1).

2. Click the View Mode pop-up menu at the bottom-left of the Media Library, and choose Full Width to expand the Media Library to the full width of the screen.

3. Right-click on the black bar at the top with column names. Turn on the Notes field so that it has a check mark next to it. Drag the heading of the Notes column (all the way to the right) so that it's next to the Name column.

4. Click the View Mode pop-up menu again, and turn off the Full Width view.

5. Move the pointer so that it's right on the border of the Name and Notes columns, and then drag the border so that the Notes column covers most of the Clip Name column, leaving only each clip's thumbnail and the first four characters of the clip name.

6. Then click the Name column header to sort by name again, and set the View mode to Player. At this point, you can clearly see the Notes column within the Media Library (see Figure 3.4), so you're ready to start typing the logging information into the notes field of each clip.

FIGURE 3.4 The Media Library showing the Notes column at the right, covering the clip name column

7. Next, select the first clip in the Unsorted Media library, and scrub around the beginning of the clip to a frame where the slate for that clip is clearly visible. The slate contains Roll, Scene, Shot, and Take information for each clip. In this production, Roll, Scene, and Take are numbered, while Shot is lettered.

8. Click the Notes field corresponding to the first clip, and then type the scene number (with a leading zero), an underscore, the Shot letter, another underscore, and the take number. It should read 03_A_1, as shown in Figure 3.5. When you're finished, press Return.

FIGURE 3.5 The slate of the first clip in the Unsorted Media library

9. Select the next clip in the Media Library, repeat steps 6 and 7 to identify the slate information, and enter it into the Notes column. It's good practice to use a leading zero whenever a scene or take number has a single digit. The result should read 04_A_3.

10. Continue this process with all of the other clips in the Unsorted Media library. If a clip has no slate, type **none** into the Notes field. If the clip is audio, type **wild**. Don't type anything for the folders.

11. Click the header of the Notes column to sort the Media Library by the notes you've just entered. The clips are now sorted by scene, shot, and take.

The Notes column is the one place in the Media Library that you can use to enter custom information about each clip. Media for highly organized projects like this narrative short benefit from the structured data that corresponds to the script notes. Other projects could use other notation schemes, but keep in mind that metadata entered into the Notes column works best when it's sortable.

Organizing Clips Using Folders

Now that you know what clips correspond to what scenes, you can organize your media even further using a combination of folders and libraries.

1. Right-click the Unsorted Media library, and choose New ➤ Folder from the context menu.

2. When the new folder appears, its name is selected to make it easy for you to rename it, which is recommended (see Figure 3.6). Type **Office Media** and press Return.

FIGURE 3.6 Entering a name for a new folder

3. Create three more folders, named **Lab Media**, **Living Room Media**, and **Hallway Media**.

4. As narrow as the Name column is, Living Room Media isn't clearly legible, so click that folder's name once to select it, type **Visit Media**, and press Return.

5. Now that you have four folders to use, click the first clip, which reads 01_B_03, in the Notes column. Then Shift+click the clip that reads 01_L_01 to select it and everything in between, and drag the selected clips into the Office Media folder.

6. Shift-click the first clip that starts with 03_ and the last clip that starts with 04_ to select the range of three clips, and then Command-click the clip that begins with 08_ to add it to the selection, and drag all of the selected clips into the Hallway Media folder.

7. Drag the clip with a note reading 13_A_03, as well as all three of the clips with notes that read "none" and two of the folders you imported (Opening Graphics Elements and Portal Graphics Elements), into the Office Media folder, too.

8. Next, select all of the clips that start with 06_ in the Notes column and drag them into the Lab Media folder, along with both of the audio-only clips (identified by their waveform icon), identified as "wild" in the Notes column.

9. Drag all clips that start with 07_ in the Notes column into the Visit Media folder.

    Now that you've organized all of the source clips, it's time to organize the assets for each scene into separate libraries and add individual sequences for each.

10. Right-click in an empty area of the Media Library, and choose New ➤ Library. When the new library appears, type **Lab Scene** and press Return. Then drag the Lab Media folder into the Lab Scene library.

11. Create two more libraries, name them **Office Scene** and **Hallway Scene**, and drag the Office Media and Opening Scene Effects Clips folders into the Office Scene library, and the Hallway Media folder into the Hallway Scene Library.

12. Click the Unsorted Media library to highlight the name, type **Visitation Scene**, drag the Visit Media folder into it, and open each library to view the folder inside. The resulting library structure should look like Figure 3.7.

Smoke 2015 added more organizational goodness in the ability to color-code libraries and folders by right-clicking them in the Media Library and choosing from the Color submenu.

There's no one right way to use libraries and folders, but a good way to think about how to use each of these organizational tools is that libraries are useful for larger collections of media that you want to browse and access all at once, while folders are useful for subdividing groups of clips that you know you want to use together within the same scene or montage.

FIGURE 3.7 All clips organized into folders according to scene

Using Folders with Thumbnails

One of the benefits of organizing your clips into smaller groups using folders is to take advantage of the thumbnail view of the viewer. If a single folder or library has too many clips, the thumbnail view can be too cluttered to be useful. However, when you place a smaller set of clips into a folder, opening that folder results in a more manageable number of clips being exposed as thumbnails, making it possible for you to organize your clips visually in preparation for editing.

1. Double-click the Lab Media folder. Its contents appear as thumbnails in the viewer. Right now, each clip is probably showing the slate to which you referred while logging.

2. Use the scrubber at the bottom of each clip thumbnail to reveal the action at the beginning of each clip so that you can see how they all fit together.

3. Drag the thumbnails in the viewer to arrange them in a plausible order — from the wide shot where the woman opens the door, to the close-up of her at the whiteboard, to the long dolly shot of her walking toward the desk, and to the medium shot of her standing in front of the green screen. The final assembly should look something like Figure 3.8.

You can automatically organize a messy set of icons in the thumbnail viewer using two commands in the Arrange submenu of the gear menu in thumbnail view: Clean Up All and Fit All.

By using folders, you can combine the column-based organization of the Media Library with the visually based organization of the thumbnail viewer while you prepare your clips for editing.

FIGURE 3.8 Rearranging the clip thumbnails to reorder them

Closing Libraries and Locking Clips

While libraries and folders both serve as containers of clips to help you organize them in different ways, there are two important differences. Libraries can be *closed* such that the contents of that library are temporarily released from your computer's active memory, taking no resources. This lets you create projects that contain an enormous amount of media, so long as you distribute the clips sensibly among a series of libraries, each one of which gives you access to a subset of clips. Additionally, the contents of a closed library are protected from changes or modifications.

To close a library, right-click it and choose Close Library from the context menu. In Figure 3.9, the Office Scene library has been closed, and its icon appears disabled in the Media Library panel. To open a closed library, right-click it and choose Open Library, or just double-click the library icon.

FIGURE 3.9 The Visitation Scene library is closed, and it appears disabled.

Additionally, you can use the Lock Clips command in the same context menu to prevent sequences or clips from being removed or changed, while allowing the contents of a library or folder to be browsed.

THE ESSENTIALS AND BEYOND

Organizing your clips is one of the most important parts of preparing to edit a project of any kind. It's important to take advantage of the Notes column, and of library and folder organization, to keep the Media Library from turning into a chaotic mess of hard-to-find media.

ADDITIONAL EXERCISES

▶ Delete the Default Library that appears at the top of the Media Library, since it's not in use.

▶ Set the View mode to Player, and play through each of the clips in the Lab Scene library to familiarize yourself with the media.

▶ Use the View Mode pop-up menu at the bottom of the Media Library to set the Media Library to Details so that you can see all of the columns. Use the column information to find the three 12-bit files in the entire collection of media you imported, then create two new folders called 12-bit Clips, one in the Lab Scene library and one in the Office Scene library, and put the 12-bit clips into the appropriate folders (the mirror and desk shots go with the Office Scene, and the long dolly greenscreen shot in the lab goes with the Lab Scene). Turn Details mode off when you're finished.

CHAPTER 4

Editing a Rough Assembly

Once you've imported and organized your source media, it's time to embark upon the first step of any edit — the rough assembly. An assembly means different things to different editors, but it's generally the stage where you start fitting clips together on the timeline in the order in which they're meant to play. For this first introduction to editing in the Autodesk® Smoke® platform, you'll begin to edit the first walkthrough of our heroine in the lab.

Topics in this chapter include the following:

▶ **Creating a sequence**

▶ **Playing and logging media**

▶ **Creating subclips**

▶ **Setting source in and out points**

▶ **Drag-and-drop editing**

▶ **Using cue marks**

▶ **Basic trimming in the timeline**

Creating a Sequence

In order to start editing, you need to create a sequence. While Smoke automatically adds a new sequence whenever you create a new project, you may want to create your own sequence in order to exercise more specific control over its characteristics, since each sequence you create can have its own settings.

Furthermore, you can create as many sequences as you like within a project and organize them however you need to. For example, you may use multiple sequences to break a project into reels, to create multiple versions of a commercial spot, or to edit scenes of a narrative project individually. Smoke provides complete flexibility when it comes to organizing your projects.

1. Right-click the Lab Scene library in the Media Library, and choose New ➤ Sequence.

2. When the New Sequence Creation dialog appears, choose the settings shown in Figure 4.1 (changing Audio Tracks to 2 Tracks and the button next to it to "Mono") and click Create.

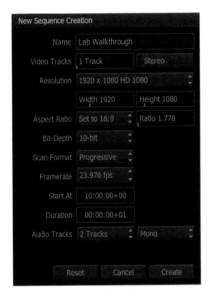

FIGURE 4.1 New Sequence Creation dialog

When creating a new sequence, keep in mind that you can choose all of these settings only when you initially create a sequence — you can't change them later. In particular, you can't change the Bit-Depth, Resolution, Scan Format, or Framerate settings later. If you choose the wrong settings for any of these parameters, your performance will be reduced, as Smoke converts each clip you edit into your sequence using a Resize or Timewarp effect. However, you can fix this after you've started editing by creating a new sequence with the correct settings and then copying and pasting all of the clips from the original sequence into the new one.

If you edit one or more clips into a sequence with frame rates that don't match that of the sequence, you'll see a warning dialog telling you what the frame-rate mismatch is and asking you if you want to proceed with the edit. Clicking Confirm will edit the mismatched clip into the sequence with a Timewarp effect automatically applied to match the clip's frame rate to that of the sequence.

Another way of preemptively dealing with clips having frame rates that aren't matched to your sequence is to use the Convert Rate command, found in the Tools tab's Utilities tab, to create a duplicate clip with a converted frame rate. Here's how you do it:

The default start time for new sequences is the European standard of 10 hours. If you live somewhere where the standard start time is 00:58:00:00, you can change this when you create your sequence. You can change the default for all new sequences in the Timeline tab of the Preferences.

1. Open the Tools tab, and then open the Utilities tab.

2. Click the Convert Rate button. You are then prompted to click a clip in the Media Library that you want to convert. Click the clip.

3. Choose a frame rate from the Convert Rate Parameter pop-up menu at the right to convert the clip to.

4. Now click a library or folder to which you want to save the converted duplicate.

   A duplicate of the clip you chose is created and converted to the frame rate you specified. The original clip is left untouched. You can now edit this duplicate into the sequence.

Editing with Thumbnails

Everyone prefers to edit in their own way. The goal of this book, however, is to show you all of the available editorial options. The following lesson starts out by walking you through a rough assembly using the thumbnail viewer.

Please note that, in all of these editorial examples, the timecode values given are for reference only — you don't need to edit your projects to be identical to the frame unless the instructions say so. Editing is a creative art. Feel free to use your own judgment as you create cut points from one shot to the next.

Setting Thumbnail In and Out Points

Each thumbnail in the thumbnail view has overlays with timecode and clip information, as well as a scrubber control at the bottom, which you saw in Chapter 2. These can be used to prep thumbnails for editing.

1. If necessary, double-click the Lab Media folder to open its contents
   into the thumbnail view. These are the clips you rearranged in
   Chapter 3. (There should be three of them, shown in the order you
   see in Figure 4.2.)

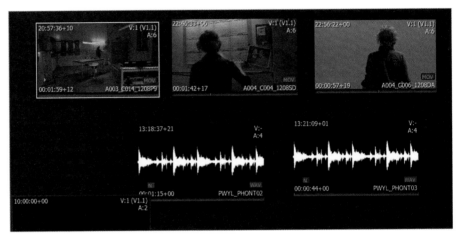

FIGURE 4.2 The three clips for this scene in the thumbnail viewer

2. Click the first clip to select it (A003_C014_1208P9, the wide shot
   toward the door), and use one of the two methods of thumbnail
   scrubbing to find the frame just before the woman opens the door, at
   the beginning of the clip. This will be frame 20:57:19+20, as shown
   by the source timecode at the upper-left corner of the thumbnail (see
   Figure 4.3).

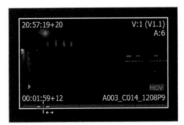

FIGURE 4.3 Finding the
first frame

These are the two thumbnail scrubbing methods:

▶ Dragging just above the thumbnail scrubber bar to scrub precisely through a smaller portion of the clip

▶ Dragging within the thumbnail scrubber bar to scrub quickly through the entire clip

3. Press the I key to set an in point at this frame, and then scrub forward in the clip to a frame where the woman has turned around (somewhere around frame 20:57:39+16). Then, press the O key to set an out point. As long as a thumbnail is selected and highlighted in white, pressing I and O will set edit points for that clip.

4. Now click the second clip (A004_C004_1208SD, the dolly shot that moves through the room), and use scrubbing with the I and O keys to set in and out points from the frame where the woman touches the pen to the calendar (22:46:37+02) to the frame where she places her hand on the podium in front of the green screen (22:47:09+09).

5. Click the third clip (A004_C006_1208DA, the medium shot toward the green screen), and use scrubbing with the I and O keys to set in and out points from the first frame where she walks into the picture (22:56:15+18) to the frame where she puts her hand back on the podium after swiping her fingers in the air (22:56:28+01).

Keep in mind that your edit points don't have to match the timecodes listed exactly. In fact, as you work along, you should focus more on following the visual instructions (find the part of the frame that looks like such and such) as opposed to trying to match the frame numbers given. You'll get a better feel for the controls that way.

All of the clips used in this project are 23.976 frames per second media. Because of this, the timecode is expressed as 00:00:00+00, with the frames separated by a plus sign. Broadcast video frame rates are expressed using the more conventional 00:00:00:00 representation.

Creating Subclips

At this point, you have three clearly defined clips, with in and out points within each thumbnail's scrubber bar (see Figure 4.4) that you can edit together.

If you've scrubbed through the rest of the media, you may have noticed that the first clip provides a reverse angle throughout the action of the entire scene. In fact, the first two clips contain overall coverage for the entire scene, so if you're trying to identify a sequence of clips that will fit together, the fact that each clip has only one set of in and out points may be somewhat inconvenient. Subclips let you subdivide longer clips into shorter ones for just this reason.

F I G U R E 4 . 4   In and out points marked for each of the three clips

1. Right-click the reverse-angle clip, and choose Create Subclip from the context menu, or press ⌘+U. A new clip appears over the top of it, with _Subclip_001 added after the name. This subclip contains only the media from the in point to the out point of the original clip.

2. Rearrange the thumbnails so that the subclip you created is first, followed by the original clip. Now that the subclip contains the range of media you want to use, you're free to set new in and out points in the original clip, so use thumbnail scrubbing and the I and O keys to set in and out points from the frame after the revolving red light over the door comes on (20:58:24+10) to the frame where the woman walks up to the podium (20:58:35+00).

3. Right-click this clip again, and choose Create Subclip (⌘+U) to create another subclip. Move the original clip down to the bottom of the thumbnail viewer to get it out of the way, and rearrange the clips sequentially, from left to right, according to the range that each clip encompasses (see Figure 4.5). To see this visually, you may want to scrub to the frame of the dolly shot where the woman opens the panel on the wall.

F I G U R E 4 . 5   Clips and subclips arranged according to scene order

Now that you've organized and subdivided your media, editing these clips together is easy.

Drag-and-Drop Editing

In this next exercise, you'll begin editing using the simplest and most obvious method possible — dragging thumbnails into the timeline. While there are more sophisticated editing techniques available, this can be a good, fast way of editing things together.

1. Drag the first clip from the thumbnail viewer to the beginning of track V1.1 in the timeline (see Figure 4.6). As you do so, you'll notice a series of red tooltips indicating which clip tracks will be edited to which timeline tracks, what new timeline tracks will be created to accommodate the six audio tracks this clip contains, and what kind of editing operation you're performing (red is the color of overwrite operations).

FIGURE 4.6 Drag-and-drop overwrite editing

When you drag a clip directly into the timeline, you edit in every track of media within that clip. In this case, the source media has six tracks of audio — some of which correspond to multiple tracks of audio, and some of which are empty. (That's just how the dailies were created.

2. Open the Options pop-up menu at the bottom left of the timeline, and choose Show Waveforms With Effects to display audio waveforms, so you can see which tracks have audio and which tracks are empty.

3. With the timeline selected, press ⌘+Equals to zoom out of the timeline, creating more room to the right for more clips.

4. Drag the positioner in the timeline ruler to the end of the first clip you edited. As you do so, a red-outlined thumbnail (named Lab Walkthrough) in the thumbnail viewer displays the current timeline frame. Continue dragging the positioner to the frame where the woman is halfway through turning away from the calendar toward the camera, as shown in Figure 4.7 (frame 10:00:18+20 in the timeline), so that you can match the action of the two clips.

FIGURE 4.7 Moving the positioner in the timeline

You can choose to display a thumbnail of your sequence in the thumbnail viewer, regardless of whether the actual sequence is in the selected folder. This floating thumbnail of your sequence appears within every selected folder while in the thumbnail view. You can choose to display or hide this floating thumbnail via the Display Sequence Viewer control in the General tab of the Preferences.

You may notice that the positioner in the timeline is locked to the tiny positioner in the Lab Walkthrough thumbnail's scrubber bar. If snapping in the timeline makes it difficult to move to the exact frame you want, you can also scrub through the Lab Walkthrough thumbnail.

5. Select the second thumbnail in the thumbnail viewer, and press Shift+I to move that thumbnail's positioner to the in point you had previously set. You can now see how this clip fits together with the next, but you'll want to scrub forward a bit to try to match the halfway point of the woman's turn in this clip to that in the timeline. This should end up being frame 22:46:39+09 (see Figure 4.8). When you do, press I to set a new in point, and then drag that clip into the timeline so that its in point lines up with the positioner.

FIGURE 4.8 Matching the in point of the second clip to the frame in the timeline

6. Move back the positioner in the timeline, and play through your new edit using the playback method of your choice (either the spacebar or JKL keys) to watch the magic happen as the two clips play together.

7. Next, drag the positioner in the third thumbnail of the viewer and the second clip you edited into the timeline to the frame where the woman is halfway through closing the panel on the wall (frame 20:58:28+14). Set an in point in the thumbnail, and drag that clip into the timeline so that it snaps to the positioner there.

8. At this point, press Shift+Z to resize the contents of the timeline to fit into its available width.

9. Now it's time to perform the last edit of this sequence. Select the fourth thumbnail in the viewer, and press Shift+I to move its positioner to the in point you set for it, which should be the frame where the woman walks into picture. Click anywhere in the timeline, and then scrub in the timeline ruler or use the JKL keys to move the positioner to a frame where the woman's position as she walks to the podium matches her approximate position at the in point of the fourth thumbnail (at frame 10:00:48+01). Then drag the fourth thumbnail into the timeline so that it snaps to the positioner, and press Shift+Z to see the entire four-clip sequence you've created (see Figure 4.9).

If the currently selected sequence is outside of the folder that contains the clips appearing within it, then a red sequence thumbnail appears within the thumbnail viewer regardless of the library or folder you've selected. You can choose whether to display this floating thumbnail via the Display Sequence Viewer control in the General tab of the Preferences.

Snapping happens only when the Snap button is turned on. However, pressing the Shift key while dragging a clip temporarily enables snapping if it's turned off, or it disables snapping if it's turned on.

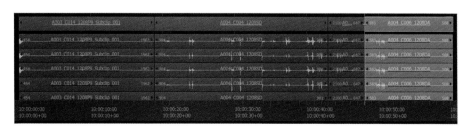

FIGURE 4.9 Your four-clip sequence so far

As you put this edit together, keep in mind that in the first pass of a rough cut, excessive accuracy is not required; you'll be tidying things up using some simple trimming in a subsequent exercise. At this point, you're almost finished, but there's one more edit left to do to get to the end of this sequence.

Dragging and Dropping an Insert Edit

If you play through the last clip you edited into the timeline, there's a frame where the woman reaches up with her arm to make a gesture with her thumb and pinky finger. (This is eventually going to correspond to a virtual computer interface, but we're not quite there yet.) There's a matching action in the reverse angle of this scene, and you can take a shortcut from having to make two edits here by insert editing the piece of the reverse shot you want in order to set yourself up for trimming the second clip you want in the timeline.

1. Use the JKL keys to play through the last clip in the timeline to find the frame where the woman reaches out to gesture. The exact frame in the timeline depends on how you edited the previous clips, but it is 10:00:57+21 in the timeline shown (see Figure 4.10).

FIGURE 4.10 Finding the woman's gesture in the timeline

2. In the thumbnail viewer, select the original reverse-angle clip from which you created the two subclips you've been editing, and scrub to find the frame where she reaches out to gesture. Notice that there's a grip who leaps out to turn on some lights on the podium, interrupting this gesture. You'll be editing after he leaves the frame (frame 20:58:50+05). Set an in point.

3. To perform an insert edit via drag and drop, click the Ripple button at the top of the timeline to turn it on (its blue on light should appear), and then drag the thumbnail for which you just set an in point into the timeline to snap to the position of the yellow playhead. Notice as you drag the clip that the thumbnails that indicate which clip tracks go where are now yellow, which is the color of ripple and insert operations (see Figure 4.11). Turn the Ripple button off again when you're finished.

FIGURE 4.11
Drag-and-drop insert editing with the Ripple button turned on

4. Press Shift+Z to fit the entire edited sequence into the timeline, and you'll see that the previous clip has been cut in half and that its second half has slid to appear after the clip you insert edited (see Figure 4.12).

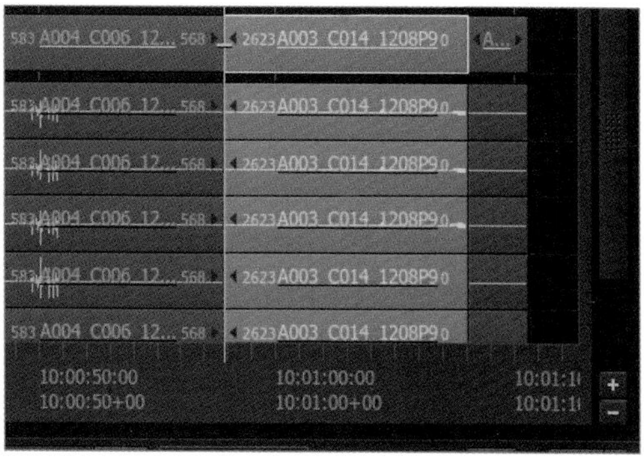

FIGURE 4.12 The result of an insert edit

Now that you've built a rough, six-clip sequence in the timeline, you're ready to start doing some simple trimming to refine what you've done.

Basic Trimming in the Timeline

Before you start trimming, you'll probably want to switch to the Player mode of the viewer, since trimming requires a more detailed look at how the outgoing frame of a previous clip and the incoming frame of a subsequent clip fit together.

Remember, the source media for this project is log encoded, so if the image appears washed out, you'll need to set the viewer to Log mode so that the scene appears the way it's supposed to look.

1. To open the Player, you can either double-click the red-outlined thumbnail in the viewer or press Option+1.

   First, you'll want to refine the edit you just made.

2. Play through the last three clips to see how they fit together. By listening to the audio, you should notice that the shot continues past the director calling "cut." You don't want to use the entirety of the clip you just edited into the timeline, so play from the beginning of the fifth clip and stop about four seconds from the point where the woman swipes her two fingers in the air (approximately 10:01:03+07, depending on the previous edits).

3. Choose Mark ➤ Add Segment Mark (Control+M) to add a marker to the clip at the frame of the positioner (see Figure 4.13). Next, open the Timeline Options pop-up menu, and choose Snap ➤ Snap Includes Marks to enable clips and the positioner to snap to whatever marks you create.

There are two kinds of markers. Cue marks (M) are placed in the timeline ruler, underneath the timeline tracks. Segment marks (Control+M) are placed at whatever segment intersects the positioner, on the track identified by the positioner's focus.

FIGURE 4.13
Placing a segment mark
on a clip

4. Click the Editorial Mode pop-up menu (to the left of the Link, Ripple, and Snap buttons), and choose Trim (or press the R key). Next, click the Options pop-up menu, and choose Focus On Trim.

   The Trim tool lets you *resize* clips, extending or shortening their in or out points. The Focus On Trim option automatically moves the positioner to whichever edit point you're trimming, so that you can see what you're doing.

5. Move the pointer to the end of the last clip in the timeline, and when it changes to a right-facing arrow, click and drag the out point of that clip to the right to make it longer (see Figure 4.14), all the way to when the woman just walks out of frame.

FIGURE 4.14
Resizing the out point of the last clip using Trim mode

6. Next, move the pointer to the beginning of the last clip, and when it changes to a left-facing arrow, click and drag the in point of that clip to the right to make it shorter. If you look at the bottom left of the viewer, you'll see two timecode displays: the first one shows the record timecode of the timeline, and the second one shows the source timecode (labeled Src) of the clip you're trimming. Drag the in point of the clip until the Src timecode display reads 22:56:31+21.

7. Play through the last clip to make sure you have the entirety of the woman's line of dialog, "Meet me at Trueberry in an hour? I need that data." If the first part of the line is cut off, adjust the in point of the clip.

8. With the last clip trimmed to the appropriate range of media, make sure the Ripple button is turned off, and move the pointer anywhere within the middle of the clip. When you see a yellow crosshairs, click and drag the last clip so that its in point snaps to the segment marker you placed on the previous clip in the timeline (see Figure 4.15). Red tooltips show that you're overwriting the last portion of the previous clip when you release the mouse button.

    At this point, it's time to start playing through all of the edits you've made to make sure they play as well as you like. You'll want to refine them for both continuity and timing using the Trim mode you've enabled.

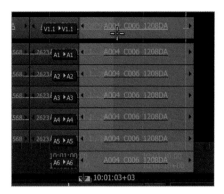

FIGURE 4.15 Overwriting one clip with another in the timeline

9. Play from the beginning of the first clip. You may have cut right in the middle of the director calling "Action," so you'll need to cut out the very first bit. Move the pointer to the very left edge of the clip, and move the trim cursor to the frame just before light from the opening door hits the wall in the darkened room. This cuts out the unwanted audio, but now there's a gap in the timeline that you need to eliminate.

10. Click in the empty part of the track, just to the left of the first clip, to select the gap. When you delete the gap, you want the rest of the clips to the right in the timeline to move to the left to fill it up, so you need to click the Ripple button to turn it on. With Ripple enabled, every adjustment you make in the timeline is done as a ripple operation.

11. Press the Delete key. An unexpected result occurs: the video clips have been moved to the left, but the audio clips have not, and now there are out-of-sync markers on every audio clip in the timeline (see Figure 4.16).

    This is not the result you wanted. It occurred because you didn't enable the *Sync Lock* buttons of each track.

12. Press ⌘+Z to undo the last operation, and Shift+click the Sync Lock button on track A1 to turn on sync lock for all of the audio tracks (see Figure 4.17). Turning on *sync lock* forces that track to keep in sync with any changes you're making to the current track, indicated by the focus point of the positioner, which is on track 1.

FIGURE 4.16 Accidentally rippling the video track but not the audio tracks

FIGURE 4.17 Turning on
sync lock

13. Now click the gap to the left of the first clip and press Delete again. This time, all of the audio clips follow the video clips in rippling to the left, closing the gap while keeping everything in sync.

14. Play through the first cut between the first and second clips in the timeline to watch the edit, which takes place just as the woman turns away from the calendar. The action in these clips is pretty well matched, and you can try different cut points by rolling the edit to another frame, in the process simultaneously changing the outgoing edit of the first clip and the incoming edit of the second clip.

15. Turn off the Ripple button. You don't want to ripple the following edit.

16. Move the pointer directly over the cut between the two clips, and when you see the roll cursor, click and drag the edit to the right to the frame where she grabs the case on the desk. As you do so, you'll see red bars on either side of the edit, which confirms that a roll is

happening (see Figure 4.18). When you're finished, play through the cut again to see how you like it, and roll the edit to another frame if you don't like the result.

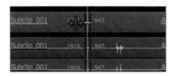

FIGURE 4.18 Rolling an edit

17. Play through the third cut of the sequence, where the woman is walking to the podium. If you edited this sequence according to the previous instructions, the few steps the woman takes toward the control panel may seem excessive. In particular, the woman takes three steps to get to the control panel in the third clip, but then she takes another two-and-a-half steps to get to the control panel in the fourth clip. The first step or so of clip 4 needs to be trimmed to preserve the momentum of the woman's stride. To accomplish this, you'll want to perform a ripple edit to trim the beginning of clip 4, while pulling all of the clips that come after it in the sequence to the left to fill the gap.

18. Turn the Ripple button on again; then move the pointer to the right of the third edit. When the left-facing trim cursor appears, click and drag to the right to trim out the first half step she takes as she enters the frame (at around 22:56:16+07), as shown in Figure 4.19.

This doesn't quite feel right, but at this point, the process of dragging the edit point is a little too coarse. Fortunately, there's a pair of keyboard shortcuts you can use to nudge a selected edit point using the currently selected Trim mode and Link and Ripple settings.

FIGURE 4.19 Rippling the incoming frame of the fourth clip

19. With the incoming frame of clip 4 still selected, press the Comma key to add frames back to the clip until you've added another half-step to the woman's stride (at frame 22:56:16+00).

   When one half of an edit is selected for a ripple operation, or an entire edit is selected for a roll operation, the Comma and Period keys let you add and remove frames one by one, allowing for more precise trimming.

THE ESSENTIALS AND BEYOND

Drag-and-drop editing and timeline trimming are essential skills for any editing project. They are particularly useful when editing with pen and tablet. Even though there are more sophisticated techniques shown in the next chapter, these techniques will continue to be useful in a wide variety of situations.

ADDITIONAL EXERCISES

▶ Use Trim mode with Ripple enabled to readjust the edit between clips 3 and 4 so that the woman takes fewer steps in the third clip and more steps in the fourth clip. Then turn off the Ripple button and try using roll edits on the edit between clips 1 and 2 and the edit between clips 2 and 3, to see if there are any other match points you might like better.

▶ Create a new sequence in the Lab Scene library named "Lab Walkthrough Alt," and edit a new sequence that starts with the wide reverse shot toward the door but then cuts to the dolly shot while the woman is writing on the calendar for a medium shot. Then edit the rest of the scene with more intercutting between the dolly and reverse shots.

◀

Shift+Comma or Shift+Period lets you perform keyboard-driven trim operations five frames at a time.

CHAPTER 5

Editing Dialog and Advanced Trimming

In this chapter, you'll take the next step and begin using a greater variety of editing commands to build a scene between two characters, this time cutting around their dialog and multiple angles of coverage. In addition, you'll begin using the many trim tools found in the Autodesk® Smoke® platform to make the small tweaks that are vital to tightening every scene and hiding your edits among the activities of the characters.

Topics in this chapter include the following:

▶ **Source/record editing using overwrite and insert edits**

▶ **Trimming for continuity**

▶ **Trimming to create split edits**

▶ **Adding cutaways with three-point editing**

Editing Dialog with the Source/Record Viewers

In Chapter 4, you did some fast editing using drag-and-drop techniques. In this chapter, you'll see how to use traditional Non-Linear Editor (NLE)-style source/record editing methods to edit together a dialog scene with full coverage in Smoke.

First, you'll need to create a new sequence:

1. Right-click the Visitation Scene library in the Media Library, and choose New ➤ Sequence. You can also click the Visitation Scene library to select it and press ⌘-N.

2. When the New Sequence Creation dialog appears, choose the settings shown in Figure 5.1 and click Create.

FIGURE 5.1 Creating a new sequence for the Visitation scene

3. When you're finished, close the Lab Walkthrough and any other red-colored sequence tabs tabs by moving the pointer over each tab and clicking the Close button that appears.

You now have a new sequence in which to begin editing.

Using Source-Sequence Viewers

So far, you've used the viewer in Thumbnail mode and in Player mode. Now you're going to use the Source-Sequence mode (labeled Src-Seq) in order to be able to load a source clip in which to set in and out points to define the range of media you want and locate the frame of your sequence where you want to edit it.

1. Click the View Mode pop-up menu, and choose Src-Seq (or press Option+2). Two viewers should appear (see Figure 5.2): a green-tabbed source viewer that shows whatever clip is selected in the Media Library and a red-tabbed sequence viewer that continues to show the frame at the positioner in the timeline. The name of each tab corresponds to the name of the selected item in the Media Library and the name of the selected sequence in the timeline, respectively.

2. Click the disclosure triangle to the left of the Visit Media folder in the Media Library to open it, and click the header of the Notes column to sort by scene, shot, and take, so that the clips are in order.

3. Click the first clip, with the note 07_A_02. Every clip in this chapter will be referred to by note rather than by clip name. This clip immediately appears in the source viewer.

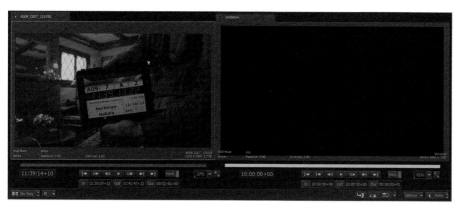

FIGURE 5.2　The Source-Sequence viewer mode

Each viewer has its own timecode displays, transport controls, and zoom and full-screen controls. Additionally, the viewer outlined in white is the currently selected viewer. In Source–Sequence mode, whenever you select a clip or sequence in the media library, the source viewer is automatically selected and displays that item.

4. Press the L key twice to fast-forward through the false start of this first take until you get to 11:39:55+07; then press K to stop. If you overshoot, press J to play in reverse and then K to stop. And you can always press K+L together to move through the clip a frame at a time or in slow motion. As you can see, the JKL keys are incredibly useful for shuttling through a clip as you begin to evaluate its contents.

5. Play through the clip until just after the director calls "Action," and then press the I key to place an in point just as the camera is pulling out from behind a wall.

6. Play through the next 49 seconds of this clip, and press the M key to place blue marks in the scrubber bar at any frame where you think you might want to cut away to something else, as shown in Figure 5.3. Ideal spots include

▶ The two women hugging at the door (11:40:03+08)

▶ The main character's friend appearing with tea (11:40:17+03)

▶ The friend saying "I had to beg a favor." (11:40:29+08)

▶ The main character saying "Thanks, I appreciate it." (11:40:36+13)

7. Set an out point just after the woman on the left says, "You can't keep skipping your classes; your TA is getting testy" (approximately 11:40:45+05).

FIGURE 5.3 Marks in the source viewer scrubber bar

8. Click the Overwrite Edit button, as shown in Figure 5.4 (or press the F10 key), to edit the portion of the clip you've defined using in and out points into the timeline at the positioner. Then press Shift+Z to fit the entire clip you've edited into the current width of the timeline.

FIGURE 5.4
The Insert Edit button (left), the Overwrite Edit button (center), and the Replace Edit button (right), which is customizable

With this clip edited into the timeline, you can see that each mark you added to the scrubber bar of the source viewer has been added as a blue *cue mark* in the timeline. Cue marks appear in the timeline ruler at the bottom of the timeline, while *segment marks* are attached to clips within the timeline. Segment marks travel with each clip, while cue marks are attached to a specific position in the timeline.

9. Move the positioner in the timeline to snap to the first mark at the frame of the two women hugging at the door, and then click the clip noted 07_B_02 (in the Notes column) to open it into the source viewer. This is a medium/close shot of the same scene from the same angle, so play through the clip using the JKL keys until you identify a frame where the position of the two women in the source viewer matches that in the frame in the sequence viewer, as shown in Figure 5.5, and then press the I key to mark an in point.

FIGURE 5.5 Matching the action of the two women hugging in preparation for editing a medium/close shot into the sequence

10. Play through the source clip until the redheaded woman closes the outer door after the woman who answered the door says "Sit down," and press the O key to set an out point, approximately 12:11:46+11. Then click the Overwrite button (F10) to edit this clip into the timeline over the top of the previous clip. Play this newly created three-clip sequence in the timeline to see how it looks, but don't worry if the second edit point is a little awkward. You'll deal with that later.

11. Move the positioner to the next cue mark to the right in the timeline by pressing Shift+down-arrow key (Shift+up-arrow key moves the positioner to the next cue mark to the left). This should be the mark you placed just as the woman walks in with the tea tray. This should be close to frame 11:40:17+03 of the source, which can be seen in the source timecode display underneath the red-outlined record timecode display at the bottom of the record viewer, as shown in Figure 5.6.

To snap clips and the positioner to markers, you must turn on the Snap button at the top right of the timeline, and you must turn on Snap ➢ Snap Includes Marks in the Options pop-up menu underneath the timeline.

FIGURE 5.6 The record viewer displays both the record timecode of the timeline and the source timecode of the clip intersecting the positioner.

12. Click the clip noted 07_D_05, play or scrub to the frame just after she spills the tea (13:05:08+09), and press I to set an in point. Then play forward to the point where the now-seated woman brings the red robot into the frame and looks at the other woman seated across from her (13:05:13+18), and press O to set an out point. For purposes of this exercise, don't worry about trying to match the continuity of this shot.

13. Press F10 (or click the Overwrite Edit button) to edit this clip into the timeline.

14. Move the positioner to the third cue mark (source timecode 11:40:29+08), where the woman on the left is about to say, "I had to beg a favor." Play forward in the same source clip (noted 07_D_05) to a frame just before the same line, "I had to beg a favor" (13:05:16+13), and mark an in point. Then play the source clip through to the end of the line "Far as I can tell, the file structure is intact" (13:05:24+06), mark an out point, and overwrite edit this clip into the timeline.

15. Play through what is now the sixth edit point in the timeline. If you've edited identically to the instructions, the edit joining "file structure is intact" and "Thanks, I appreciate it" is a bit jumbled and doesn't fall on that last cue mark you placed.

16. Click the bottom handle of the last cue marker in the timeline, and press Delete to get rid of it. Markers are both selectable and draggable, if you want to move a marker to another frame.

17. Use JKL or scrub in the timeline or sequence viewer to identify the frame right at the end of the word "intact." Then click the clip noted

07_C_01 in the Media Library to open it into the source viewer, and
mark an in point at the very frame before the redheaded woman in
the reverse shot smiles and says "Thanks" (12:24:11+14). Then play
forward and mark an out point just after the line "People are asking
about you" (12:24:16+07). Do an overwrite edit to put this clip into
the sequence.

18. At this point, play through your eight-clip sequence to see how things
are lining up, as shown in Figure 5.7.

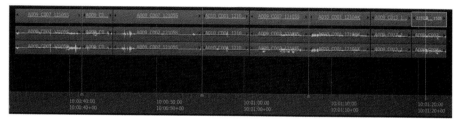

FIGURE 5.7 The roughly edited Visitation sequence

Watching the sequence, you'll undoubtedly see several edits where the clips on
either side are either out of sync or awkwardly cut together. That's OK because
now you're going to use the various trimming tools in Smoke to refine this edit.

Trimming for Continuity

Throughout this sequence, you have full coverage of the scene from a variety of
angles. Using clip 07_A_02 as the master shot, you've edited insert shots to call
attention to key moments and direct the viewer's eye. However, small variations
in each performance conspire to make these different angles of coverage fit
together imperfectly. With the overall scene edited together, it's time to use the
various trim modes.

1. Move the positioner to the beginning of the second clip in the
timeline (at approximately 10:00:07+22), and play from the second
clip to the third to see how it looks. You should notice a continuity
break as the woman coming into the entryway is suddenly inside the
house.

2. To make sure that each clip's audio trims along with its video, check
that the Link button is turned on.

3. Press the R key to select Trim mode (or choose Trim from the Edit Mode pop-up menu). Then press Option+4 (or choose Trim View from the Viewer Mode pop-up menu). When you select Trim View, the playhead immediately jumps to the nearest edit point, and the viewer changes to show the initially two-frame Trim View mode (see Figure 5.8), which shows you the outgoing frame to the left and the incoming frame to the right, along with some custom controls for adding frames to or removing frames from either side of the edit point.

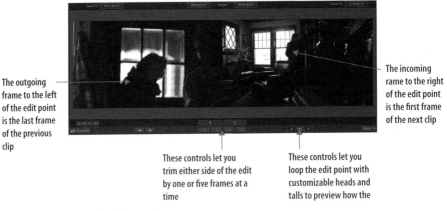

The outgoing frame to the left of the edit point is the last frame of the previous clip

The incoming rame to the right of the edit point is the first frame of the next clip

These controls let you trim either side of the edit by one or five frames at a time

These controls let you loop the edit point with customizable heads and talls to preview how the

FIGURE 5.8 Trim View mode

> You can also use the Trim tool to double-click an edit point, both to select it and to open Trim View mode.

If you're not positioned on the correct edit point (between the second and third clips), you can use the up- and down-arrow keys to jump the positioner, and the selection, from one edit to the next on the timeline.

With the trim mode selected and the trim view open, you need to choose which part of the edit you want to trim. You can ripple the sequence by trimming the outgoing or incoming half of the edit, or you can roll the edit by choosing both sides together. There are three ways you can set this up (seen in Figure 5.9):

▶ In the trim view, click the left-hand frame (adjust outgoing), the center point between both frames (roll), or the right-hand frame (adjust incoming).

▶ If you're a keyboard jockey, press P (adjust outgoing), left bracket (roll), or right bracket (adjust incoming).

▶ In the timeline, click to the left of an edit point (ripple outgoing), on top of the edit point (roll), or to the right of the edit point (ripple incoming).

Here's another thing to keep in mind: unlike some other applications, the trim options you set up don't always ripple the sequence when you're adjusting the outgoing or incoming half of an edit. If you want to ripple rather than overwrite or open up a gap, you need to turn on the Ripple button.

FIGURE 5.9 Yellow indicators show whether you're rippling the outgoing half (left), rolling the whole edit (center), or rippling the incoming half (right).

4. Click the Ripple button to turn it on. The trim indicators in the timeline should turn yellow to indicate that you're rippling rather than resizing.

5. Select the outgoing half of the edit by clicking the left image in the trim view, pressing P, or clicking to the left of the edit point in the timeline. A yellow line should appear to the left of the edit point being trimmed, and the left frame indicator of the Trim View should also appear highlighted in yellow.

6. Having selected the part of the edit you want to trim, there are four ways you can perform the necessary trimming to fine-tune the edit.

   ▶ Click the +5 button 13 times.

   ▶ Press Shift+Period 13 times to add frames in five-frame increments (the Comma key subtracts frames).

   ▶ Click the outgoing half of the edit in the timeline, and drag to the right until the outgoing frame count at the end of the clip you're adjusting reads 2597.

   ▶ You can also use the JKL keys to play forward or backward, and the edit point will trim to the new position of the positioner whenever you stop.

If you're trimming by dragging in the timeline, you can hold the Shift key down while dragging to disable snapping temporarily if it's on and getting in the way or temporarily enable snapping if it's off and you need it.

7. Evaluate your adjustment by clicking the Trim View play button (see Figure 5.10) or pressing the spacebar, which will loop the playback of this edit repeatedly until you stop. Don't use the JKL keys to do this, since doing so will actually trim the edit. This adjustment should look fine, although you should feel free to fine-tune this if you want to experiment with the different methods available to trim. When you're finished, press Command+Shift+A to deselect the edit point you were working on.

FIGURE 5.10
The Trim View play button loops the edit point to let you see how the edit plays from one clip to the next.

8. Now that you've rippled the sequence, the cue markers in the timeline no longer make sense, so ⌘+click all three remaining cue markers to select them, and press Delete to eliminate them.

9. Next, play through the third and fourth edits of the sequence — from the end of the third clip to the beginning of the fifth clip in the timeline. Notice that while the continuity from the third to the fourth clip is plausible, the cut from the fourth to the fifth clip shows the woman picking up the red robot thumb drive twice. This is easily corrected using one of the other trim modes.

10. Choose Slide from the Editorial Mode pop-up menu (or press D). When in this mode, you can drag a clip in the timeline to the right and left while simultaneously adjusting both of its edit points in order to leave no gap between it and the neighboring clips in the sequence.

    Before you use Slide mode to trim the next clip, it's important to understand that if Ripple is enabled, Slide mode will work differently than you may be used to in other applications. To help you keep this in mind, the Slide cursor will be color coded to let you know whether you're sliding with Ripple turned on (yellow) or off (red).

    ▶ With Ripple turned on, sliding a clip will ripple the outgoing edit of the clip to its left, altering the duration of the overall sequence from that clip forward (see Figure 5.11).

FIGURE 5.11 Sliding with Ripple turned on ripples the sequence forward, before, and after.

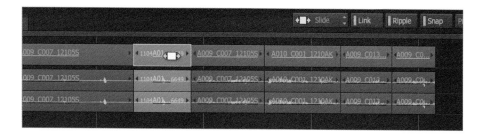

▶ With Ripple turned off, sliding a clip will roll that clip's incoming and outgoing edit points, so that the duration of the clips to the left and right of it will be changed, but the overall duration of the sequence will not (see Figure 5.12).

FIGURE 5.12 Sliding with Ripple turned off leaves the overall sequence duration unchanged, before and after.

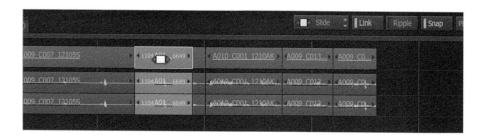

11. Click the Ripple button to turn it off, because you want to slide this clip forward without rippling the rest of the sequence in order to improve the continuity of the outgoing edit. The Slide item in the pop-up menu and the cursor should turn red to show that Ripple is disabled.

12. Double-click the middle of the fourth clip to enable the trim view. You should now see four frames in the viewer (see Figure 5.13), representing the outgoing and incoming frames of both edit points that you'll be adjusting with this operation.

FIGURE 5.13 The trim view, showing (from left to right) the outgoing and incoming frames of the first edit side by side and the outgoing and incoming frames of the second edit side by side

13. With all of this set up, drag the center of the selected clip forward until the position of the woman's hand holding the red robot in the third frame matches that of the fourth frame (see Figure 5.14).

FIGURE 5.14 Matching the position of the woman's hand at the outgoing edit using a slide operation and the trim view

14. Click the Trim View play button to see how the two edits connecting these clips play together, and continue to tweak the adjustments using the Comma and Period keys to fine-tune the position of the clip you're sliding frame by frame, in order to match the movement of the woman's hand from one frame to the next. A good place to stop is just before the woman begins to say "You owe me for this" in the next clip (source timecode 11:40:23+23).

As you can see, Slide mode is a fast way for changing how three clips fit together in a single step, but there are even more trim tools available for fine-tuning your edits.

Trimming to Create Split Edits

In this next series of operations, you'll use Trim and Slide modes, as discussed in the previous exercise, and you'll also use Slide mode and the Roll operation to start creating split edits to make the scene flow more smoothly. You'll start by tightening up the edit a bit.

1. Play through the fifth and sixth clips. The dialog of the sixth clip in the timeline is extraneous and can be cut to speed up the exchange. Use the JKL keys to move the positioner to the frame just before the line "Far as I can tell, the file structure is intact," and stop.

2. Press Control+M to place a segment marker on that clip at the positioner.

3. Press R to enter Trim mode, turn the Ripple button on, and then click the incoming half of the fifth edit and drag to the left until the marker snaps to the edit point (see Figure 5.15).

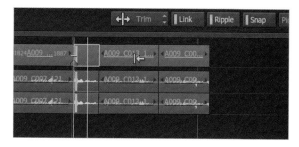

FIGURE 5.15 Rippling to cut out a line of dialog

4. Play this edit, and you'll probably notice that the pause between the lines spoken by the woman holding the red robot is too long. Press P to select the outgoing half of the edit, and then press Shift+Comma three times to ripple the outgoing frame to just after the line "anything off of this."

5. Next, press] (Bracket) to select the incoming half of the edit, and use the Comma and Period keys to trim an appropriate number of frames before the line "I had to beg a favor…" in order to create a smooth-playing edit.

    As you can see, you can use the P, [, and] keys along with the Period and Comma keys to select and trim edit points in the timeline, even if the trim view is not currently displayed.

6. Using the JKL keys, play through the line "As far as I can tell, the file…" and stop before the words "structure is intact." Press Control+M to add a segment marker at this point.

    This edit is a good opportunity to create a split edit, moving the video edit separately from the audio edit, to refine the cut and help the dialog and performance to flow more seamlessly.

7. Turn off the Link button, because you want to adjust the video without also adjusting the automatically linked audio that accompanies it. Then turn off the Ripple button and press A to enter Selection mode. Move the pointer over the middle of the second edit from the end until the Roll cursor appears, and then drag the edit point so that it snaps to the marker on this clip, as shown in Figure 5.16. Use the JKL keys to review this edit to see how it plays.

FIGURE 5.16 Rolling the video separately from the audio by disabling Link and Ripple

The split edit you created plays well, but now there's a bit of a pause between the line and the redheaded woman's response.

8. Turn the Link button back on, because you'll want to slip the audio and video together. Press S to enable Slip mode, and then double-click the second-to-last clip to open the trim view.

   With this set up, you'll use the Slip tool to change the content of the clip so that the redheaded woman's line starts earlier, without changing anything else about the edited sequence.

9. Click the -5 button twice (or possibly once, depending on your particular cut) to slip the clip contents to the left (you could also press Shift+Comma or drag the clip with the Slip cursor); then use the Trim View play button or press the spacebar to preview the change you just made. Feel free to fine-tune it by slipping the clip left or right by however many frames are needed until it feels right to you.

10. Play through the last two clips in the timeline.

    Two lines of dialog are joined by an edit: "People are asking about you" and "You can't keep skipping your classes." To make the scene a bit more dynamic, you'll overwrite the previous line with the more forceful second line, but then you'll edit the visuals to cut at a different frame than the audio.

11. Play through the second-to-last clip, and stop just after the red headed woman says "Thanks, I appreciate…." Press A to choose Select mode, and then drag the last clip until its in point snaps to the frame of the positioner (see Figure 5.17), overwriting the line "People are asking about you."

FIGURE 5.17 Overwriting the end of a clip in the timeline

12. Play both clips around this edit. There's too large a pause in between the two women's lines to play well, so turn the Ripple button on, press R to enter Trim mode, then double-click the edit point between both clips to open the trim view, and use the controls to tighten up first the outgoing half of the edit and then the incoming half of the edit, so it sounds like one woman is interrupting the other.

With this done, the dialog sounds convincing, but the motion of the arm holding the red robot now has poor continuity. The solution to this will start with another split edit, but this time you need to create room in the last clip to find a good frame for continuity.

13. Turn off the Link and Ripple buttons; make sure Trim mode is enabled, and double-click the edit between the last two clips to open the trim view. Now drag the last edit to the right until just after the line "You can't keep skipping your classes" but before "your TA is getting testy." Play through the result using JKL, and use the Comma and Period keys to fine-tune this edit frame by frame until it's right between these lines.

The delay between the audio and video edits looks great, but now the continuity is even worse. It turns out that the performer's business with the red robot in each angle of coverage doesn't match, so you'll need to look to editing another clip into the timeline with better continuity.

Adding Cutaways with Three-Point Editing

The previous exercise left you with a nice split edit that cut away to a clip with poor continuity. In this last exercise of the chapter, you'll use three-point editing to add a better clip and use the same technique to add an additional cutaway as you continue to refine this scene.

1. First, select the clip noted 07_D_03 in the Media Library to open it into the source viewer, and play through to find the line "Your TA is getting testy." Mark an in point at the beginning of "Your...."

2. Now move the positioner so that it sits over the last frame in the timeline, and press the X key to set in and out points to match the duration of that clip, as shown in Figure 5.18.

3. Now press F10 (or click the Overwrite Edit button) to edit the source clip into the sequence.

   You've just made a three-point edit, where three edit points are used to edit a clip into an automatically defined space of the timeline. Technically, you've already been making three-point edits by setting in and out points in the source viewer and using the positioner in the timeline as the third point to define where the incoming clip should start.

When using the X key (Mark In/Out Around Selection) to add sequence in and out points that match a clip, whichever clip is on the track indicated by the focus of the positioner is the one used to set the points.

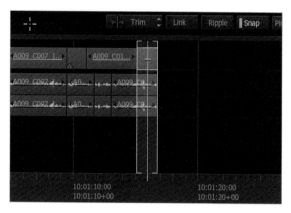

FIGURE 5.18 Marking in and out points around a clip to make a selection

In this case, you've only defined where the incoming clip should start via a source viewer in point, and because you've set in and out points in the timeline, Smoke automatically calculates how much of the source clip to edit into your sequence.

4. Play through the last two clips. The continuity of the woman's arm now works because it's cut off in the last clip, and the line readings almost match, but there's a fast way of fixing the dialog.

5. If necessary, press R to enable Trim mode, make sure both Link and Ripple buttons are turned off, and then ⌘-click the incoming half of the audio edits for the last audio clips on tracks A1 and A2 (see Figure 5.19).

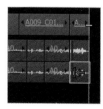

FIGURE 5.19
Selecting incoming audio edit points in preparation for a trim operation

6. Now move the positioner in the timeline to the preceding edit, and press E to trim the selected edit points to the positioner (see Figure 5.20). Play through the last three clips in the sequence to review the result.

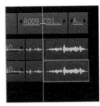

FIGURE 5.20
Using the Trim To
Positioner command (E)

The Trim To Positioner command (E) automatically moves any selected edit point to match the location of the positioner. It is a powerful command for making quick adjustments when you've identified a target frame using the positioner.

7. Play through the fourth and fifth clips again. Now that you've created some sophisticated edits at the end of the sequence, this edit may not seem as smooth as it could be.

8. Select clip 07_C_01 in the Media Library to open it into the source viewer, and move the source positioner to frame 12:23:53+23, which is the last frame of a close-up shot of the red robot just before it's lowered out of the frame. Press O to mark an out point.

   Now you know the last frame of the close-up that's available, but you want to figure out how much of this clip you want to edit into the sequence to cover the desired section. You can figure this out automatically by *backtiming* the edit using a different edit points setup with three-point editing.

9. To identify where in the sequence you want to edit the incoming clip, use the JKL keys to play through the fifth clip in the timeline and stop the positioner after the word "wasn't" and just before the phrase "…sure I was going to be able…"

10. Press O to set an out point in the timeline, press the up-arrow key to jump the positioner back to the previous edit, and press I to set an in point (see Figure 5.21).

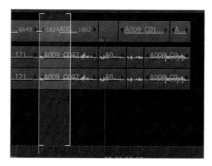

FIGURE 5.21 Defining in and out points in the timeline for the incoming clip

11. You want to overwrite the video but leave the audio alone, so click the A1 and A2 source/destination controls to disconnect these tracks from the operation (see Figure 5.22).

FIGURE 5.22 Disconnecting the audio source/destination controls so that only video is edited into the timeline

12. With all of this set up, press F10 (or click the Overwrite Edit button) to automatically edit the appropriate duration of the clip in the source viewer into the section you've defined in the sequence by aligning the source out point with the sequence out point.

13. Play around the clip you've just edited into the sequence, and observe that the woman's hand in the static shot is very still compared to the movement of her hand in the previous shot. This is a good opportunity to slip the content of the insert shot to a range of media with better continuity.

14. Press S to choose Slip mode, and double-click the clip you just edited to open the trim view. Drag the clip to the right, use the Period or Shift+Period key shortcuts, or click the +1 or +5 trim viewer button to slip the clip so that the woman's arm moves up for the first few frames of this clip, as shown in the left two images of the trim viewer (see Figure 5.23).

FIGURE 5.23 Slipping the clip to match the arm motion at the incoming frame

Use the spacebar or Trim View play button to loop through the edit until you're happy with the continuity of motion from one shot to the next, and then play through the entire edited sequence to see what you think. Feel free, at this point, to use what you've learned to fiddle with the current set of edits. There's a lot left to fix and refine.

THE ESSENTIALS AND BEYOND

The exercises in this chapter have covered a wide spectrum of source/record editing and trimming techniques, all of which are common operations that with practice you'll find yourself using every day.

ADDITIONAL EXERCISES

▶ Play through the second and third clips, and notice that the woman answering the door says "sit down" three times the way it's now edited. Trim or re-edit this edit so that she says it only twice — once as an invitation and then a second time with urgency.

▶ When you feel comfortable with the techniques shown in this chapter, go ahead and edit the second half of the scene using the remaining clips. On your first pass, edit for continuity of dialog and edit in every single line of the scene.

▶ After you've cut the second half of the scene, trim it down to tighten the performances and see what lines you can eliminate to pick up the pacing of the scene. Don't forget that you can choose different takes to even out the performances and cut out lines of dialog by editing the audio and video at different places.

CHAPTER 6

Adding Transitions and Timewarp Effects

So far, you've done a variety of cuts-only edits using the various assembly and trimming tools found in Autodesk® Smoke® software. In this chapter, you'll learn how to create transitions, such as dissolves, between two clips. Additionally, you'll be introduced to some simple uses of the Timewarp effect, by using it to improve the timing of the opening sequence of edits in this movie.

Topics in this chapter include the following:

▶ **Importing the opening scene**

▶ **Adding and editing dissolves**

▶ **Creating dissolve-to-color transitions**

▶ **Creating and customizing wipes**

▶ **Retiming a shot using Timewarp**

Importing the Opening Scene

In this chapter, you'll begin using effects to help refine your edit. In order to focus on effects rather than editing, you'll begin with a previously edited rough cut of the opening scene of the movie.

1. Select the Office Scene Library in the Media Library to choose where to put the sequence you're about to import, then open the Conform tab, click the Conform Task pop-up menu (with the gear icon), and choose Load New FCP XML/AAF/EDL from the context menu. The File Browser panel appears.

2. At the bottom of the Media Import dialog, a set of tabs lets you choose settings for the imported project. Click the EDL Import Options tab, and then click the "Resolution From Project" button

to change it to "Select Resolution," and check to make sure the settings are correct. The resolution should be set to 1920×1080, with Set to 16:9, 10-bit, and Progressive selected. When you're done, click Import.

3. Use the Bookmarks pop-up menu to navigate to the directory bookmarked in Chapter 2, which contains your downloaded book media. Open the Scene EDLs folder, then select the Opening Scene.edl file, and click the Load button.

4. Click the Set Directory browser, and click the Up Directory button to navigate to your media, then click the set button at the bottom right of this window.

5. If green checkboxes don't immediately appear in the status column for each of the media items in the conform list, then open the Match Criteria pop-up menu and make sure that Source Timecode and Framerate are checked on, and File Name is unchecked (off).

6. Click the pop-up arrow at the right of the Link Selected button, and choose Link Matched Sources from the pop-up menu. Every clip in the imported EDL should now be linked to the downloaded project media (see Figure 6.1). Open the Timeline panel.

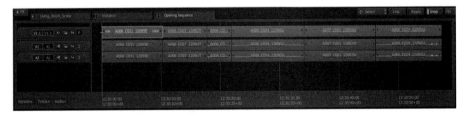

FIGURE 6.1 The imported Opening Scene timeline

7. Play through the sequence to see what you'll be working with. Using this sequence as your starting point, you'll now begin to refine this edit using effects inside of Smoke.

Adding and Editing Dissolves

The opening scene begins with a four-clip sequence of shots that visually establishes some key information that sets up (a) that our main character is a physicist studying a particular subject, and (b) that the technology throughout the movie depends on high-tech contact lenses. Since this is a visual montage, dissolves will help blend these clips together and smooth out the sequence.

1. Make sure that no clips are selected in the timeline (press ⌘+Shift+A to deselect everything). Then use the up- or down-arrow key to jump the positioner from edit to edit until it's on the first edit, between the first two clips.

2. Add a dissolve by doing one of the following:

   ▶ Click the FX tab to open the FX Ribbon, and then click the Transition button and click Dissolve (see Figure 6.2).

FIGURE 6.2   The Dissolve transition button in the FX Ribbon

   ▶ Right-click the edit point between the two clips on the timeline, and choose Add Dissolve from the context menu.

   ▶ Press ⌘+T to add a dissolve to the edit at the focus point of the positioner or a selected edit point, or press Shift+⌘+T to add a dissolve to the edit of every clip in every track ending or beginning at the positioner or selected edit point.

   A transition appears as a centered dissolve, with the default duration of 10 frames. The default transition duration, alignment, interpolation, and wipe type can be changed in the Timeline panel of the Preferences window. Notice also that when a transition in the timeline is selected, the FX Ribbon shows most of the parameters and controls that you can use to adjust the transition, as shown in Figure 6.3.

The focus point of the positioner is used to determine to which clips on which track a transition is applied. The Page Up and Page Down keys let you move the focus point up and down to different tracks of the timeline.

FIGURE 6.3   Transition controls in the FX Ribbon, excluding the Delete button

3. You can use the Duration field in the FX Ribbon (or any number fields in Smoke) as a virtual slider to extend or reduce the dissolve's duration. Click in the Duration field of the FX Ribbon, and drag to the right until the duration is 00:00:02+00. The transition in the timeline widens to match.

   If you know exactly how long you want a transition to last, you can change the duration numerically using the onscreen calculator.

4. Click the transition Duration field, and use the cursor to enter – 24 into the onscreen calculator (see Figure 6.4). The result is to subtract 24 frames from the current value of 48 frames (2 seconds), changing the duration to 24 frames, or 1 second of screen time. As you can see, the calculator can be used to add or subtract values from the current setting or to use calculations to update the value of a numeric field.

FIGURE 6.4
Using a subtract calculation to enter a number, rather than an absolute value

5. Use the JKL keys to play around with this transition. It's still a fairly fast dissolve relative to the slow pan of the two clips, so turn off the Link button (if necessary), zoom into the timeline, press the R key to enable Trim mode, and position the trim cursor to the left of the transition object in the timeline and drag it farther left to make the transition longer (see Figure 6.5), until the Duration field shows 3 seconds. Notice that you've just created an asymmetrical dissolve, where one side of the transition is longer than the other.

FIGURE 6.5 Extending
a transition in the timeline
using the Trim tool

6. Move the positioner back to the center of the edit. Then move the
   pointer over the middle of the transition and you'll see the Slide
   cursor; use it to drag the entire transition over to the right so that it's
   more centered (see Figure 6.6). As you drag the transition, you can
   see the level of transparency in the dissolve that coincides with the
   edit point in the viewer. This is one way of fine-tuning the balance of
   a transition around an edit point. You should also notice that a dark
   line at the top of the left half of the transition object shows you the
   halfway point.

FIGURE 6.6 Sliding a
transition in the timeline using
the Trim tool

7. At this point, you decide that you want the audience to linger on
   the text of the *Many-World Physics* book on the wall, so click the
   Transition Alignment pop-up menu in the FX Ribbon (currently
   set to Custom) and choose From Cut to move the transition so that
   it starts on the edit point and extends into the second clip. The
   Transition Alignment menu is a fast way to realign an edit to a precise
   location.

   If you play through the dissolve, you can see that it looks pretty
   good, but there's an even finer degree of control you can exercise
   over the way this dissolve plays by using the dissolve editor.

8. Click the Editor button in the FX Ribbon, or double-click the dissolve object in the timeline to open the dissolve editor. By default, the dissolve editor doesn't show you much more than the FX Ribbon does. However, you can expose a powerful method of customizing dissolves using the Animation curve.

9. Click the Animation button at the left of the screen. When it opens, click the Filter tab at the right of the Curve Editor box, then turn on Animated, choose Exp & Col (expand and collapse) and Show All from the two pop-up controls underneath the Animated button, then choose Animated from the Auto Frame pop-up control, and turn on Filter Tang. All of these settings set up the Curve Editor to automatically display all animated curves and control points, and, in fact, you should be able to see the Dissolve Mix curve now. (Another way of doing this more simply, when only one property is animated, is to click the Frame All button.)

    By default, dissolves in Smoke have a nice, smooth acceleration ramp applied to them, resulting in a pleasing fade from the outgoing image to the incoming image. You can use the Bezier handles of the curve to customize the acceleration of this fade further to give more weight to the beginning or end of the transition.

10. Pull the top-right and bottom-left Bezier handles of the curve to the right so that the outgoing portion of the curve is a very gradual slope and the incoming portion of the curve is very steep (see Figure 6.7). A good goal is to try to have the book image linger until a sudden finish to the dissolve coincides with the rack focus shifting from the back wall to the woman's face by using the transport controls to play through the dissolve (indicated by a blue-gray bar in the scrubber bar of the viewer).

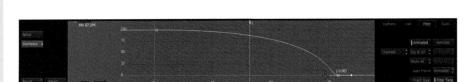

FIGURE 6.7 Adjusting the transition curve in the dissolve editor

11. When you're finished adjusting the curve, click the EXIT button to return to the timeline.

    Since this dissolve is so elaborate, it might be worth copying it to the second edit in the sequence, because you want to put a dissolve there too.

Using the Add Points tool in the Tools pop-up menu, you can add more control points to a dissolve's curve if you really want to fine-tune the fade. However, this can be overkill for speedy dissolves.

12. Right-click the dissolve, and choose Copy (or select the dissolve and press ⌘+C). Then right-click the second edit and choose Paste Dissolve (or move the positioner to the second edit and choose Option+V). A duplicate of the dissolve you created appears.

    Playing through this second dissolve shows that the effect is wildly inappropriate because it obscures the extreme close-up of the woman's eye that's meant to show the high-tech contact lenses (after you composite them in, of course). You could simply remove it by pressing ⌘+Z to undo, but there are several easy ways to eliminate dissolves.

13. Do one of the following to eliminate the second dissolve:

    ▶ Right-click the dissolve and choose Delete.

    ▶ Select the dissolve and press the Delete key.

    ▶ Move the positioner to the edit with the dissolve and press Control+V.

14. Deciding that you want a dissolve on this second edit after all, move the positioner back to the second edit, press ⌘+Shift+A to deselect everything, press ⌘+T to add a default dissolve, and change the duration to 00:00:01+12.

    Keeping in mind that the curve you applied to the first transition might come in handy later, there's an easy way to save a dissolve's curve profile for easy application.

15. Select the first dissolve you added to the timeline, and click the Editor button in the FX Ribbon.

16. When the dissolve editor opens, click the Save button to open the Save Dissolve panel.

    By default, each type of timeline effect can be saved for future recall into a subdirectory specific to that effect inside your project in the Smoke database.

17. Type **Lingering Incoming Fade** into the text field at the bottom, and click the Save button (see Figure 6.8). When the dissolve editor appears, click the EXIT button to return to the timeline.

FIGURE 6.8 Buttons to save and recall dissolve curves

18. Press the down-arrow key or click the Next Transition button in the viewer transport controls to move the positioner to the third edit in the sequence. Then add a default dissolve, and click the Editor button in the FX Ribbon.

19. Click the Load button; then click the Lingering Incoming Fade icon in the browser, and that curve profile is immediately applied. It even automatically fits itself to the new duration of this dissolve.

20. Play through the dissolve. The saved curve profile doesn't really suit the short duration, so exit the editor and press Command-T to overwrite the previous transition you created with a new one.

Now that you've seen the most commonly used transition other than a cut, it's time to take a look at some of the other transition options that Smoke provides.

In the previous exercise, the goal was to add motivated transitions to a naturalistic progression of coverage in a narrative scene. However, if your goal is to add more energetic or stylized transitions, Smoke has other options you can apply.

1. First, duplicate the Opening Scene sequence in the Media Library by right-clicking it and choosing Duplicate from the context menu (or selecting it and pressing ⌘+D). Rename this sequence by clicking the name once and briefly pausing; when the text is highlighted, type **Trailer Cut** and press Return.

2. Open Trailer Cut, and delete all of the transitions from the timeline.

3. Now add a dissolve transition to the first edit, and set the duration to 2 seconds.

   Now you're back to having a plain- old dissolve. However, this time you want to build a more exciting sequence by shortening each clip and using dissolve-to-black transitions (eventually accompanied by grinding pulses of music, one would imagine).

4. With this new transition selected, click the To/From Colour button in the FX Ribbon.

5. A Colour Picker dialog appears, set to black by default (see Figure 6.9). You could elect to use the vertical red, green, and blue sliders to choose a color, or click the Pick button to use a color picker cursor to sample a color from an image in the viewer, but since you actually want black, simply click OK.

FIGURE 6.9 The
Colour Picker dialog

The FX Ribbon updates to show additional controls for the dissolve-to-color transition, which is currently set to black. In the timeline, you can see that the previous single dissolve has changed to two dissolves — one for the outgoing clip and one for the incoming clip — each of which has individual durations (see Figure 6.10).

FIGURE 6.10 Dual dissolve
transitions for a dissolve-to-color
effect

6. Play through the transition. Right now it's a bit slow, but there are some interesting things you can do to jazz it up.

7. Zoom into this transition in the timeline, press R to enter Trim mode, and turn on the Ripple and Link buttons (if necessary).

8. Double-click the edit point (not the transition) to open Trim view. Then shorten the outgoing clip by −34 frames (as indicated by the left trim frames indicator). Next, drag the left end of the transition to the right to shorten the outgoing portion of the transition to four frames. If snapping is getting in your way, you can press the Shift key to turn snapping off temporarily while you drag to trim.

If you play through this transition, you'll have more of a crash to color, but the transition is still too gradual, so perhaps a dissolve to white would be more interestingly abrupt.

9. To change the color to which this effect is dissolving, click the narrow white color swatch in the FX Ribbon. The thin color swatches are presets, but you can click the larger color swatch to open the Colour Picker. Then click the Replace button to confirm the change, and the color swatch to the right of it changes to show that it's updated. Play through the transition, and you'll see that both sides have been updated to white.

10. To change the acceleration of the transition to make it more abrupt, you'll want to edit its curve. Double-click the first half of the transition to open the Curve Editor, open the Animation editor to display the Dissolve Mix curve, and edit the Bezier splines of the curve to resemble Figure 6.11, with a gradual slope in and an abrupt slope out. Click EXIT when you're finished.

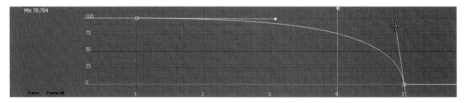

F I G U R E 6 . 1 1 Dissolve curve with gradual in and abrupt out

11. To finish this effect, double-click the second half of the transition to open the Curve Editor and edit the Bezier splines of the curve to resemble Figure 6.12, with an abrupt slope in and a gradual slope out. Click EXIT when you're finished, and play through the transition.

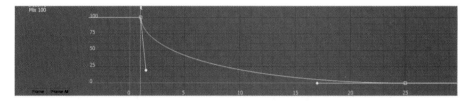

F I G U R E 6 . 1 2 Dissolve curve with an abrupt in and a gradual out

Now you have a sudden flash to white with a slow burnout bridging the transition between the shortened first clip and the second clip.

Creating and Customizing Wipes

Another form of stylized transition that you can apply in Smoke is the wipe, which takes a wide variety of customizable forms.

1. Play through the second clip until you reach the point where the focus racks from the wall to the woman's face, and press Control+M to place a segment mark at the first frame in which her face is in focus. Press R to get back into Trim mode, turn the Ripple and Link controls on, and trim the incoming frame of the second clip to shorten it, bringing the marked frame where her face is in focus to about nine frames before the end of the incoming transition.

2. Now use the trim cursor to ripple the outgoing frame of the second clip to omit the last half of that clip where the woman rolls her eye back. When you're finished, turn the Link and Ripple controls off, and press A to choose the Select mode.

   At this point, you'll add another transition, but it's time for something different — it's time to apply a wipe.

3. Move the positioner to the second edit, press Shift+⌘+A to deselect everything, and then click the Transition ➤ Wipe buttons in the FX Ribbon.

   By default, a horizontal wipe appears using the default transition duration specified in the preferences. This transition is not very exciting, so it's time to customize the effect.

4. By default, the selected wipe exposes a set of General controls in the FX Ribbon that let you invert the wipe and choose how opaque the wiped part of the screen is. However, clicking what the tool tab refers to as the "Garbage Mask Quick Selector" pop-up menu, you can choose from among four sets of controls: Softness controls that let you feather the center of the wipe, Axis Offset controls that let you change the center point of the wipe, and Transition controls that let you change how the transition is centered in the timeline, as well as what its duration is.

   Smoke comes equipped with 254 standard SMPTE wipe patterns. However, the default list showing each one by number isn't particularly illuminating.

5. Click the Presets button to open up the wipe presets browser. Click the Titles button in the upper-left corner to change the browser to Proxies mode. The list updates to show a set of numbered thumbnails corresponding to each available wipe pattern (see Figure 6.13). This includes, if you scroll down, the infamous heart wipe.

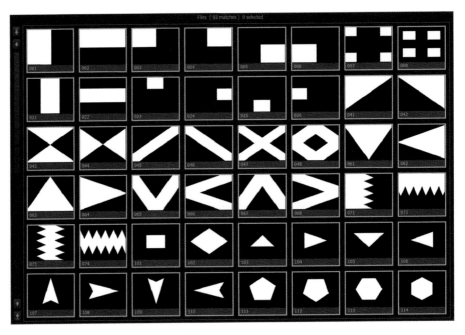

FIGURE 6.13 Wipe pattern proxies

6. Click pattern 062 and then click Confirm when you're asked if you want to replace the current setup, and the timeline reopens with that pattern loaded into the wipe. The current pattern number appears to the right of the Pattern button you clicked.

   This wipe pattern is certainly more interesting, but it's still a clear wipe pattern that may or may not appeal to everyone. Fortunately, there's more that you can do to bend this transition to your will.

7. Choose Softness from the wipe transitions pop-up menu within the FX Ribbon and set the Offset slider to 50. Playing through the wipe

now shows that you've nearly created the equivalent of a directional dissolve.

The wipe is looking good, but you might wish for the hard V shape to be a gentler U sort of curve. Fortunately, every wipe pattern in Smoke is actually an editable shape, called a Gmask, which can be easily customized.

8. With the wipe transition selected, click the Editor button in the FX Ribbon (or double-click the wipe transition) to open the transition editor.

The transition editor has all of the controls for manipulating the shapes that make up each wipe pattern. There are a lot of controls in here, but in the following steps you'll focus on adjusting the softness (using the Offset slider) and changing the Gmask using the spline controls in the viewer.

9. If necessary, choose Fit from the Zoom pop-up menu, so that you can see the entire image in the viewer.

10. Use the left- and right-arrow keys to move the positioner to the very center of the transition so that you can clearly see the shape being used for the wipe.

11. Choose Add Points from the Tools pop-up menu to the right of the transport controls (see Figure 6.14).

FIGURE 6.14 Adding two control points to the Gmask being used to create the wipe effect

12. Click on the surface edge of the shape (colored orange) to add control points at the top and bottom halfway points of the V of the shape. A plus sign on the cursor shows you that you're about to add points to the Gmask.

13. Now choose Select from the Tools pop-up menu, and edit the two control points and Bezier handles that you've just created by dragging them in the viewer to look like the shape in Figure 6.15.

     It is possible to animate a wipe via keyframes set throughout the length of the effect. This allows you to create some extremely elaborate and creative transitions with the wipe tool.

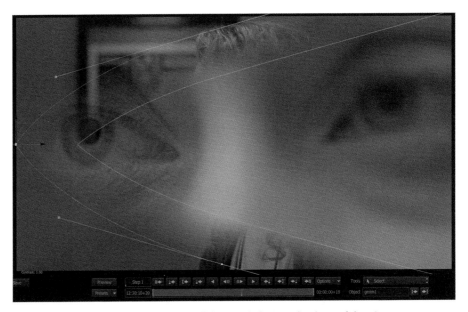

FIGURE 6.15   Altering the shape of the Gmask changes the shape of the wipe.

14. Click EXIT to go back to the timeline and play through the wipe to see how it looks.

As you can see, there are all kinds of interesting ways that you can customize wipes for creative effect. For now, that's a sufficient tour of the creative possibilities of transitions in Smoke. It's time to go back to the narrative edit of this scene and fix a shot using the Timewarp effect.

Retiming a Shot Using Timewarp

Another way of addressing the timing of your edit is to literally retime the clips that you're using. In this next exercise, you'll learn how easy it is to create high-quality slow motion in Smoke using the Timewarp effect.

1. Reopen the Opening Scene in the timeline, and play through the second clip. Halfway through the second clip, the actor blinks and rolls her eye back (waiting for the director to give a verbal cue that he's completely forgotten about).

   This defeats the purpose of the clip, which supposedly was to provide a lingering introduction to this character as she stares forward at a computer display. Fortunately, you can retime this clip to play in slow motion, extending the duration that the woman is looking forward. Since there's so little motion, this effect shouldn't give itself away.

2. Select the second shot in the timeline, and click the FX ➤ Time Warp buttons (see Figure 6.16). If the FX Ribbon is closed, you can press Control+Tab to summon a floating FX Ribbon at the position of that clip in the timeline.

FIGURE 6.16 Adding a Timewarp effect using the FX Ribbon

   This opens up the Timewarp controls in the FX Ribbon, as shown in Figure 6.17.

3. Move the positioner to the very beginning of the transition on the second edit, and then drag the Speed percentage control in the FX Ribbon to the left, slowing the speed of the clip and retiming the media within this clip until the woman remains looking straight ahead at the frame of the positioner (around 54 percent).

◄

With Anchoring set to both Start and End, trimming clips with both Ripple and Link on will ripple the video, but not the audio, necessitating that you resync the audio in a second step.

FIGURE 6.17 Timewarp controls in the FX Ribbon, excluding the Reset and Delete buttons

You should notice that the Anchoring pop-up menu is set to start, which means that as you make this adjustment, the in point of this clip is locked at its current position in the timeline, and your speed change is altering the frame at the out point. You could also change this setting to End, which would lock the frame at the out point and readjust the frame appearing at the in point of this clip. As you make this change, the duration of the clip in the timeline stays the same, which keeps all subsequent clips in the timeline in sync with where they were before you altered this clip's speed. If you want this clip's speed alteration to affect its duration, you can set Anchoring to Start and End, and turn the Ripple and Link controls on prior to adjusting speed.

4. Play though the second clip again, and you can see that you've created a linear timewarp such that the entire clip plays at the same slow-motion speed. However, you might notice that the woman's blinking eye in the third clip is now out of sync with the woman's blinking eye in the slow-motion second clip.

5. Move the positioner forward through the second dissolve until it sits on top of a frame where the woman's eyelids are almost closed in the outgoing clip. Then turn off the Ripple button, choose Slip mode, and slip the third clip to the right to position a frame of the woman's eyelid almost closed in the incoming clip at the positioner, as shown in Figure 6.18. Play through the result, and nudge the third clip using the Comma or Period key with the Slip tool as necessary to achieve a smooth-looking result.

Rendering Slow-Motion Effects

The quality of the real-time slow motion you've just added to the clip is good, but there's still an odd quality to the motion. This can be improved using the Timewarp Rendering Option in the Frame Interpolatation Menu under the Timewarp Mode pop-up menu. This, in turn, opens up the topic of rendering in Smoke, because advanced timewarp effects can be render-intensive. You can play render-intensive effects in real time to get a preview, but you won't necessarily be seeing them at full quality.

FIGURE 6.18 Lining up eye blinks for continuity

The default Timewarp Rendering Option setting is Mix, which blends together a range of frames for each slow-motion frame in a timewarped clip in order to smooth out the potential jittering that can result. With the default value of 0, no mixing is taking place, but you can specify the number of frames before and after each frame of media that are mixed together to the optimal number that's appropriate for the speed percentage you've applied and the media you're working on.

1. Change the Mix parameter to 1.5. Most recent iMacs, Mac Pros, and Macbook computers should be able to play a speed effect using Mix in real time.

RENDERING EFFECTS IN THE TIMELINE

When you click the Render button, you cache a preprocessed version of that clip to the specified storage volume for that project. Smoke keeps track of all of the rendered media in a project when you save and quit, so that it reappears when you reopen the project. However, updating a rendered effect always flushes the previously cached render, requiring you to rerender the clip.

The playback quality should be quite good. However, for the ultimate in high-quality slow-motion processing (for some clips), Smoke is also capable of optical flow processing, which essentially does automatic warping to generate brand-new frames.

2. Click the Timewarp Rendering Option pop-up menu, and choose Motion. Then choose Full Res from the Quality pop-up that appears to the left. This effect, unlike Mix, is more computationally intensive, and requires rendering. Click the Render Sel button (Render Selection) at the left of the FX Ribbon. A progress dialog appears, showing you how quickly the render is proceeding and giving you the option to cancel. How fast this effect renders depends entirely on the speed of the machine you're using and on the speed of your designated storage volume.

   When the render is done playing through the second clip should reveal flawlessly smooth motion. Figure 6.19 shows the difference between using Mix and Motion to process slow motion on the woman's blinking eye. While both effects smooth out the motion, the Mix option blends a bit of her eyelash into a frame where it shouldn't be visible, whereas Motion generates sharp, correct-looking frames.

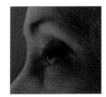 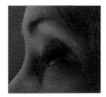

FIGURE 6.19 Mix (left) and Motion (right) slow-motion processing compared

Later on, when you learn how to use Gmasks, you'll superimpose two versions of the same clip processed with different slow-motion processing options and mask unwanted artifacts in a Motion-processed clip with corresponding parts of a Mix-processed clip.

   Keep in mind that Motion processing isn't always the best choice. Clips that have several moving subjects that cross one another in opposite directions can result in undesirable artifacts when the Motion option attempts to warp the frame. In cases where Motion processing doesn't work optimally, you can switch to Mix processing to see if you can get a better result.

THE ESSENTIALS AND BEYOND

Transitions and timewarps are staples of editorial and are an easy way to dip into the wider world of timeline effects that are available in Smoke. These effects will be covered in more detail in the coming chapters.

ADDITIONAL EXERCISES

▶ Open the Trailer Cut sequence, and continue the process of shortening each clip in this sequence to contain only the most active bits of performance. Use the Timewarp effect to add more urgency to some clips by speeding them up, or experiment with slow motion or even reverse speed to see if you can assemble a creative take on this scene that's all your own.

▶ Use the Slip tool on the fourth clip to find the most active segment of the actor's performance, and then apply a new Timewarp effect, set the Timewarp Type pop-up menu to Strobe, and play through the clip to see what the effect is with the default value. Next, try setting the Timewarp Type pop-up manu to Constant, and the Timewarp Rendering Option to Trail, experimenting with different Pre and Post frames to see what motion effects you can create.

▶ Finally, try adding more creative versions of the dissolve-to-color and wipe transitions to the third, fourth, and fifth edits in this sequence, experimenting with different colors and adjustments to the wipe settings described earlier in this chapter.

CHAPTER 7

Using Timeline Effects

In the last chapter, you experienced your first introduction to timeline effects through the use of the dissolve and timewarp effects. In this chapter, you'll learn how to use the power of the 2D Transform and Action tools in your Autodesk® Smoke® installation to build some rough composites in order to determine how two sets of superimposed clips should cut together.

Topics in this chapter include the following:

▶ **Editing superimposed clips**

▶ **Creating a picture-in-picture effect using 2D Transform**

▶ **Tracking a superimposed clip to match a background**

▶ **Editing and keying a superimposed greenscreen clip**

Creating a Picture-in-Picture Effect Using 2D Transform

This scene has several multilayer composites. While the final shots will be extravaganzas of layered effects, as you initially edit the scene, you'll often want to start by creating a simple placeholder composite so that you can figure out the timing of the different layers and see how well they'll fit together before you start the really time-consuming part.

However, an advantage of Smoke is that your placeholder effects can actually be much nicer-looking representations of the eventual composites than a piece of text that reads "VFX HERE." In particular, by learning how to use the timeline effects, including the versatile 2D Transform and Action effects, you'll be able to create effects that will be convincing enough to give your first test viewers a clear idea of what is to come.

Editing Superimposed Clips with the Source-Destination Controls

Before you get started, you need to lay the superimposed clips with which you'll be working into multiple video and audio tracks.

1. Right-click the Opening Scene sequence and choose Duplicate from the context menu, and then rename the resulting sequence to be **Opening Scene C07**.

2. Open this new sequence, click the Track+ button underneath the patch panel area to add a new video track, and then click the Audio+ button twice to add two new mono audio tracks (see Figure 7.1).

FIGURE 7.1 The Add Track buttons under the timeline patch panel

Option+clicking Audio+ adds a stereo audio track, while Command+clicking the Track+ button adds a new track below the positioner's focus point. You can also right-click the Version+, Track+, and Audio+ buttons to find additional commands in the context menu.

3. Whenever you add a new track, the focus of the positioner automatically moves to that track. In this case, you don't want the focus to be on audio track A4, so press Page Up four times to move it to track V1.1. (Page Down moves the focus of the positioner down.)

4. Press Option+2 to set the viewer to Source/Sequence mode, and then find and click the clip noted as 13_A_03 in the Media Library to open it into the source viewer.

5. Play through the man's clip, and set an in point where his two fingers are first extended (01:03:10+05). Then set an out point at the frame where he finishes swiping with two fingers the second time (01:03:23+12).

   In the movie, the character's finger swiping corresponds to a heads-up display that needs to be composited to be seen.

6. Play through the fifth clip in the timeline to the frame where the woman's two-finger swipe is almost finished (19:54:32+11 relative to the source timecode). This is where you want the man's videoconference clip to appear.

Up to now, you've only edited clips into video track V1.1 and audio tracks A1 and A2. This is a common way to work, given the plethora of trimming options available to you. However, once you start getting into compositing and the assembly of complex layered montages, you'll need to start editing clips into multiple timeline tracks. The green source-destination controls in the patch panel area let you control into which tracks clips are edited.

7. Press Page Up to move the focus of the positioner to video track V1.2, and notice how both the green V1.1 source control and the red P (for Primary) button move up (see Figure 7.2). Moving the positioner up and down also reassigns the source-destination controls that determine into which video track an incoming edited clip is placed.

FIGURE 7.2 Reassigning the positioner and video source control to track V1.2 (timeline shown zoomed in)

The sequence viewer shows the source timecode of any clip on the same track as the focus of the positioner. If the focus is on a video track with no clip at that location, no source timecode will be visible.

Before you make this edit, however, take a quick look at the timeline and notice that the green A1 source control is connected to the destination control of track A1. Every time you open a clip into the source viewer, the tracks within that clip create an equal number of green source controls, and you need to reassign source A1 to another destination audio track if you don't want to overwrite whatever is currently in timeline track A1.

8. Click within the source control of track A3, and drag to the left or right until it shows the green A1 source (see Figure 7.3). If the source clip had more than one audio track, then dragging to the right would cycle among all of the available sources. (Most of the clips provided for this book have six audio tracks.)

FIGURE 7.3 Reassigning audio source control A1 to timeline track A3

9. Now, with source V1.1 assigned to V1.2 and A1 assigned to A3, press F10 to overwrite the marked portion of the clip in the source viewer so that the in point aligns with the playhead's focus (see Figure 7.4).

F I G U R E 7 . 4 Editing a superimposed clip into the sequence

Now that this clip is in place, it's time to turn it into a floating video window.

Using the 2D Transform Effect

If you click the FX button at the upper-left corner of the FX ribbon (you may have to click the FX tab at the upper-left corner of the timeline area to see it), you can see the many timeline effects that are available for you to apply to clips in your edit. Smoke 2015 adds many more timeline effects than there were in previous versions of Smoke, and many of them work differently than their equivalents in previous versions. In this exercise, you'll start out by using the 2D Transform tool, which is a multipurpose transform tool that has options for both 2D and 3D transforms and stabilizing. In the following exercises, you'll use this tool to resize and reposition the clip of the man to appear as a video window.

1. Move the positioner so that it intersects the clip you edited into track V1.2, select it, and then click the FX ➤ 2D Transform button in the FX Ribbon.

   The FX Ribbon immediately updates with a 2D Transform box that appears to the right of the default Format Options and Pre-Processing boxes, and an arrow points down from the 2D Transform box to a row that contains the default Axis subset of 2D Transform parameters. These are useful for altering the position, scale, and rotation of the clip and changing which filter these transform operations is used to process. You'll start by using these controls.

2. Using the FX Ribbon controls, drag the Scale X parameter to the left to shrink the clip to a value of approximately 60. (The Scale Y parameter is automatically locked to the same value.)

   As soon as you make this adjustment, you'll notice that the shrunken image is not composited against the lower clip; it's surrounded by black. What gives? It turns out that in order to see a clip composited against other clips, you need to take an additional step.

3. Click the Comp box at the top left of the FX Ribbon to select it (see Figure 7.5), then click its On button to enable it. The Comp effect, which always appears at the end of the string of timeline effects that you apply in the FX Ribbon, is a set of controls that you can use to turn clip compositing on and off, as well as for setting different blend modes and choosing whether a composite is premultiplied or not.

FIGURE 7.5 The Comp effect must be turned on for a superimposed clip to be composited against other clips underneath it in the timeline.

4. Select the 2D Transform box again, and then drag the Pos (position) X parameter to move the clip to the left (around -280), and drag the Pos Y parameter to move the clip up (around 100).

   As you make this adjustment, you can now see the underlying clip in track V1.1 showing through. However, you can make this composite a bit more integrated by playing with transparency.

5. Select the Comp box again, choose Screen from the Blend Mode pop-up menu, and drag the Transparency parameter to the right so that it's about 20 percent.

   At this point, the image should appear something like Figure 7.6. Play through the clip and see how it looks.

FIGURE 7.6 The repositioned and rescaled superimposition

The transform and compositing bring the clip of the man into the scene by making room for the woman's over-the-shoulder position, but while the result is acceptable for a very rough cut, you can do better using the 2D Transform editor.

6. Select the 2D Transform button and click the Editor button on the FX Ribbon to enter the 2D Transform editor. Once again, the composited effect disappears, and the currently selected clip is surrounded by black. In order to see your full composite within any effect's editor, you need to click the View pop-up at the bottom left corner of the editor, and choose Context ➤ Primary Track from the menu. Once this is done, the full composite should appear.

7. Choose Fit (if necessary) from the Zoom pop-up menu to fit the entire available area of the frame into the viewer. At first, the 2D Transform editor's viewer is showing the low-contrast look of the log media.

8. Click View (see Figure 7.7) to display the View controls, and then choose Logarithmic from the Image Data Type menu to set the viewer to display the clip in Log mode. When that's done, click View again to return to the main 2D Transform editor controls.

FIGURE 7.7 The viewer controls in the 2D Transform editor contain the Zoom control, the Tool pop-up, and access to the Grid, View, and Pan/Tilt controls.

There are several sets of parameters in an effect editor's viewer that you view by clicking a button and dismiss by clicking the same button again to turn them off. These include Grid, View, Setup, and Animation.

Now that you can see what you're doing, it's time to make a few more adjustments to marry this clip more convincingly into the scene. Despite its name, the 2D Transform editor actually lets you work in a "2.5D" compositing environment, so long as the Transform Type control is set to Perspective (to the left of the transform parameters).

9. Drag the Y rotation control to the right to tilt the image in about 12 degrees. Once the Y rotation control has been altered, you can see an onscreen rotation control in the viewer that exposes all three axes of rotation (see Figure 7.8). Try adjusting the clip's rotation with this control so that the X rotation is about 5 degrees and the Y rotation is about 15 degrees.

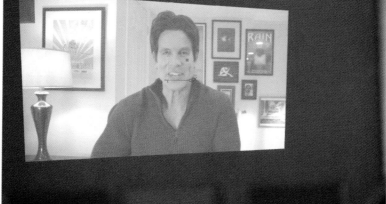

FIGURE 7.8 The transformed picture-in-picture effect

10. With the screen tilted in, it now seems a bit close to the left edge, so drag the X position parameter to the right so that the X position is about –191. Notice that adjusting the position exposes the onscreen position control, which you can also use to reposition this layer.

11. Play through what you've done so far to see how much more integrated this clip is to the rest of the scene.

    There's more to be done, but when you get to the end of the clip you're compositing over at present, the next clip appears, for which the current effect is completely unsuited. You need to fix this before moving on.

12. Click Exit to go back to the timeline.

13. Press Control+down-arrow key to move the positioner to the next transition or edit point in the timeline on any track.

14. With the positioner at the in point of the next clip in the sequence and the focus over the superimposed clip, press Control+V to add an edit to the superimposed clip. This automatically adds a cut to both the video and audio when the Link button is enabled (see Figure 7.9).

> Just pressing the up- or down-arrow key moves the positioner to the next edit point on the track at the position of the focus. Pressing Control+up- or down-arrow key jumps the positioner among all edit points on all tracks.

FIGURE 7.9 Adding an edit to a clip using Control+V

15. Now click the vertical scroll bar and drag to the left to make every track in the timeline taller. Keep dragging until the tracks are tall enough for you to see the dark gray TR (transform) proxies attached to the superimposed clips; a CO (comp) proxy should be visible on the first clip, but is hidden on the second because it's too narrow (see Figure 7.10).

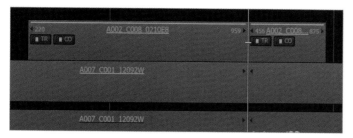

FIGURE 7.10 Taller timeline tracks reveal the 2D Transform effect proxy that lets you copy and delete timeline effects.

16. Drag the TR proxy from the second superimposed clip down to the bottom of the display until you see a little trash can cursor (see Figure 7.11) to delete it. With it gone, the CO proxy should appear.

FIGURE 7.11 Deleting an effects proxy from the timeline

Alternately, you can right-click the 2D Transform box in the FX Ribbon, and choose Delete to remove the currently selected timeline effect, or you can Option+click a timeline effect's button in the FX Ribbon to delete that effect.

At this point, the clip looks like a video window, but it doesn't move along with the camera motion of the scene. Although the 2D Transform node is great for making simple scale, pan/tilt, and rotation adjustments, and while it *can* do stabilization to steady a wiggly shot (via the controls in the Stabilization tab), it can't do match-moving. Fortunately, there's another effect you can use to accomplish this.

Stabilization and Motion Tracking

To convincingly make our floating video window match the wandering camera movement of this scene, you'll need to use the transform and tracking controls of the Action effect.

1. Select the first clip in track V1.1 again, Option+click the 2D Transform effect you'd originally applied to delete it, and then click the FX ➤ Action button in the FX Ribbon.

The FX Ribbon updates with an Action effect, which is a multipurpose effect that lets you create 2D and 3D transforms, do match-move operations, create sophisticated digital relighting composites within a 3D environment, add 3D text, create lens flares, and composite using advanced keying features (which you'll see later in this lesson), all with a single effect.

While the FX Ribbon shows you a simple subset of Action parameters that you can adjust, the full power of Action must be harnessed within the Action editor.

2. Turn off the Comp effect at the right of the top row of FX Ribbon controls. The Action node has its own control for enabling compositing, found at the right of the bottom row of controls, labeled Use Back. When using the Action node, you need to turn on Use Back to enable this clip to be composited against lower clips on the timeline. You'll lose the screen effect you had before, but the Action editor has a complete set of blend mode controls that you can use instead, so that's okay.

3. You've lost your video window transform, so recreate it now using the set of Axis controls found in the FX ribbon (if you don't see them, choose Axis from the third pop-up menu from the left in the bottom row). Set Pos X to –191, Pos Y to 99, Rot X to 5, Rot Y to 15, and Scale to 60 (as seen in Figure 7.12). Remember that you can click any parameter field and use the pop-up calculator to edit numerically.

FIGURE 7.12 The FX Ribbon after replacing the 2D Transform effect with the Action effect

4. With that accomplished, click the Editor button at the left of the FX Ribbon, or double-click the Action box found in the upper row of the FX Ribbon.

By default, the Action editor appears, showing the contents of the Action Bin, which are a series of nodes you can connect together to create various effects. The Action editor encompasses an incredibly deep amount of functionality, of which this chapter merely scratches the surface.

To give you a simple overview, the controls at this top level of the Action editor (seen in Figure 7.13) are organized in a left-to-right fashion, with each successive column of buttons exposing different sets of controls. The buttons all the way at the left expose alternate controls for setting up your environment:

FIGURE 7.13 The top level controls of the Action editor

Setup   For choosing preferences

Animation   The keyframe and curve editor

Priority   A list for determining which clips are on top and which are at the bottom for compositing.

The next row of buttons to the right select different sets of primary Action controls:

The Action Bin   For choosing Action effects nodes

Media   For accessing each clip's main keying and compositing controls

Object   The Action editor's transform and tracking controls that you used previously

Source   Controls affecting motion blur

Output   Controls over stereo rendering and other image rendering controls

Analyzer   Other advanced tools

5. Before doing anything else, set the Viewer to Log so you can see things closer to the way the clips are supposed to look. Each effect's editor has independent Viewport settings, so moving from one effect to another means you have to set things back up to the way you want them to be.

Using the Action Schematic

The Action Schematic is a node-based effects tool that lets you expand what's possible within the Action editor. The schematic is designed to let you connect multiple nodes to one or more images, with each node applying individual operations to the scene such as digital lighting effects, 3D transformations, or the creation of 3D text objects. When you add a series of operations together, you can create some very sophisticated effects.

   Axis nodes, in particular, let you transform images in different ways, and you can combine multiple Axis nodes in order to use a simple X, Y position adjustment in one Axis node to alter a motion track performed in another Axis node.

6. Click the View button to open the View controls that let you customize the editor Viewport (seen in Figure 7.14), and then choose 2-Up from the Layout controls at the bottom. This splits the Viewport into two halves. Click View again to go back to the Object controls.

FIGURE 7.14   The View controls let you adjust how the Viewport is configured.

7. With the left Viewport selected and highlighted in white, find the View pop-up menu at the bottom left of the interface (not to be confused with the View button you just used). Click it and choose Action Schematic from the menu.

   This exposes the Action Schematic, which is a vital yet often hidden set of controls in Smoke that lets you do a variety of compositing tasks including transforms, digital relighting, lens flare effects, 3D Text, and many other powerful effects. For simple effects, it's often not necessary and so it's hidden by default. However, by opening it up, you've positioned yourself to exercise more control over this transformation.

For now, you should notice that the axis1 tab over the transform parameters corresponds to an Axis node named axis1 in the Action Schematic (seen in Figure 7.15). This is because all of the parameters found in the Object page of controls correspond to the Axis node in the schematic. This Axis node holds the position and rotation data you set up on the timeline controls.

FIGURE 7.15 The axis1 node in the Action Schematic corresponds to the axis1 tab of the Object controls in the Action editor.

8. Click the Action Bin button to expose the Action Bin, which contains nodes that you can use within the Action Schematic to create different effects.

9. Drag an Axis node from the Node Bin to the Action Schematic, and then drag a connection line from the middle edge of the axis2 node onto the axis1 node. They should end up connected, with an arrow pointing towards the axis1 node (see Figure 7.16).

10. Double-click the axis2 node, and the Object controls reappear, this time with an axis2 tab, showing that you're now adjusting the axis2 controls.

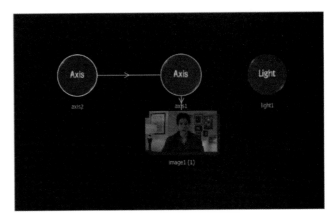

FIGURE 7.16 Connecting a second Axis node to the first one in the schematic

11. Click the Object button to open up the axis, tracking, and blending controls for Axis 2. This one page of controls will let you accomplish everything you need to do to create this effect.

12. Move the positioner all the way to the left of the Timebar, then check that the pop-up menu underneath the Stabilizer button is set to Track, and click the Stabilizer button to open the stabilization controls (see Figure 7.17).

FIGURE 7.17
The Stabilizer button

Your view is now set back to 1-Up inside the Stabilizer. The entire bottom of the interface now contains the stabilization controls, which you can use either to track a feature for match-moving or to motion-stabilize the current clip to eliminate unwanted motion, depending on the setting of the pop-up menu underneath the Stabilizer button that you checked in step 12.

In this case, you'll be match-moving the current clip of the man in the floating window to follow along with the dynamic camera motion of the background clip in track V1.1. When you're using the Axis stabilization controls, whichever clip is in the next-lower track of the timeline is the one you'll be tracking, which makes sense in most compositing situations.

13. Choose Fit from the Zoom pop-up menu so that you can see the entire frame. Since the image in the Viewport is being shown too lightly, click the View button, choose Logarithmic from the Image Data Type menu, and then click View again to go back to the stabilization controls.

14. Drag the tracking box in the viewer down so that it's over the left corner of the middle chair against the far wall (see Figure 7.18). This feature is out of focus. When tracking, you typically want to choose a clear, high-contrast feature. In this case, however, beggars can't be choosers, since camera and subject movement obscure the only other possible tracking features in this clip.

In this example, you're using only a single tracker, but it's possible to use two trackers to track rotation as well as position by clicking the Tracker 2 button to reveal the second tracker and its controls.

FIGURE 7.18 Positioning the tracking box

15. After you've positioned the tracking box, check that the Direction pop-up menu to the right of the Analyze button reads Forward, and click the Analyze button.

16. Watch as the box tracks the out-of-focus chair back, but as soon as the tracker loses its way and starts wandering across the screen (and it will), click the mouse to stop the track.

Tracking went well for a while, but the focus must have gone just a little too soft and the tracker lost the feature.

17. Click the Reset button at the bottom right, and then click Confirm when prompted.

    Sometimes, starting from the beginning of a clip makes it hard to find a feature that will track accurately. Fortunately, you have the option to track in reverse.

18. Click the Direction button (to the right of the Analyze button) so that it reads Backward; then move the positioner all the way to the end of the scrubber bar and drag the tracking box to the left corner of the right-most chair against the wall, which is now in slightly better focus (see Figure 7.19). Click Analyze.

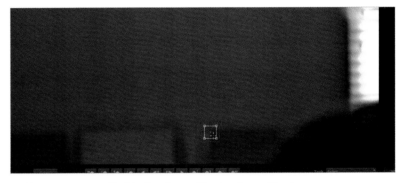

F I G U R E   7 . 1 9   Positioning the tracking box for tracking in reverse

19. Watch the track carefully, because one of two things will happen depending on exactly how you positioned the tracker in the viewer. Either (a) the track will lose its way just before the woman's arm comes up, or (b) the woman's arm will come up and occlude the tracked feature, knocking the tracker off to one side. In any event, as soon as this happens, click the mouse to stop the track.

    In either case, this is not an altogether uncommon problem to have, and there's an easy method for switching features mid-track that you can use to rescue the situation.

20. Move the positioner back to the last frame where the track was accurate. In the tools pop-up menu select Offset Reference (Figure 7.20). Press and hold Shift+Ctrl and move the Reference box to drag the tracker to the original feature you wanted to track, the left corner of the middle chair back. A dotted white line should be seen connecting the last good track position and the new reference location.

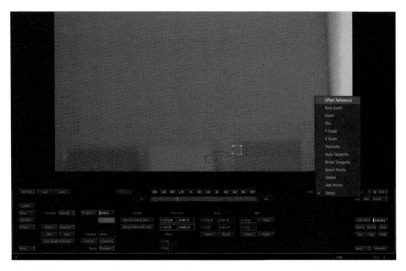

F I G U R E   7 . 2 0   Using the Offset Reference control to change the feature you're tracking mid-track when a feature becomes obscured

21. Click Analyze, and you should notice that while the red tracker is following the new feature you chose, the motion path being constructed by all of the tracking points in the viewer continues from where it left off, with the result being a smooth, continuous motion track following the motion of the camera.

    If the tracking area you chose doesn't work very well, you can always drag the positioner back to the last accurate frame of tracking, choose Offset Reference again, reposition the tracking box again, and click Analyze to see if you have better luck. You can do this as many times as you need to until you get a good track.

22. When you're finished, click the Return button.

    Now that you've returned to the main Axis controls, you can see that you've got a problem. The motion tracking you did has overwritten the transform you created to create the floating window effect. If you play through the clip, you can see that while the video window is now moving along with the underlying clip, the position has been changed to match the tracker so that it's now at the bottom of the screen. You need to offset this.

23. Select Axis 1 from the schematic and reveal its Object menu. You can now reposition the screen back in place where you had it originally in the upper-left of the screen. You will notice that the image is now

tracking with the scene underneath and, with the Offset Axis in place, you can adjust the image in the shot without affecting the track data, since it is being performed on the parent Axis 2 (Figure 7.21).

FIGURE 7.21 The almost-final floating window effect

24. To add the final touch, either double-click the image1 node (the node with the thumbnail of the clip) or click the image1 tab in the Object controls to expose the Blending and Surface controls.

25. Choose Screen from the Blend pop-up, and set the Transparency control to 19 percent.

26. Click the Exit button to return to the timeline, and play through the clip to view the final effect.

The floating window in which the man's message plays should now follow along with the camera's motion perfectly, providing a convincing temporary composite that will work until the final composite is created later.

Editing and Keying a Superimposed Greenscreen Clip

In the next exercise, you'll use the Modular Keyer in the Action Effect to do a temporary greenscreen composite in order to determine the range of media in a background plate that you want to accompany this clip in the final composite. After all, you can't really start compositing until you know which parts of what clips you want to use together.

1. Make sure the Link button is turned on, press R to choose Trim mode, and drag the end of the very last clip to the right until the woman pauses what she's doing and starts to turn to her right, camera left (see Figure 7.22). Cut the clip midway through her head turn (around frame 755 according to the clip out point frame count shown in the timeline). Press A to choose Select mode when you're finished.

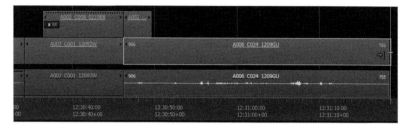

FIGURE 7.22 The new out point of the last clip

2. Press Option+2 to put the viewer into Source-Sequence mode, and open the clip noted 01_G_01 into the source viewer. Then play through this clip until you find a frame that matches the action of the woman in the previous clip (17:19:58+00), and mark an in point. Then play forward until you hear the director read the line "Surprised?" and mark an out point just afterward (frame 17:20:04+23).

3. Click the Timeline Layout button at the bottom-right corner of the timeline to reset the height of every track, and notice that there are now four source controls in the patch panel area.

   The source audio clip has six audio tracks, of which tracks 1 and 2 are a mixdown, track 3 is a boom microphone, and track 4 is a lavalier microphone. For simplicity, you'll be using the mixdown tracks, although you could elect to use one or the other microphone track if a particular microphone had better quality. The only reason you're seeing the additional source controls now is that there are more audio tracks in this sequence, and you'll have to deal with patching the audio source-destination controls to get the audio you want.

4. Click and drag the source controls (in green) of audio tracks A1 and A2 so that source A1 corresponds to destination track A1 and source A2 corresponds to destination track A2. Then click the destination controls (in gray) of audio tracks A3 and A4 to disconnect them from the source, as shown in Figure 7.23. Now you're set up to edit only audio into the first two tracks of the timeline.

FIGURE 7.23 Patching the source-destination controls for multiple audio tracks

5. Move the focus point of the positioner to track V1.2, and press F10 (or click the Overwrite button) to edit the source clip you've just set up into the timeline on a superimposed track. Having the greenscreen clip on track V1.2 creates a gap on track V1.1 that you'll use to place the clip that'll be showing through underneath.

   If you look at the FX Ribbon, you may notice that a Resize effect has automatically been added to this clip. This happens when the clip you're editing into a sequence either (a) has a larger frame size than that of the sequence or (b) has a different bit-depth than the sequence. In this case, the sequence was set to 10-bit processing, but the clip you've edited (encoded using Apple ProRes 4444) is a 12-bit clip, so the Resize effect was added to convert the bit-depth.

6. Select the clip noted 01_B_03 in the Media Library to open it in the source viewer, and play forward to just after the point where the woman holding the air gun says "Surprised?" (10:46:33+15).

   At this point, it's difficult to set proper in and out points because you don't know quite how the background clip will play along with the foreground clip. Fortunately, there's a keyboard modifier that you can use to sync the source and sequence positioners together while scrubbing playback using the mouse. Having both the source clip and sequence scrub together lets you easily see how they line up.

7. Press F7 to switch to the record viewer, and then press the down-arrow key to jump the record positioner to the end of the clip in the sequence.

Press F6 to select the source viewer so that the keyboard shortcuts control the source transport controls. Press F7 to select the record source viewer.

8. Now press and hold Shift+Ctrl while dragging the source positioner to the left, watching both the source and record viewers, and stop when you reach the beginning of the greenscreen clip in the timeline. At this point, press F6 to select the source viewer and press I to set an in point in the source clip.

9. Press F7 to switch to the record viewer again, and then press Page Down to move the focus point of the positioner to track V1.1. You may be wondering why you didn't just move the focus point to this track right away, so play forward through the sequence (see Figure 7.24), and notice that now the record viewer shows only black.

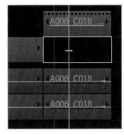

FIGURE 7.24 No video clips above the focus of the positioner are shown during playback.

The focus point does more than just determine into which track incoming clips are edited. It also lets you exclude superimposed video clips from the currently rendered composite.

10. Press the X key to mark timeline in and out points to fit the gap that intersects the positioner on track V1.1, and then press F10 (or click the Overwrite Edit button) to edit the clip of the woman in the mirror onto the timeline using a three-point edit.

Getting Started with Keying

At this point, the two main clips necessary for creating the effect of the woman's counterpart from another dimension appearing to her are roughly in place, and you can begin creating a preliminary greenscreen key, again using the Action timeline effect, so you can actually see both clips sandwiched together in order to better align the action in one with the action in the other.

1. Move the positioner to track V1.2 so that you can see the greenscreen clip in the record viewer, select the clip, and then click the FX ➤ Action button to add an Action effect to it.

   With the Action box selected in the FX Ribbon, a row of Axis controls appears, similar to those that appear when you apply a 2D Transform effect. However, with the Action effect, these controls are just the tip of the iceberg.

2. Turn on Use Back at the far right of the FX Ribbon (see Figure 7.25), in order to enable compositing with the clip below via the Action effect.

FIGURE 7.25 The Use Back button enables compositing using the Action effect.

3. Click the Editor button or double-click the clip in the timeline to open the Action editor.

   As before, the Action editor appears showing the contents of the Action Bin, which are a series of nodes you can connect together to create various effects. However, what you want to do is to create a quick and dirty greenscreen composite so you can see how the two layers will stack together. The next few steps will walk you through how to set up the Action editor for keying.

4. Click the Media button to open up the Media list, which shows you all of the media (clips) that can be effected using the controls of the Action editor.

   In this exercise, you're concerned only with the Media list, which exposes the source clip as a row in a list with cells (arranged as columns) that act as controls that let you apply keying, color correction, blur, retiming, drop shadow, and cropping to your clip. A series of pop-up menus just to the left of the Media list let you control how your media is connected to the Action editor.

5. To begin creating a key, double-click the K column corresponding to the Source clip (seen in Figure 7.26).

FIGURE 7.26 Clicking the K cell to open the Modular Keyer editor

Immediately, you can see the Modular Keyer's schematic, and a brand new bin of nodes for compositing. This is the Modular Keyer editor, which is an advanced keying environment that's useful for any keying task you might have. When you double-clicked the K cell for the source clip, the Modular Keyer editor was opened up. This means that you're now two editors deep into the Action environment. However, it's easy to get back.

6. Click the Return button at the upper-left corner of the control area.

    You are now returned to the Media list. If you click the Exit button, you'll go back to the timeline, where you can continue editing, but you're not going back just yet. Notice how the K cell you double-clicked before now contains MK, which tells you that you've enabled the Modular Keyer for that clip. Notice also that the image in the viewer is a strange blend of the front (top) and back (bottom) clips in the timeline. This is because you've added a keying effect, but you haven't set it up properly yet, so you're seeing a half-finished composite. It's now time to start putting this effect together properly.

7. Double-click the MK cell to reopen the Modular Keyer editor.

    In its current state, the Modular Keyer isn't very useful, so you'll need to customize the environment so you can begin working. You should note that everything you learn about working within the Modular Keyer will also apply later on when you begin using ConnectFX.

8. Choose 2-Up from the Viewport Layout pop-up menu at the upper-left of the control area to divide the Viewport into two regions.

9. Choose MK Schematic from the View pop-up menu all the way at the upper-right of the control area to display the default node structure you'll use to create your keying effect.

10. Double-click the *MasterK* (*Master Keyer*) node in the schematic at the left to open the keyer controls. The Master Keyer node is the heart of the Modular Keyer editor, and double-clicking this node exposes its controls along the bottom of the interface. Double-clicking any node in the schematic will open that node's particular set of controls at the bottom.

11. Next, click anywhere within the right frame of the Viewport to select it so that it's highlighted in white, and then choose Master Keyer Result from the View pop-up menu (or press F4). This shows you the state of the image as it's being output by the MasterK node. At this point, the interface is set up and ready for you to begin working (see Figure 7.27).

FIGURE 7.27   Screenshot of Modular Keyer setup

 NOTE   The Action editor will be discussed in much greater detail in Chapter 9 in the context of using it within ConnectFX. One of the advantages of using the Action node is that whatever timeline effects you create can be perfectly converted into ConnectFX node trees for more detailed effects work later on.

The node tree shown in the schematic at left displays a pre-made set of operations that constitute the most common tools for creating a key in Smoke.

Each node is an individual compositing operation, and they act upon the image one at a time from left to right. The Front, Back, and Key In nodes at the far left represent the clips in the timeline; the Front and Key In nodes represent the current clip you're working on, and Back represents all clips underneath the current one in the timeline. You should notice that the Back node is also attached to the green Back input of the Result node.

These all connect to the red "front," the green "back," and the blue "matte" inputs at the left of the MasterK node, which is the heart of this entire operation. The Master Keyer node, within the Modular Keyer environment, is the most powerful and flexible keyer in Smoke. Unlike some channel keyers, which are specifically engineered for keying out blue or green, the Master Keyer is useful for keying any hue to turn it into a region of image transparency.

The MasterK node's blue "matteOut" output is connected to a set of three nodes connected one after the other below: the 2D Histo (histogram), Matte Edge, and GMask nodes. These three nodes are set up to let you make further alterations to the key being generated by the MasterK node, adjusting its contrast, altering it with Matte Edge tools, and using a garbage mask to refine the resulting matte that will define transparency in the final composite (in this exercise you'll only use the Matte Edge node).

The MasterK node's yellow "result" output is then connected to the red "front" input of the Result node. The Result node represents the final result of the keying operation you're creating in the Modular Keyer editor, and combines the red front image with the green back image using the connected matte image. Since the MasterK node does spill suppression (to eliminate green fringing) in addition to creating a matte, connecting its "result" output to the Result node means that you'll be using the automatically spill-suppressed version of the image in the final effect.

Pulling a Greenscreen Key

Since everything is already set up for you in advance, all you need to do to get started using the Master Keyer is to sample the image using the two color pots shown in Figure 7.28.

FIGURE 7.28 The primary
and secondary color pots

1. Move the positioner all the way to the left of the Timebar, then click the left Key Colours color pot; then position the sample cursor over the greenscreen to the right of the hair at the woman's shoulder and drag over a small portion of green to sample the greenscreen (see Figure 7.29). The color pots both turn green to show which color you've sampled, and the Spill control also turns green to show which color is automatically being suppressed in the image in order to eliminate any possible fringing.

FIGURE 7.29 Sampling the first region of the greenscreen

You could continue working to refine this key using the Front CC selection of the Result Output pop-up menu (showing you the RGB image), but it's probably easier for you to work on the matte by viewing it directly.

2. Choose OutMatte from the Result Output pop-up menu to the right in the MasterK controls. Alternately, you can leave the Result Output pop-up set to Front CC, and press F4 to toggle the left Viewport pane between the Result and the OutMatte.

A grayscale image of the OutMatte takes the place of the color image, and you can see that the green portion of the background immediately turns black (representing areas of transparency), but the initial key is so broad that parts of the woman's face and the background of the image that should be white (representing solid areas of the image) are being affected, so this result needs to be refined.

3. Click the highlight of the woman's right cheek (camera left); three sliders appear (see Figure 7.30). If only two sliders appear, then click in the gray area outside the viewer to dismiss them and try sampling a different area of her left cheek.

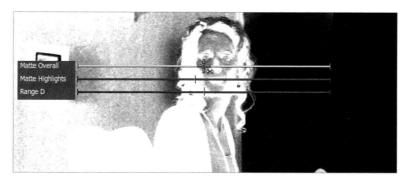

FIGURE 7.30   Sample adjustment sliders for fine-tuning the matte

Holding the Option key down while moving the pointer over an image being keyed with the Master Keyer dynamically shows whichever matte adjustment sliders are available to manipulate that region of the key.

These are matte adjustment sliders, and which sliders appear depends on the part of the key you clicked. The Master Keyer is smart enough to display contextually only the sliders that will help you to refine the region of the key that you clicked, so clicking on the woman's cheek shows you the three sliders that will adjust that area of the matte — Matte Overall, Matte Highlights, and Range D.

The topmost sliders are always the ones that have the greatest effect on the matte, while sliders closer to the bottom have decreasing influence and are typically used to refine small details. The Matte sliders (Overall, Highlights, and Shadow) adjust the entire matte, whereas the Range sliders (A, B, C, D, and E) adjust very specific areas of the matte. The best way to get the hang of these controls is to play with them.

4. Drag the Matte Overall slider to the left until the woman's face and the wall behind her are opaque, but there is still plenty of transparency among her strands of hair. There will be unwanted transparency in the hair on top of her head, around a picture frame on the wall, and you'll start to lose transparency in the greenscreen, but that's okay. You can't do everything with one slider. A solid wall is the most important part of this adjustment.

5. Drag the Matte Highlights slider to the left until the hair on the top of the woman's head is completely opaque. You'll lose some more transparency in the greenscreen area, but again, that's okay. These sliders work one step at a time.

6. Drag the Range D slider to the left until the lightest strands of the woman's hair over the greenscreen become a bit more solid. The end result of the last three adjustments should resemble Figure 7.31.

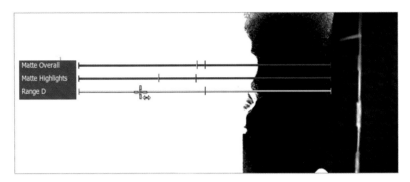

FIGURE 7.31 First refinements of the greenscreen key

Each of the matte adjustment sliders works similarly: pulling the slider to the left makes that region more opaque, while pulling the slider to the right makes that region more transparent. At this point, you should be able to see that the solid regions of the matte look pretty good, but the transparent area is looking a little ragged, lacking a clean, continuous black area of transparency.

Because this scene was shot in a hurry, the lighting crew wasn't given enough time to hang and light a truly seamless greenscreen. As a result, the values of green are all over the place, so a single sample is unlikely to do the job. Since this is the reality more often than not, there are Patch controls available using the Sampling pop-up that let you sample additional areas of the image to improve the matte. A good place to start adding patch samples is any area of the matte where adding a garbage mask would be inconvenient; examples include areas close to her hair or around her moving arm and hand. After all, there's no point killing yourself to fine-tune an area of a matte that you can easily crop out with a simple shape.

7. Choose Patch1 from the Sampling pop-up menu at the right of the Key Colours patch controls, and then click and drag over the gray opaque area within the crook of her elbow. The Patch1 button next to the Range and Soft fields should light up, and if the pop-up menu to the right says "Analysis," click it and choose Black instead to make sure that the Patch1 sample is being used to add transparency (see Figure 7.32).

FIGURE 7.32 Adding to the matte using the Patch controls

8. While Patch1 is selected, you can continue sampling more parts of the greenscreen; drag two or three times above her arm and within the gray opaque areas of the doorway next to her head, and just at the upper-camera left corner of the doorway. Eventually, you should be left with only a minimum of solid fringing on the greenscreen immediately surrounding her head and arm, as shown in Figure 7.33.

FIGURE 7.33 The matte after refinement using the Patch1 controls

9. There's still a gray area corresponding to a portion of the greenscreen on the back wall around her hand, and it appears to have a distinct range of color, so choose Patch2 from the Sampling pop-up menu, and drag around the light gray area (not the tape, which turned yellow in the light and so is now hard to key). After several drags, you're probably close to eliminating this light-gray area of the matte, but still not quite there. Fortunately, there's another control you can use.

10. Drag the Range parameter to the right of the Patch2 button to the right to further eliminate the remainder of the fringing on the wall (a value somewhere around 1.81 may do the job).

    Each Patch control has range and softness sliders that let you adjust their influence on the overall matte. Furthermore, each set of patch samples can be individually refined and turned on and off, so organizing additional refinements that you're not sure will work into a separate patch is a good idea, because you can always resample or turn the patch off if it doesn't work out.

11. At this point, there's just that tape on the wall. Choose Patch3 from the Sampling pop-up menu, and drag right on top of the tape to sample it. It'll likely take several drags, but once there are just a few bits of tape left on the wall, drag the Patch3 Range parameter (to the right of the Patch3 button) to the right until you strike a good balance between eliminating the tape and retaining the edge detail of the woman's hair. If necessary, you can also drag the Soft parameter to the left to eliminate any last bits of the tape intruding into the matte.

12. Now it's time for one last bit of refinement. Choose Matte from the Sampling pop-up menu, and then hold down the Option key and hover the mouse over where her hair passes in front of the greenscreen until you see the Matte Overall, Matte Shadows, Range B, and Range D sliders. Adjust these sliders to either the left or right until you feel that you've struck a good balance between the translucence beside each lock of hair and the solidity of the individual strands. Unfortunately, you'll find that the better her hair looks, the more of that tape on the wall will intrude back into the matte.

13. Before you move on, be sure to set the Result Output pop-up to Front CC, to make sure that the composite will be correctly assembled.

    At the end of this process, you'll still have some holes on the desk, but don't worry about those now. For now, here's one last matte refinement technique before we go.

14. Click the Matte Edge node in the schematic to expose its controls (seen in Figure 7.34), and then click the right side of the Viewport and choose Matte Edge Result from the View pop-up. This lets you see the matte you want to work on.

While refining a matte using the Matte and Range sliders, it's always a good idea to take a look at the matte itself. It can be easier to spot and fix holes using the Matte and Range sliders in Matte view. Press F4 to go back to viewing the result.

▶

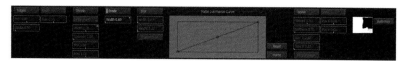

FIGURE 7.34 The Matte Edge controls

15. Click the Erode button to enable the Width parameter, and drag Width to the right to see its effect on the Matte. The Matte Edge node has several categories of matte adjustments that you can apply. If you like, you can experiment with the Erode, Edges, Shrink, and Blur parameters by turning on the category you want to work with and manipulating the parameters underneath.

    Feel free to continue experimenting with and refining this matte, but at this point you should have a good enough key for compositing the two clips that will be going together to make an editorial decision. We'll revisit more advanced keying techniques in Chapter 9.

16. Click the Return button to get back to the main Action controls, and then click the Exit button to go back to the timeline. Now you can see the clip in track V1.1 showing through, but it's completely misaligned and will require some adjustment to fit correctly.

17. Select the background clip in track V1.1 of the timeline, and click the FX ➤ 2D Transform button to add a 2D Transform control. You'll be able to make all of the adjustments you need from the FX Ribbon above the timeline.

    One of the reasons the background clip is so puzzlingly off is that a mirror was used to extend the distance of the actor from the camera on a relatively small stage. This was done in order to match the distance that an actual duplicate of the actress standing in the next room would be from the camera in order to make the composite simpler. However, you need to reverse the image because of the mirror's reflection.

18. Move the positioner near the end of the clip, and click the lock button next to the two scale parameters to turn it off. Then click the Scale X parameter, use the Calculator to enter -100, and click Enter. The image should be reversed, with the duplicate holding a dart gun aimed at the seated woman.

19. In the final shot, you'll want to see more of the lab showing through the dimensional doorway, so drag the Position X slider to the right to slide the background over until the podium is just peeking through. Then drag the Position Y control to the right to raise the background plate a bit, cheating the shot to make the alternate more visible. At this point, the result should look something like Figure 7.35.

FIGURE 7.35 The finished temporary composite

20. The resulting composite in the timeline is likely too processor-intensive to play in real time on your computer. So, with the background clip selected, click the Render button in the FX Ribbon, and when the progress bar finishes, play through the clip to enjoy your hard work.

Clearly this isn't the final effect; the "doorway" effect hasn't yet been built, the foreground plate has a magenta tinge because of the aggressive spill suppression, and the desk needs some work, but you and your test viewers will certainly know what's going on, and if the result needs trimming, you can use the Slip tool to change the timing of the duplicate with the dart gun in relation to the seated woman's reaction. On the other hand, you've pulled a really good key that you'll be able to use later in the final composite.

THE ESSENTIALS AND BEYOND

As you've seen, the Action timeline effect encompasses a wide range of sophisticated compositing tools, many of which are shared with the more in-depth ConnectFX compositing environment you'll see in the next chapter. For this reason, although you've used Action in this chapter to create temporary effects while you edit, there are many situations where you can create finished effects right in the timeline.

ADDITIONAL EXERCISES

▶ In this chapter, you created a picture-in-picture effect for the first portion of the superimposed video chat clip that corresponds to the fifth clip in the timeline. Now use the same techniques to integrate the last portion of the superimposed clip (in which the man concludes his message) with the sixth clip.

▶ The beginning and ending of the superimposed picture-in-picture effect come up abruptly, so add transitions to the beginning of the first superimposed clip and the end of the last superimposed clip in order to bring the "floating video window" into and out of the frame.

▶ In the fifth clip, the woman raises her fingers to play the video on the floating window, but the superimposed clip appears to be in front, rather than behind where it's supposed to be. Edit a duplicate of the fifth clip into a new track on top of the superimposed clip of the man, add an Action effect to it, and use the Modular Keyer to turn the wall in the distance transparent, while leaving the woman's hand and arm solid, so that her hand appears to pass in front of the floating window.

CHAPTER 8

Introduction to ConnectFX

In this chapter, you'll create your first simple composite using ConnectFX, the powerful node-based compositing tool integrated tightly within Autodesk® Smoke® software. When you need to do something more complicated than what can be easily accomplished using timeline effects, ConnectFX (CFX) provides an environment within which you can create intricately detailed multilevel composites. In addition, there are many more effects tools available within the CFX editor that you can use to fix problems and create visual magic.

Topics in this chapter include the following:

▶ **Applying ConnectFX to a clip**

▶ **Understanding the CFX editor**

▶ **Looping and extending clips using the MUX node**

▶ **Dealing with log-encoded media in CFX**

▶ **Assembling a process tree**

▶ **Match-moving with the 2D Transform node**

▶ **Rotoscoping with the GMask node**

▶ **Changing the Blend mode and adding blur**

Applying ConnectFX to a Clip

In this section, you'll take the first step toward putting together a composite using ConnectFX. You will accomplish this by editing together the principal clips you want to use onto the timeline and then sending all of them to the ConnectFX editor as the starting point of your node tree:

1. Launch Smoke, and open the Opening Scene sequence that you worked on in Chapter 7.

2. Before you do anything else, delete the two transitions that are on either side of the third clip in the timeline since these will interfere with this exercise. You'll put these back in later.

3. Press Option+2 to put the viewer into Source-Sequence mode, and then select the EyeInterface clip to open it in the source viewer, as shown in Figure 8.1. (It should be in the Opening Graphics Elements folder of the Office Media folder inside the Office Scene Library.)

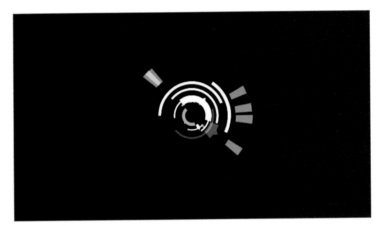

F I G U R E   8 . 1 The EyeInterface clip that you'll be using to create an animated contact lens effect

Source: Design and animation by Brian Olsen at Splice Here

4. Play through the EyeInterface clip from the beginning, and you'll notice that the graphic zooms up from nothing. Mark an in point at the first frame where the graphic is at its full size (00:00:00+14).

5. Move the positioner in the timeline to intersect the third clip, make sure the positioner focus is on track V1.1, and then press X to set in and out points to match the third clip. Remember, you can move the focus up and down by dragging it directly in the timeline, by clicking the video track indicator button all the way to the right in the timeline patch panel area, or by pressing Page Up or Page Down.

6. Press Page Up to move the focus to track V1.2, and press F10 (or click the Overwrite Edit button) to edit the `EyeInterface` clip into clip V1.2. It's not long enough to cover the entire duration of the third clip, but that's OK; you'll deal with this later.

7. Now Shift+click both the third clip in track V1.1 and the superimposed clip you just edited into the timeline to select them both. Then click the FX button to open the pop-out Video Effects menu, make sure that the Selection As Flowgraph check box is checked, and click the Create ConnectFX button.

  The ConnectFX editor opens, and the two clips you selected appear within, automatically assembled into a node tree within the ConnectFX Schematic that creates a simple composite that's equivalent to what was in the timeline. This tree can be seen in Figure 8.2.

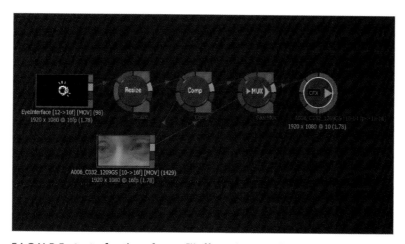

FIGURE 8.2 Creating a ConnectFX effect using two selected clips in the timeline

In the following sections, you'll use these two clips to create the effect of the animated contact lenses, which provide a heads-up computer display for this character throughout the rest of the movie.

Understanding the CFX Editor

The ConnectFX editor is divided into several sections, some of which were briefly discussed in Chapter 2. In this section, you'll get a more detailed view of the different areas of the CFX editor that you'll be using to create and refine effects in Smoke.

The Viewport

By default, the Viewport at the top contains the ConnectFX Schematic on the left and a viewer on the right that shows the CFX output result. Both of these are within a 2-Up display. You can drag any border between each viewer in the display to resize it. For example, dragging the border shown here lets you create more room for nodes at the expense of shrinking the viewer (see Figure 8.3).

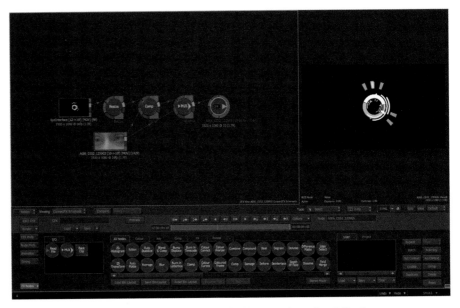

FIGURE 8.3   The ConnectFX Schematic and CFX output viewer in a 2-Up view

The Viewport Layout pop-up menu at the bottom-right of the Viewport lets you choose from several multi-pane layouts (see Figure 8.4).

> The same keyboard shortcuts that let you choose different viewer layouts also let you choose different Viewport layouts in the CFX editor. Option+1 through Option+4 let you choose the 1-, 2-, 3-, and 4-Up layouts.

FIGURE 8.4   Different options available for the Viewport

You can alter the contents of any pane by clicking within it to select it and then choosing another option from the View pop-up menu that's at the bottom-left of the Viewport. An accompanying zoom control lets you resize the currently selected pane. If you're creating a complex node tree or doing 3D compositing, it can help to have multiple schematics and viewers showing different angles of the composition, but the exercise in this chapter can be easily accomplished using the default 2-Up view.

FX Node Bins

Underneath the Viewport are the FX node bins (see Figure 8.5), which contain every type of node that's available for doing compositing and effects work. The first tab contains every single node that's available for use in the ConnectFX Schematic, but other tabs expose subsets of these nodes that are specific for a particular use.

FIGURE 8.5   The ConnectFX nodes

If anything else is being displayed at the bottom of the CFX editor, you can always show the FX nodes again by clicking the FX Nodes button underneath the Viewport to turn it back on. Turning it off reveals the parameters of the currently selected node in the ConnectFX or Action Schematic.

The I/O Node Tab

The I/O tab to the left of the node bins, shown in Figure 8.6, contains three types of nodes, each of which serves a very different purpose.

FIGURE 8.6   The I/O node bin

> Create your own tab containing a custom subset of nodes by clicking the + button at the right of the existing tabs; you are immediately prompted to name the tab. Drag whatever nodes you want to add to it from other tabs onto the tab you created.

These nodes are special in that they provide the source of the image-processing pipeline described by the node tree of the ConnectFX Schematic. Following is a description of each node:

Read File   *Read File nodes* add clips to the CFX processing pipeline directly from the filesystem, not from the Media Library like typical clip nodes that are created when you select clips in the timeline to create CFX. Because Read File node clips reference files in the Finder directly, overwriting files in the Finder results in those clips being automatically updated within your CFX composite, which makes it easier to build composites that use media generated by other applications that might get updated frequently, such as 3D renders going through multiple iterations. Clips that you add to a CFX composite from the Media Library are clip nodes, and they reference the linked media that you've imported into Smoke, which cannot be overwritten in this way without permanently damaging your Smoke database.

MUX   Adding a *MUX node* to a clip node lets you create freeze frames, and provides options to extend the beginning and end of clips using either freeze frames or ping pong looping (which you'll use in the next exercise). The MUX node can also switch between multiple inputs as a cut or a dissolve.

Back Clip   Adding a *Back Clip node* to the beginning of a node tree provides a way of dynamically reading in whatever clips are in the timeline underneath the current ConnectFX clip's composite. This is useful if you know the clips in video tracks underneath your CFX clip are going to change or be re-edited and you want those changes to automatically be included in the current composite. The Back Clip node is also essential when you're applying ConnectFX to a gap as an *adjustment segment* that works as an otherwise blank layer that applies its adjustment to all clips falling underneath it. (Some applications refer to this as an adjustment layer.) You'll learn more about adjustment segments in Chapter 11.

> You can double-click any Read File node that's currently selected in the ConnectFX Schematic to relink it if it's disconnected or to choose a completely different clip for that node to read into the composite.

Node Parameter Editor

The bottom area of the CFX editor changes based on the node you've selected within the ConnectFX or Action Schematic. For example, if you double-click the Resize node, you'll see the parameters shown in Figure 8.7.

FIGURE 8.7 The Parameter editor

Additionally, a row of buttons at the left of this area (see Figure 8.8) lets you expose different editors that can be used to alter other aspects of your composited effect.

FIGURE 8.8
Buttons that let you
open additional CFX
editors

To access any of these additional sets of controls, click the corresponding button to turn it on. To go back to displaying the node parameters of the currently selected node or the FX node bins, click that button again to turn it off.

CFX Prefs and Node Prefs

The *CFX Prefs button* provides access to Rendering settings for enabling proxies and hardware acceleration, environmental preferences governing which panes of the Viewport output audio, and the operation of schematics.

The *Node Prefs button* gives you access to the operational preferences of nodes, such as the Action node, that have them. For example, when an Action node is selected, you have access to the resolution and bit depth of that Action node's internal compositing environment: its rendering, anti-aliasing, and motion blur settings. You also have access to node-specific preferences, as well as to adaptive degradation settings that let you specify which processor-intensive operations to disable temporarily when making interactive adjustments. For more information on Action node preferences, see Chapter 9, "Using the ConnectFX Action Node."

Animation Editor

The *Animation editor* is a curve editor that you can use to graphically edit keyframes that have been applied to different node parameters for creating animated effects.

You don't have to use the Animation editor to animate effects, because the Node Parameter editor exposes keyframing controls that let you place effect keyframes within the CFX scrubber, located underneath the transport controls.

However, if you are keyframing an effect, the Animation editor gives you a much more precise environment for making careful adjustments.

Timing Editor

Clicking the *Timing button* shows you a miniature timeline containing only the clips that are used in the current CFX composite in a stack that lets you adjust each clip's temporal offset relative to the current composite. This lets you see the current duration of the CFX composite, shown by the in and out points, as well as the overall duration of unused clip media falling outside this duration.

Additionally, you can do some simple editing using Trim mode to make individual clips shorter or longer and Slide mode to change the range of each clip's media that appears within the composite.

Looping and Extending Clips Using the MUX Node

If you play through the entire composite using the available transport controls or their keyboard equivalents, you should notice that the animated contact lens graphic cuts off near the end, leaving only the underlying close-up of the woman's eyes. You need the graphic to be the same length as the actor's close-up for this composite to work. To deal with this, you'll need to use the MUX node, found in the I/O tab, to extend its length by looping it using a ping pong operation:

1. First, drag the nodes in the ConnectFX Schematic to space them out a bit. In particular, create a space between the EyeInterface Clip node and the Resize node immediately to its right. When working, it's always a good idea to keep your nodes tidy and organized.

2. Click the FX Nodes button, if necessary, to open the node bins again.

3. Drag a MUX node out of the I/O tab and into the ConnectFX Schematic, moving it onto the red link line that connects the EyeInterface node to the Resize node, and dropping it when the line highlights in yellow as shown in Figure 8.9.

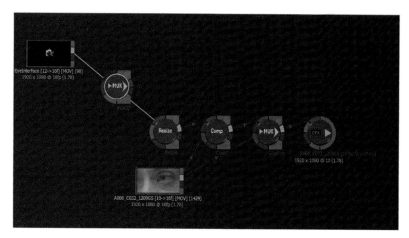

FIGURE 8.9 Connecting the MUX node to a Clip node

The node is inserted between the Clip node and the Resize node, which means that the MUX node intercepts the EyeInterface animation being read in, processes it, and feeds the result to all of the other nodes in the schematic.

4. Double-click the MUX node to expose its parameters at the bottom of the CFX editor. Turn on the Active button in the FX Range group.

   The FX Range controls let you set up whether anything appears before the beginning or after the end of the current range of image data being imported for that clip.

5. Click the left pane of the Viewport, then choose CFX Result from the View pop-up (or press 0). This lets you see the end result of the entire composite, as output by the CFX node at the end of the schematic's process tree. This is necessary to see why the next few steps are important.

6. Drag the positioner around the end of the Timebar, and you should be able to see that the EyeInterface clip ends before the end of the composite, leaving the close-up of the woman's eye. For this composite to be successful, the duration of the EyeInterface clip must match that of the underlying clip you're compositing it into.

7. Drag the positioner in the Timebar to the last frame where the EyeInterface graphic is visible. Then drag the To parameter's slider to the left, moving the out marker for the looping effect you're about to create to coincide with the last frame of the animation (this should be frame 82).

Using the From and To parameters, you can choose a specific range of media to loop using the MUX node's Before and After options.

8. Click the After pop-up menu, and choose Ping Pong. The settings should appear as they do in Figure 8.10. Now if you play through the entire range of the composite, you can see that the EyeInterface animation plays forward and, when it reaches the end, starts to play backward to cover the gap left by the end of the animation.

The second option, Ping Pong+, provides another option for playing media back and forth as a loop; it allows the last (or first) frame of a clip being looped using Ping Pong to be played twice: once as the clip plays forward, and once as the clip plays backward.

FIGURE 8.10   The MUX node's parameters

At this point, if you scrub through the timebar, you may notice that while the clip begins to loop back and forth, it suddenly switches back to the woman's eye for some reason. It turns out that the composite was created with a MUX node just before the CFX node that's attempting to preserve the gap.

9. Click the MUX node labeled "GlueMux" (each node's label appears in gray at the bottom-right corner of the node), and then press the Delete key to eliminate it. This leaves a gap, so click the yellow output of the Comp node, and then click the Red input of the CFX node to connect them together again. Now, the EyeInterface animation should play all the way through the composite.

Now that you've found a creative way of matching the duration of the graphic to that of the woman's close-up, it's time to start compositing these elements together.

Dealing with Log-Encoded Media in CFX

All of the media in this program is log-encoded, which makes the clips themselves appear to be low contrast and colorless. So far, you've dealt with this by setting the different viewers in Smoke to display in Log mode, which normalizes the image to appear as it should in the sRGB of your monitor or the Rec.709 colorspace of an external monitor connected via an AJA or Blackmagic video interface.

However, when you're compositing in ConnectFX, you'll often want to normalize the image data itself so that various processes work better. For example, you may get better results from the Stabilizer or from the Master Keyer nodes if you use them on media with higher contrast and a wider range of color. This can be set up in the clips that need it.

1. Double-click the Clip node of the woman's close-up to open its parameters at the bottom of the CFX editor.

2. Click the RGB LUT button at the left of the screen, choose Log To Lin from the Conversion LUT Type pop-up menu, as shown in Figure 8.11, and click the Active button to turn this effect on (if necessary).

FIGURE 8.11 Using the RGB LUT options in a Clip node to normalize a log-encoded clip for CFX compositing

From this point forward, the image data of the woman is not log-encoded, and you can work with it as you would any other video image. However, if the ultimate goal is to export a log-encoded version of the finished program, then you'll want to alter the settings of the CFX node that outputs this composite back to the sequence in the timeline.

3. Double-click the CFX node to show its parameters, click RGB LUT, set its Conversion LUT Type pop-up menu to Lin To Log to change the final composite to Log.

Now, the log-encoded media coming into Smoke is normalized so you can work on your composite with the media looking as it should, before re-encoding the output of the composite to match the log media in the rest of the sequence.

Assembling a Process Tree

The *process tree*, or *node tree*, as shown in Figure 8.12, which was created by Smoke to combine the two clips you had superimposed in the timeline, is a standard way of creating a composite.

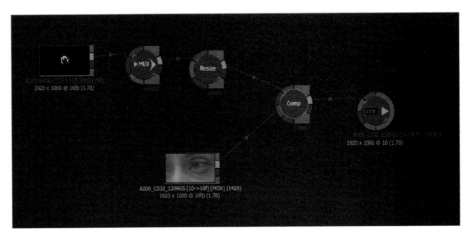

FIGURE 8.12 The current state of your ConnectFX process tree, rearranged for clarity

Pretty much every node tree works from left to right, with Clip nodes adding media to the composite. Then a progression of nodes, connected via *links* (the lines with arrows pointing to the right), apply specific adjustments to process the image data being propagated along each branch of the tree. In this example, the EyeInterface clip is processed by the MUX node and then processed by the Resize node.

When two or more nodes need to be combined to create a new image, a multi-input node, such as the Comp, Action, or Blend & Comp node, is used. In Figure 8.12, you can see that the post-resized EyeInterface clip and the woman's close-up are both fed into a Comp node, which is an easy way to combine two images.

Once you've added all of the nodes necessary to create your final effect, the last node of your process tree is linked to the CFX node, which is always the last node, because it's what feeds the final result back to the Smoke sequence in the timeline as a clip. If the CFX node is not connected, there will be no effect.

The Comp node is a fairly simple compositing too, so let's look at it first.

1. Double-click the Comp node.

    You can see that it has a relatively simple set of controls. Two sets of Input Controls let you set how the matte, clamping, premultiplication, and transparency of the image connected to the top red input (a tooltip shows that it's Input 1 if you move the pointer over it) are handled, and how the same parameters for the bottom red input (labeled Input 2) are handled. A second set of controls to the right lets you control how the images are blended together.

2. Click the Blend Mode pop-up menu and choose Screen. The black parts of the EyeInterface clip should immediately turn transparent as the two images are composited together.

Like I said, simple. However, let's make things a little more complicated by replacing the Comp node with another node that has even more options, the Blend & Comp node.

3. To disconnect the Comp node that you don't want, click and drag to draw a red line across the red lines that connect the Comp node to the other nodes to the left in the tree, as shown in Figure 8.13. Then draw another red line across the link connecting the Comp node to the CFX node.

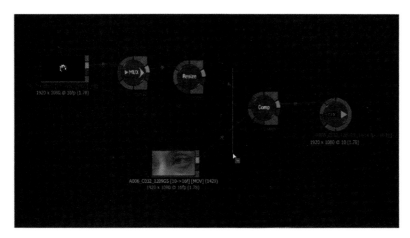

FIGURE 8.13 Severing link lines to disconnect nodes by drawing a line across them

4. To delete the Comp node, click to select it, and then do one of the following:

▶ Select a node, and press the Delete key.

▶ Right-click one of the selected nodes, and choose Delete.

▶ Drag one of the selected nodes down to the bottom of the screen until the trash can cursor appears and drop it.

Now that you've removed the unwanted Comp node, it's time to add its replacement, in this case the Blend & Comp node.

5. Turn on the FX Nodes button; then hover the pointer over the node bin and press the B key. All nodes that don't start with the letter *B* are grayed out, making the Blend & Comp node easier to see (see Figure 8.14).

If you happened to disconnect two or more nodes from a tree and you wanted to select them all in order to delete them, you can Shift+click one node and all nodes attached to it will be automatically selected.

FIGURE 8.14 Highlighting nodes starting with the letter *B* by pressing the B key

6. Drag the Blend & Comp node into the ConnectFX Schematic pane of the Viewport, and drop it onto the space left by the deleted Comp node. Before going any further, we're going to examine the node connections that appear in Figure 8.15 in more detail.

FIGURE 8.15 Inputs and outputs of the Blend & Comp node

Each node has a set of input tabs on the left and a set of output tabs on the right. Each of these inputs and outputs is color-coded:

Red Tabs   Front, the image data you're passing from one node to the next.

Blue Tabs   Matte, a channel containing transparency data created by a GMask or a curve, although any grayscale high-contrast image can be used as a matte.

Green Tabs   Back, a special image channel that appears as a layer behind all of the front channel layers. The Back channel also serves as the channel to be tracked when using stabilization within the Action node.

Yellow Tabs   Nodes output image data via a yellow output tab. Many nodes also output a separate blue Matte tab as well, so that one node processes both the Image and Matte channels.

Gray Tabs   Some nodes, such as the Depth of Field node, have additional special inputs that are colored gray. In the case of Depth of Field, the middle gray tab lets you input a z-channel depth matte for use in defining artificial camera defocusing based on distance from camera.

Hovering your pointer above a node's tab displays a tooltip explaining exactly what the tab does. In the case of the Blend & Comp node, there are five input tabs: Front and Matte, Front2 and Matte2, and Back. These inputs let you layer one image with its matte on top, a second image and its matte underneath, and a third back image appearing at the very bottom, compositing up to three images in total.

7. Connect the yellow output tab of the Resize node to both the top Front and Matte input tabs of the Blend & Comp node, and then connect the yellow output tab from the woman's close-up to the green Back input tab of the Blend & Comp node using any of the four following techniques:

   a. Click the output tab of one node, and then click the input tab of another node to create a link automatically (see Figure 8.16).

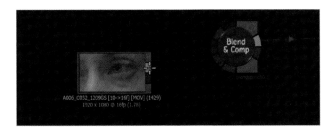

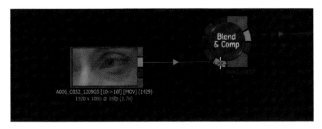

FIGURE 8.16   Clicking two tabs to create a link, before and after

b. Drag a link from one node's output tab onto another node's input tab (see Figure 8.17).

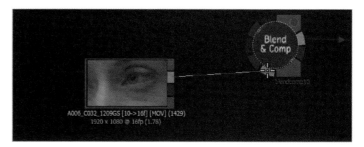

FIGURE 8.17 Dragging a link from one tab to another

c. Hold the Option key down while dragging a node, and touch that node's output tab to another node's input tab to "kiss" the nodes, creating a link (see Figure 8.18).

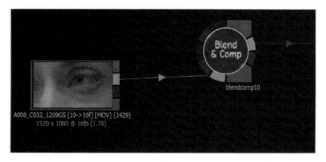

FIGURE 8.18 "Kissing" two nodes while holding the Option key to create a link

d. While dragging a node, press Shift+Option to display a connection "arm" that makes it easier to connect one specific node's input to another node's output. Holding Option and pressing Shift repeatedly toggles this handle among a node's Front, Back, and Matte inputs.

In a departure from previous versions of Smoke, it's not necessary to connect each image's output tab to *both* the Front and Matte input tabs; connecting to the Front input tab is enough. Other nodes, such as the MasterK node used for keying, *require* the Matte input tab to be connected because those operations need the matte of the image (even if it's completely opaque) to be calculated into the composite being made. However, if you really don't want to have to connect the matte input, you can turn off the matte of either input using the Blend & Comp node's controls.

8. Connect the Blend & Comp node's yellow output tab to the red CFX input tab.

9. Connect the output of the Resize node to the red front input of the Blend & Comp node.

10. Click the Blend & Comp node and change the Blend mode under the Result Output section to Screen.

11. Lastly, click the right pane of the Viewport to select it, and set the View pop-up to Blend Comp Result (or press F4) so that you can see the result of the Blend & Comp node that's still selected. Then move the positioner to the first frame of the timeline.

When you're finished, the node tree and result viewer should look something like Figure 8.19.

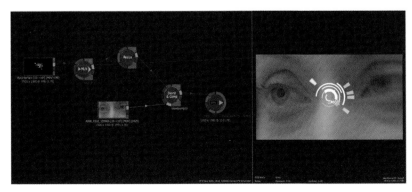

FIGURE 8.19 The EyeInterface graphic composited against the woman's close-up using the Blend & Comp node

Match-Moving with the 2D Transform Node

So now you have your composite. However, the EyeInterface animation needs to be match-moved to follow the camera's motion so that it looks like it's actually attached to the woman's face and then transformed to fit inside the woman's eye before you can create a convincing effect. This can all be accomplished using the 2D Transform node.

1. First, open the FX Nodes bin and drag a 2D Transform node into the ConnectFX Schematic; then hold the Option key down and touch its red front input tab to the yellow output tab of the woman's close-up node to create a link.

2. Double-click the 2D Transform node to open its parameters at the bottom of the CFX editor, and then click the Stabilization tab to expose the Stabilizer parameters and controls.

3. Click the Enter Stabilizer button to open the stabilizer, and then choose Fit from the viewer's Zoom pop-up menu so that you can see the entire image.

4. Drag the top (red) tracker box to the inner corner of the woman's camera-left eye, and then drag the bottom (green) tracker box to the inner corner of the woman's camera-right eye.

5. Make sure that the positioner is at the beginning of the timeline and click Analyze. The tracker boxes should follow along with the woman's eyes as the camera pans across her face, leaving a series of tracking points that form a motion path, as shown in Figure 8.20.

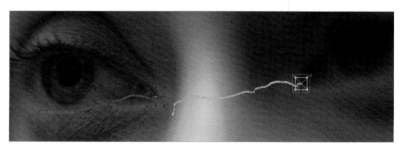

FIGURE 8.20 The motion path formed by the tracking points created by stabilization

You should notice that there are dips in the motion path that correspond to every time the woman blinks. Scrubbing along the timeline should confirm this. These could cause unwanted twitches in the track, but fortunately they're easy to remove.

6. Click the Animation button at the left to open up the Animation editor. A series of hierarchical disclosure triangles inside of the light-gray graph in the middle show every parameter available to the current scene.

7. Click the triangles to the left of tracker1 and tracker2 to view the parameters within, and then click the triangles to the left of the Shift parameters for tracker1 and tracker2 to reveal the graphs for each tracker.

8. At this point, the unwanted bumps in the graph can be hard to see, so do the following to resize and pan around the data:

   ▶ Hold Control+Option down and drag with the pointer in the Animation editor to zoom and resize the graphs. Drag up to zoom into the Y-axis to make it easier to see the bumps.

   ▶ Hold Control+Command down and drag with the pointer to pan around the Animation editor, moving the data around.

   You should zoom and pan around the graph until it looks something like Figure 8.21.

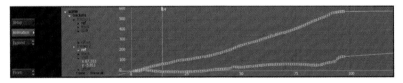

FIGURE 8.21 The Shift parameter in the Animation editor lets you see the tracker's results.

Scrubbing with the positioner in the Timebar, to find the motion path dips where she blinks in the Viewport, can also help you to find the corresponding keyframes via the Animation editor's positioner, which mirrors it.

9. Now that you can find the bumps in the tracking data, choose Delete from the Tools pop-up menu underneath the viewer, and then click the Shift parameter in the Animation list to select that curve and drag a bounding box around the clump of control points at each bump to delete them (see Figure 8.22).

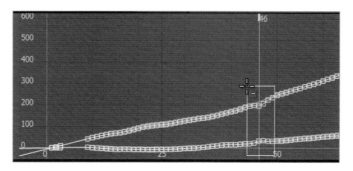

FIGURE 8.22 Deleting tracking points from each selected Shift graph using the Delete tool

10. Do this for the Shift parameters of tracker1 and tracker2, and you'll end up with a smoother graph where the motion data is automatically interpolated wherever you deleted the unwanted tracking data (see Figure 8.23).

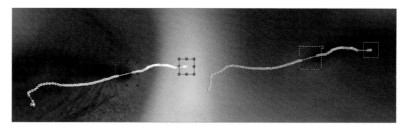

FIGURE 8.23 A smoother motion path after deleting unwanted tracking data

11. Click the Animation button again to toggle it off and go back to the Stabilizer controls, and then click the Return button to go back to the CFX editor.

12. Break the link connecting the 2D Transform node to the woman's close-up, and then drag and drop it on top of the red link between the Resize node and the Blend & Comp node to insert it into the EyeInterface branch of the process tree.

    You may need to rearrange the node tree again to keep things neat. When you're finished, the node tree should look something like Figure 8.24.

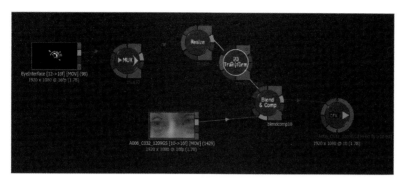

FIGURE 8.24 Moving the 2D Transform node into the CFX Schematic.

13. Double-click the 2D Transform node to open the controls in the Stabilization tab, and click the Invert Stabilization button to transform the EyeInterface animation to follow along with the camera motion that you analyzed in the previous steps.

With Invert Stabilization off, stabilization transforms the image to eliminate motion in the frame. With Invert Stabilization on, stabilization works as a Match Move operation instead.

At this point, if you don't see both input images composited in the viewer at the right, then click the right pane of the Viewport and press the 0 key to set it to display the CFX Result.

14. To position the graphic to be better lined up with the woman's eyeball, you need to transform the EyeInterface animation a second time. Open the FX node bins, and drag a second 2D Transform node into the graph, connecting it to the left of the first 2D Transform node so that the red and blue links go from the Resize node to the Front and Matte input tabs of the new 2D Transform node, which connects to the Front and Matte input tabs of the 2D Transform node that has the tracking data (see Figure 8.25).

Technically, you could do both of these operations within a single 2D Transform node, but if you don't apply the offset to position the graphic *before* the 2D node that's applying the tracking operation, then the Match Move operation won't work correctly and you'll notice the track drift. But there's an added benefit, as this node structure will make it easy to use the original 2D Transform node to match move the rotoscoped matte you'll create in the next exercise.

> Use keyboard shortcuts to activate different views in the currently selected Viewport pane. Press F4 to see the currently selected node's result, press 0 to see the CFX node result, and press Control+Esc to see the ConnectFX Schematic.

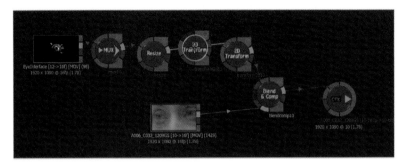

FIGURE 8.25 Adding a second 2D Transform node to reposition and scale the EyeInterface graphic

15. Click the new 2D Transform node to open its parameters, and use the Position, Rotation, and Scale controls to position the EyeInterface animation to match Figure 8.26 so that it looks like the animation is right on top of the woman's iris.

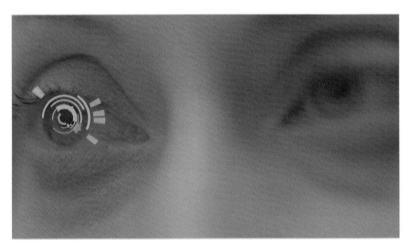

FIGURE 8.26 Transforming the EyeInterface animation

Now, if you scrub through the timeline, the animated EyeInterface graphic should follow along.

WHAT IS THE PURPOSE OF THE RESIZE NODE?

You'll recall that when editing a clip into a sequence, if the clip has a different frame size or bit depth than the sequence, a Resize effect is added. When that clip was selected in the timeline to create a ConnectFX composite, the Resize effect appeared as a node.

At this point, you may be wondering why you need to add the 2D Transform node when there's already a Resize node. That's because the Resize node only alters the overall resolution and bit depth of an image; it's not for rescaling or repositioning an image to a specific set of coordinates in the composite.

Some nodes that have multiple inputs require that each linked image have the same resolution and bit depth. For this reason, Smoke automatically adds Resize nodes to make the resolution of every image being read in identical.

Rotoscoping with the GMask Node

Now that the graphic is following along with the woman's eye movement, the challenge is to make it look like it's actually inside her eyelid. This is not necessarily simple, because she is blinking, so any solution you use must be animated as well. Fortunately, Smoke has a powerful rotoscoping and mask-drawing tool in the GMask node.

1. Click the FX Nodes button and hover the pointer over the All Nodes bin; then press G to isolate all nodes that start with *G*, and drag the GMask node into the ConnectFX Schematic underneath where the second 2D Transform and Blend & Comp nodes connect. You're going to use this GMask to rotoscope the woman's eye and create an alpha channel to crop the EyeInterface layer, and you'll probably want to drag the Blend & Comp and CFX nodes to the right to make some room.

   At this point, the node tree is getting a bit big. Fortunately, the two methods of zooming and panning you used in the Animation editor also work in any pane of the Viewport:

   ▶ Hold Control+Option down, and drag with the pointer to zoom in and out. Drag right to zoom in, and drag left to zoom out.

   ▶ Hold Control+Command down, and drag with the pointer to pan around.

You can zoom and pan schematics, viewers, graphs, and even the timeline using these keyboard modifiers, so they're good to remember.

When rearranging nodes, Shift+clicking a node selects both that node and all upstream nodes to the left of it, making it easier to drag long branches of nodes around the schematic. Control+Shift+clicking a node selects both that node and all downstream nodes to the right of it.

2. Connect the GMask node so that the process tree resembles Figure 8.27 by creating the following links:

   a. Link the yellow output tab of the woman's close-up to the GMask node's red Front input tab. (You can link a single output to as many inputs as you like, but you can attach only one link to an input.)

   b. Link the GMask node's yellow output tab to the blue Matte input tab of the Blend & Comp node.

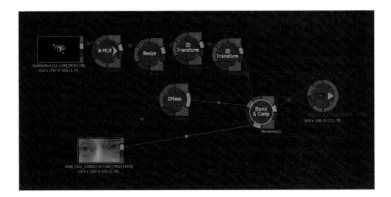

FIGURE 8.27 Attaching the GMask node

Here's the reason you're connecting the GMask in this way. By attaching the image of the woman's close-up to the GMasks's Front input, you're setting up a reference image to trace while drawing the mask. Meanwhile, attaching the matte from the GMask to the Blend & Comp node's topmost Matte input (which matches the Front input the graphic is connected to) lets the GMask node's output act as an alpha channel for the EyeInterface clip.

Basically, you're using the woman's close-up to draw a mask while applying it to the EyeInterface layer. This ability to use each of the separate color and matte channels propagated through the Smoke node tree for a different purpose is one of the great advantages of node-based compositing.

3. To prepare for drawing a mask where you want it, make sure the positioner is at the beginning of the timeline. Then click the GMask node to show its controls, click the right Viewport pane, and choose GMask Inputs Front (F1) to view the Front input while drawing with the GMask tools. It's also a good idea to Control+Option drag in the viewer to zoom into the woman's camera-left eye to make it easier to trace it in detail.

   Be aware that the controls for creating and animating masks (as shown in Figure 8.28) appear only when a viewer is selected. If a schematic is selected, these controls will be hidden. Furthermore, you can see mask shapes and control points only when you're viewing the GMask inputs (to trace a Front input image) or GMask Results (to modify a GMask relative to its final effect).

FIGURE 8.28 The GMask object controls appear only when a viewer is selected in the Viewport.

4. To begin drawing a mask, do one of the following:

   ▶ Click the Add button (see Figure 8.28) to add a new draw object.

   ▶ Choose Draw Shape from the Tools pop-up menu underneath the Viewport.

   ▶ Press Shift+C.

5. Click to add points to trace the inside of the woman's eyelid. Smoke uses familiar Bezier drawing controls for creating masks:

   ▶ Click to add a new control point with an automatically calculated curve relative to the last point you drew.

   ▶ Click and drag to add a control point and adjust its curvature using Bezier handles.

   ▶ Click the first point you created to close a mask.

   ▶ Drag control points to modify the shape, or drag any point's Bezier handles to customize the curve.

▶ Add or delete points, or modify Bezier handle tangents, using alternate tools found in the Tools pop-up menu underneath the Viewport.

▶ Alternatively, pressing and holding the Shift key lets you draw a freehand shape. Draw all the way back to the first point you drew to close shapes drawn in this way. You can also draw freehand sections while drawing shapes the conventional way.

When you're finished, the mask should look something like Figure 8.29. Keep in mind that whenever you draw a mask that will need to be animated, it's good to use the fewest number of control points that you can get away with. Also, you're principally concerned with where the eyelid will move over the EyeInterface animation.

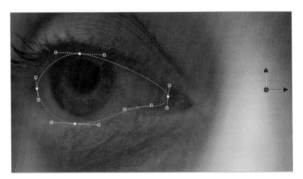

FIGURE 8.29 The initial mask

6. To wrap up the initial state of this matte, you may notice that the edge where the GMask cuts off the graphic is a bit hard. Raise or lower the Offset parameter to offset the softness of the mask, softening this edge until it looks right (the controls can be seen in Figure 8.30).

FIGURE 8.30 The Outside and Colour parameters let you invert the mask when necessary, and the Offset parameter lets you feather the edge.

This is a good start, but now that you have the initial state of the mask drawn, you'll take advantage of the fact that the eye doesn't really change shape (except for three blinks) to save some time using motion tracking. The GMask node is one of several with built-in Stabilizer controls for match-moving masks to follow a moving target, and you'll use that feature now.

7. Make sure the positioner is at the beginning of the clip, and then click the Stabilizer button, drag the tracker box over the inner corner of the woman's camera-left eye, and click the Analyze button, just as you did in the previous exercise. There's no camera rotation, so one tracking point will be just fine. Click Return when it's done.

   Play through the clip, and you'll see that the mask you just drew is now tracking nicely to follow the camera's motion. Now all you need to take care of are the frames where the woman blinks, easily accomplished using the GMask's keyframing tools, as shown previously in Figure 8.28.

8. For maximum efficiency, tackle this simple rotoscoping job in the following steps:

   a. Click the right pane of the Viewport to select the image you're working on. You should notice that the Timebar switches from displaying the tracking keyframes to being devoid of keyframes; you're now ready to start keyframing the shape.

   b. Move the positioner to the frame just before each blink starts, and click the Set Key button to create a keyframe. Then move the positioner to the frame just after each blink ends, and click the Set Key button to create another keyframe. At the end, you should have two keyframes defining the first frame before and the last frame after each blink, at which the mask should remain in its initial position. Keyframes appear as light blue lines within the timeline (see Figure 8.32).

   c. Now turn on the Auto Key button. This puts Smoke into a mode where every adjustment you make creates a new keyframe. Be very careful what you do when Auto Key is turned on.

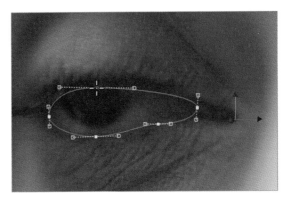

FIGURE 8.31 Creating two mask keyframes at the beginning and end of each blink

d. Move the positioner to the frame of each blink where the eye is most closed. (Her eye is never quite closed on camera because the blinks are so fast.) Drag the mask control points to shorten the top of the mask to follow the movement of the eyelid (see Figure 8.32). You've just created an animated change from the open-eye mask keyframe to the closed-eye mask keyframe.

FIGURE 8.32 Adjusting the mask to follow the blink

e. Move the positioner frame by frame through the blink, and readjust the mask wherever there's a gap between the mask and the contour of the upper eyelid. It's a good rule of thumb to "divide by two." In other words, start out by placing new keyframes halfway between every two keyframes, which you've already created, to see if Smoke's shape interpolation will take care of the rest.

f. Do this for each of the three blinks in this clip. When you're finished, you should have keyframes in the timeline that look something like Figure 8.33.

FIGURE 8.33 Placing the fewest number of keyframes you can to animate the mask to match each blink

9. You should now be finished with the eye mask, so turn off the Auto Key button.

10. With the viewer selected in the Viewport, press 0 to set the View pop-up menu to the CFX Result so that you can see the overall composite, and choose Fit from the Zoom pop-up menu to see the entire frame.

    At this point, you're seeing exactly what you want: the GMask is limiting the graphic to the inside of her eye, as shown in Figure 8.34.

Leaving Auto Key on accidentally is one of the most common mistakes you can make; there's nothing like placing an unwanted keyframe when you don't realize it to make you wonder what you're doing wrong. Always turn off Auto Key when you're finished keyframing an effect.

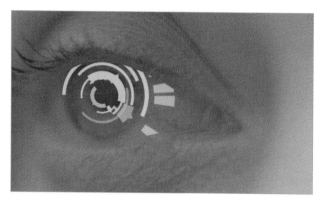

FIGURE 8.34 The state of the image when viewing the CFX Result

However, there will be other instances when you draw a shape with the GMask node and end up with the opposite of what you wanted. When this happens, you need to turn on the Outside button and change the Colour parameter to 0. Three controls define how each mask object interacts to define image transparency:

Outside This control determines whether a matte is created outside or inside the mask you've drawn.

Colour This control determines whether the mask creates a region that's transparent or opaque.

Opacity This control determines how transparent or opaque the feathered edges of a mask are.

Changing the Blend Mode and Adding Blur

At this point, the EyeInterface animation follows along with the woman's eye, sitting inside her eyelid very convincingly. However, it still looks like a computer graphic rather than an integrated part of the scene. To finish the illusion, you'll use the controls of the Blend & Comp node, as well as a Blur node, to create a more organic effect.

1. Click the Blend & Comp node to show its controls, and then click the right Viewport and press F4 to view the current node's output.

   There are three sets of controls corresponding to Input 1 (currently connected to the EyeInterface branch of the node tree), Input 2 (currently connected to the video clip), and Result Output, which is currently disconnected.

   The Blend & Comp node is an extremely powerful node; not only does it let you composite three images together all at once, but it also provides a multitude of Blend mode (or Transfer mode) options, individual color-correction controls for each layer, and color-correction controls affecting the overall output. In other words, it gives you a lot of bang for the buck.

2. Click the Blend Mode pop-up menu corresponding to the left-most Blend Mode controls, and choose Spotlight Blend (see Figure 8.35).

FIGURE 8.35 The Blend Mode pop-up menu corresponding to the mix of Input 1 and Input 2

Each Blend mode is a different way of mathematically combining the different inputs to blend with one another. Spotlight Blend is a proprietary Autodesk operation that combines both the dark and light portions of two images in a way that seems very natural for a variety of situations, such as when trying to give the illusion of a reflection or a material that's semi-opaque.

3. This looks good, but the effect is still a bit in-your-face, so drag the Transp (transparency) slider to the left to around 40 percent to make the Overlay effect even more translucent.

4. Now, to give a bit of color to the contact lens effect, drag the Input 1 color-balance control toward the blue edge of the wheel, until the Gain parameters read something like "Red = 82, Green = 103, Blue = 130."

    The color-balance control, or color wheel, of each input is meant to let you add subtle color adjustments for making two composited layers match more convincingly. Here, though, it's a useful creative tool. At this point, the effect as shown in Figure 8.36 is looking quite nice. But there's just one more thing you need to do to nail the effect.

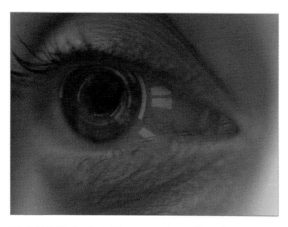

FIGURE 8.36 The contact lens effect after using the Overlay, Transparency, and Color-Correction features of the Blend & Comp node to customize the composite

The last aspect of the EyeInterface animation that gives it away as being artificial is that it's a bit too sharp, and it doesn't go out of focus along with the rest of her face when the camera moves. Adding a Blur node lets you take care of both issues at once.

5. Click the FX Nodes button, and hover the pointer over the All Nodes bin. Then press B to isolate all nodes that start with *B*, and drag the Blur node onto the red link connecting the last 2D Transform node's yellow output tab and the Blend & Comp node's top Front input tab, as shown in Figure 8.37.

If you need more room for the ConnectFX Schematic, you can set the Media Library's View Mode pop-up menu to Hidden.

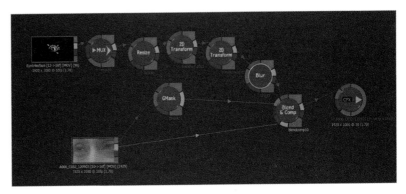

FIGURE 8.37 Connecting the Blur node between the 2D Transform and Blend & Comp nodes

6. Double-click the Blur node in the ConnectFX Schematic to open its parameters. By default, the Blur node is set to Gaussian, which creates a soft, smooth blur effect. Drag the Width slider to the right to increase the amount of blur from 1.00 to 2.00, just enough to knock the edge off the graphic's sharpness.

7. To get a before-and-after look at the effect that the Blur node is having on the image, click the Bypass button (at the right of all of the parameters) off and on again. Every node has a Bypass button that can be used to disable a node's functionality without deleting it from the node tree.

   The Blur node is extremely flexible. By default, the width and height of the blur are locked proportionally, and the matte is also locked to the same value. Turn off Proportional or Lock To Front to adjust these parameters independently. Furthermore, there are separate parameters to blur the X and Y dimensions of the red, green, and blue channels individually. You can also switch among different types of blur.

8. Choose Defocus from the Type pop-up menu, and drag the Width slider left to about 6.00. The Defocus blur simulates an optical blur with bokeh characteristics, as seen through a camera's lens. Additional controls cover the size, shape, and rotation of simulated bokeh and the type and amount of simulated blooming. They can provide a more natural-looking effect when matching genuine lens blur.

Adding just a bit of blur makes the effect seem more like part of the scene, but the shallow depth of field in this shot causes different regions of the image to go out of focus when the camera pans. You can simulate this by keyframing the Blur node.

9. Scrub the positioner through the timeline until you reach frame 12:30:19+22, and then stop. This is the point at which the woman's camera-left eye starts to go out of focus. Click the Animation button to view the Animation graph, and click the Set Key button to place a keyframe.

10. Scrub the positioner forward to frame 12:30:20+08, which is when the woman's camera-right eye just comes into focus, turn on the Auto Key button, and turn off the Animation button to see the blur parameters again. Raise the Front Width parameter to around 12. Now the simulated contact lens goes out of focus as the camera pans over.

Playing the Effect

At this point, the effect is a bit too processor-intensive to play in real time, so you'll need to render it to see it play back.

1. Click the Render button. A dialog with a progress bar shows you how long this render will take.

2. When the progress bar concludes, click the Exit CFX button to go back to the timeline.

3. Play through this clip in the timeline to see how it looks.

THE ESSENTIALS AND BEYOND

While this chapter merely scratches the surface of what's possible using ConnectFX, the techniques shown here are the foundation upon which everything else that you'll do rests. It's important to master the basics of node-based compositing before you move on to more complicated exercises.

ADDITIONAL EXERCISES

▶ The exercises in this chapter create a contact lens effect in one eye. Use the same techniques, applied using the same EyeInterface graphic, to apply another animated contact lens to her other eye.

(Continues)

THE ESSENTIALS AND BEYOND *(Continued)*

Here are some tips:

▶ Don't import another EyeInterface layer; pull another link out of the yellow output tab of the EyeInterface node and connect it to another MUX node.

▶ Also, see which nodes you can duplicate to save yourself some effort.

▶ Finally, connect the second animated contact lens branch of the node tree by reconnecting the video clip to the Bland & Comp node's green Back input tab, and then connecting the second contact lens branch to the now unused Front2 and Matte2 input tabs of the Blend & Comp node.

CHAPTER 9

Using the ConnectFX Action Node

Having used the basic tools available in the ConnectFX Schematic, it's time to delve even deeper and explore the possibilities afforded by the Action node. The Action node is the heart of the Autodesk® Smoke® 3D compositing environment, and it provides a wholly separate node-based environment for detailed keying and multilayered compositing. It is, in fact, a second stage of compositing that works hand in hand with the ConnectFX Schematic, enabling you to build even more sophisticated effects.

Topics in this chapter include the following:

▶ **Moving timeline effects into CFX**

▶ **Introducing the Action node**

▶ **Multilayered keying in action**

▶ **Adding media to a CFX composite**

▶ **Building a multilayer composite in action**

▶ **Working on the pre- and post-action image**

▶ **Using simple color correction to match layers**

Moving Timeline Effects into CFX

In this chapter, you'll finish the work you started in Chapter 7. You'll use the capabilities of the Action node to finish creating the effect of a dimensional doorway opening up between the lead character and her doppelganger from an alternate reality. For those of you who've seen "The Place Where You Live" on the web, this is a simplified version of the original effect created by Smoke veteran Brian Mulligan.

1. First, duplicate the Opening Scene C07 sequence you completed in Chapter 7, and rename it **Opening Scene C09**.

2. Open this new sequence, and press Shift+Z if necessary to fit the entire sequence into the available width of the timeline.

3. Turn the Link button off, and Command+click the two superimposed video clips at the very end (see Figure 9.1).

FIGURE 9.1
Selecting the last two composited clips to create a ConnectFX effect

4. Click the FX button, make sure the Selection as 3D Comp check box is turned on, and click Create ConnectFX.

   The ConnectFX environment opens up, and a node tree representing the two-clip composite from the timeline appears in the ConnectFX Schematic. When you first enter CFX, you'll find a riot of nodes that are the result of Smoke automatically converting your timeline effects to equivalent CFX. However, Smoke tends to overdo these conversions by adding more nodes than are strictly necessary. Simplify the node tree by doing the following:

   a) Delete the Resize and 2D Transform Nodes at the left, the two MUX nodes, and the last Action node at the right.

   b) Select the remaining action node, and press Control+N to add another media connection.

   c) Reconnect the remaining nodes to look like Figure 9.2 b.

   This ends up making the visual result of the composite a bit of a mess, but this is a necessary step to simplify this composite and make the end result as elegant as possible, so you'll take care of these issues later.

If the node tree is offset, you can hold the Control+Command buttons down while dragging within the gray area of the ConnectFX Schematic to pan around, moving the node tree to the center.

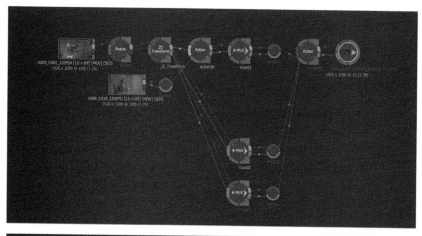

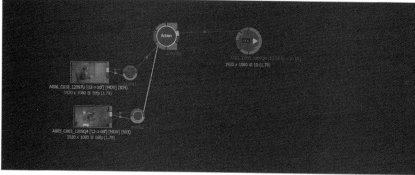

FIGURE 9.2 The ConnectFX Schematic of your two-clip composite

With Selection as 3D Comp chosen, composites that were originally done using timeline effects are converted to a ConnectFX tree using an Action node. You also have the option to preserve the timeline effects you created previously by choosing Selection as Flowgraph. With this option, the effects used in the timeline will simply be converted to nodes within ConnectFX.

Introducing the Action Node

The *Action node* is an integrated "compositor within a compositor" that lets you perform more complex multilayer operations than those allowed by the Blend & Comp and Comp nodes. Although it's represented within the ConnectFX Schematic as a single node, this one node actually contains its own

Action Schematic, its own bin of Action nodes, and a Media list and Object editor unique to the Action node. Using the Action node, you can do the following:

- ▶ Create multiclip composites that go well beyond the Front/Front2/ Back inputs of the Blend & Comp node.

- ▶ Incorporate color-correction operations, Axis transforms, and Blend mode operations without the need for additional ConnectFX nodes.

- ▶ Create more intricate greenscreen keys using the Action node's Modular Keyer Schematic.

- ▶ Transform layers in full 3D space with 3D object support and lighting. (The Blend & Comp node is a 2D compositing operation only.)

- ▶ Integrate 3D camera tracking data from other applications.

- ▶ Import multilayered Photoshop files.

- ▶ Create 3D text objects.

And the list goes on. In short, the Action node is a multipurpose tool for taking care of a wide variety of tasks involving multiple image inputs.

In the following exercises, you'll use the Action node to finish building the effect of the dimensional doorway, refining the greenscreen work you did in Chapter 7, inserting a fake wall, and building the effect of an energy portal opening up. Before getting started, though, it's time to take a brief tour of the Action environment so that you can find your way around.

The Action Node Structure

Looking at the Action node, you should notice that it's different from the other nodes you've used in ConnectFX in that it has red and blue media inputs (see Figure 9.3) instead of Front and Back input tabs. It also has a green Back input tab and a yellow output tab for video and a blue output for matte data.

Each Action input lets you connect an image for compositing within the Action node. You can select an Action node and press Control+N to add as many inputs as you require to composite however many layers you need. You can connect images of varying resolutions to the different inputs of an Action node.

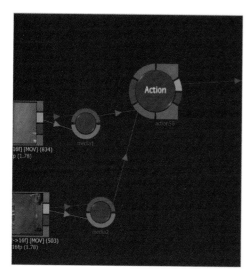

FIGURE 9.3 The Action node with two media inputs

There's one thing you need to know, however, about the Action node. Each small, round input has separate Front (red) and Matte (blue) tabs, which let you link different images to the Front and Matte of a single media input. For example, you can connect a video clip to the Front and a GMask to the Matte. However, when linking different images to the Front and Matte tabs of a single input, both images need to have the same resolution and the same bit depth. Otherwise, the input will display a red dot (see Figure 9.4), which shows that the two connected images are incompatible.

FIGURE 9.4
A red dot on an
Action input shows
that the two images
connected to it have
different resolutions
or bit depths.

If you see a red dot, you can use the internal Resize and RGB LUT controls of the clip nodes to make both images the same. The Resize controls let you change the output resolution, and the RGB LUT controls let you change the bit depth. You'll see how to do this in one of the exercises later in this chapter.

The Action Environment

To open the Action environment, you can either select the Action node itself or select any of the media inputs. Depending on the last thing you did when working with an Action node, either the Media list or the Object editor will appear.

As important as the Media list is, you'll also want to open up more panes in the viewport to see the Action Schematic.

1. Choose 4-Up from the Viewport Layout pop-up menu.

2. Click the upper-right pane to select it, and choose Action Schematic from the View pop-up menu (or press Escape). This shows you the node structure that's internal to the Action node.

3. Select the lower-right pane, and choose CFX Result from the View menu (or press 0). This shows you the final result of the overall composite, so that you can see what you're doing within the context of the overall composite. Set the Zoom pop-up menu to Fit.

4. Select the lower-left pane, and choose Action Output1: DefaultCam (or press F4). This option sets the selected viewport to display the output of the currently selected node, letting you see the isolated results of the node on which you're working.

   With the viewport set up in this way, it should look something like Figure 9.5.

▶

If you want more room in any pair of panes in a 4-Up viewport, you can position the pointer at the border between any two or at the intersection of all four viewports, and drag to resize them.

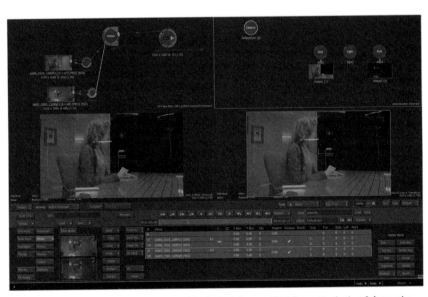

FIGURE 9.5 The viewport set to (clockwise) ConnectFX Schematic, Action Schematic, CFX Result, Action Output1: DefaultCam

The Media List

If necessary, click the Media button to open the *Media list*, which is the heart of the Action node. While its rows and columns can be a bit daunting to read at first, learning what to look for is key to understanding how the different Action node controls fit together. The Media list displaying the current composite appears in Figure 9.6, and it contains five rows that correspond to each of the Action node's inputs: B for the green background input tab and two pairs corresponding to the Front and Matte of the media1 (1F and 1M) and media2 (2F and 2M) inputs.

F I G U R E 9 . 6 The Media list showing a row for every image that's connected to an input of the currently selected Action node

The currently selected media input in the ConnectFX Schematic corresponds to the currently selected rows in the Media list. The Name column shows the name of the image or alpha (A) connected to each input; the K column is used for accessing the Modular Keyer Schematic; the CC column is used for accessing the built-in color-correction controls. Additional columns show the parameters for adjusting X and Y blur, slipping the media forward or back in time, adding a shadow blur, enabling Gaussian blur, dividing a premultiplied image, and cropping the top, bottom, left, and right of an image.

At the left of Figure 9.6, a pair of thumbnails shows the front and matte of the selected rows. To the right of that, a series of pop-up menus and buttons let you copy, paste, and delete media inputs, as well as turn the Front, Back, and Matte on and off.

The Object Editor

Click any node in the Action Schematic to open the *Object editor*, which exposes the editable parameters associated with the selected node. As with the ConnectFX Schematic, different parameters and controls appear when you select different nodes in the Action Schematic. The layout of these controls will no doubt remind you of the controls found in the timeline Axis control. This is because the timeline effects in Smoke are based on the Action node.

Priority List

Click the Priority button to open the *Priority list*, available when the Media list or Object editor is selected. It shows a simple list of every input that's connected to the Action node. Each input's position in the list indicates whether it's in front of or behind other input images; the higher an input is in the list, the farther forward in the composite it appears. In Figure 9.7, you can see that the image of the woman sitting at her desk appears in front because it's at the top of this list, while the image of the mirror is composited behind this layer since it appears at the bottom of the list.

F I G U R E   9 . 7   The Priority list in the Action node

Controls at the right (see Figure 9.8) let you reorder each item in the stack to change which clips appear in front of the others. In particular, you can select an item on the list, and use the Bring To Front and Push To Back buttons to move the item in front of or behind other layers in the Action composite. Other commands let you automatically sort the list by each input's Z-depth (if you're working with 3D objects and layers), sort the list by objects and GMasks, create groups of objects, and cut, copy, and paste objects in the list.

F I G U R E   9 . 8   Controls for reorganizing input objects in the Priority list

Right now, the order of the layers in this composite is backwards; you want the shot of the woman at the desk to be in front.

1. Select the Image1 layer.

2. Click the Bring To Front button.

The CFX Result image immediately improves as the woman at the desk becomes more solid.

The Priority list is necessary in the Action node because the Media list isn't organized by priority, and the Action Schematic doesn't provide a graphical indication of what's on top. Furthermore, if you begin to arrange layers in space using Z-depth within the Action Schematic, you may experience visual anomalies if the layers in the Priority list don't match the actual Z-depth of the composite. This is the reason for the Z-Sort button, which automatically sorts the layers in the Priority list based on their Z-depth. The Analyze button automatically keyframes layer order to match animated changes in Z-depth that you create.

The Action Schematic

The *Action Schematic* is a node-based view of the compositing operations within the Action node (see Figure 9.9). It is designed to apply operations to the media inputs, *not* to determine the hierarchy of composited layers — that's done with the Priority list. Accordingly, its structure is very different than that of the ConnectFX Schematic. Whereas every node of a process tree in the ConnectFX Schematic is connected, from left to right, in a linear series of sequential operations, the Action Schematic is instead composed of individual,

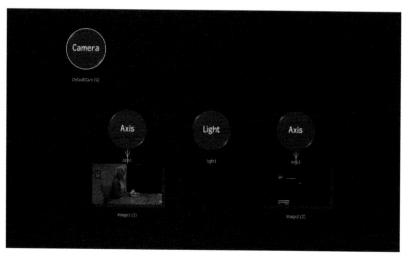

FIGURE 9.9 The Action Schematic, cleaned up

disconnected branches. Right now, there's one branch for each media input that's connected to the Action node. Each branch consists of a *surface*, which represents the image coming in via one of the media inputs, and a number of *Axis* nodes, which let you transform the surface to which they're connected in various ways. In the Action Schematic, nodes act upon other nodes.

Clicking the Action Bin button shows a set of nodes that appear only in the Action schematic. Many of these are nodes that are not available in the ConnectFX Schematic, such as the Texture, Lighting, and Map nodes. Furthermore, the mechanics of working with nodes in the Action Schematic are a bit different, as you'll see in subsequent lessons in this chapter. For example, Action nodes don't have either input or output tabs. Instead, links are dragged from within any node to the top of any other node to create a connection.

By default, Action nodes that were automatically generated from timeline effects that were converted into ConnectFX can be a bit messy. You should clean this up before proceeding.

1. Option+drag the top node of each branch of nodes in the Action Schematic to move them together, until they all appear in the available space, as shown in Figure 9.9.

2. If necessary, you can Control+Option+drag to zoom out to create more room and Control+Command+drag to pan around the Action Schematic.

The Modular Keyer Schematic

Click the Media button to open the Media list, and notice that an MK appears in the K column of the 2F and 2M layers. This tells you that there's a Modular Keyer effect applied to this layer, which is in fact the greenscreen key you created in Chapter 7.

Double-click the MK, and the viewport changes to the MK Schematic, which currently displays a node tree that is the equivalent of the timeline effect you created (see Figure 9.10). This is yet another dedicated environment — one used for creating highly detailed keys using all of the keying tools available in Smoke, including a few not available in other schematics, such as the Matte Blend node for combining multiple Modular Keyer nodes more easily.

The MK Schematic currently shows a preset node tree that immediately provides most of the tools you'd use to create a highly detailed key, including a Master Keyer node automatically connected to the Front/Back/Matte of the relevant inputs of the Action node; a set of nodes for post-processing the matte generated by the keyer, including the 2D Histogram, Matte Edge, and GMask nodes; and a Colour Curves node preprocessing the Front image before it's

The Start Mode pop-up menu provides a way to reset the MK Schematic to different preset node trees that are useful for a variety of keying situations.

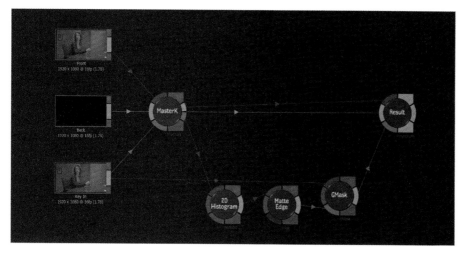

FIGURE 9.10   The automatically created node tree in the Modular Keyer Schematic

fed into the Master Keyer in case you need to make any color adjustments to improve the key.

To exit the MK Schematic, click the RETURN button.

Node Preferences for Action Nodes

When an Action node is selected, clicking the Node Prefs button gives you access to the resolution and bit depth of that Action node's internal compositing environment and its CG Rendering, Anti-Aliasing, and Motion Blur settings (see Figure 9.11).

FIGURE 9.11   The Node preferences of an Action node

Two other tabs provide access to Action Schematic–specific preferences, as well as Adaptive Degradation settings that let you specify which processor-intensive effects to disable selectively when making adjustments in order to improve interactivity while you work. Click the Node Prefs button again to exit these controls.

Basic Compositing in Action

Now that you've gotten the tour, it's time to dig in and start using these tools to create cinema magic. The following exercises are going to take you through a series of fairly complex operations, so we'll focus on taking things one step at a time.

Adding a Fake Wall

It's time to do something about that big hole in the wall to the woman's left. Eventually, there'll be a dimensional doorway there, but for now you need to create the illusion that there's an actual office wall there by adding another clip to the ConnectFX Schematic.

1. If necessary, turn off the Hidden option of the Media Library pop-up menu to display the clips available in your project.

2. Select the Action node in the ConnectFX Schematic, and create a new media input by doing one of the following:

   ▶ Press Control+N.

   ▶ Click and hold the New Media button in the Media list above the Front/Matte thumbnails, and choose New Input.

   A new input appears, labeled media3. You should also notice that an additional pair of rows appears at the bottom of the Media list with the name colored red to show that they're disconnected.

3. Scroll down the Media Library, and open up the Office Media and Portal Graphics Elements bins, which contain the additional media elements that you'll be using for this exercise. Then drag the Wall_Plate_111 clip to the schematic to add it. You may need to zoom out and pan up to create a bit of room in the ConnectFX Schematic.

   This is a still photograph of the wall of the set, taken after the shoot, for the express purpose of having a clean plate to use for the doorway opening effect. Of course, it's the wrong size and has completely different lighting, but you have Smoke, so you can fix that in post.

4. Hold the Option key down, and drag the media3 input to touch the Wall_Plate_111 clip's yellow output, connecting the yellow media

output to the red media input tab, and the blue matte output to the blue media input tab (do this for the mirror shot of the standing woman, as well). When you're finished, the node tree should resemble Figure 9.12.

Connecting the blue matte outputs of these two clip nodes automatically outputs solid white mattes for each clip, which correspond to the bottom white half of those thumbnails. This ensures these clips are solid in any compositing operation.

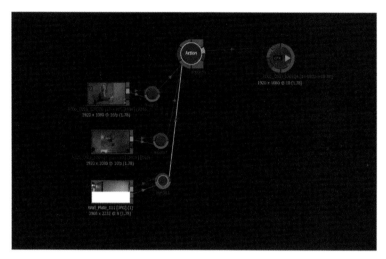

FIGURE 9.12 Connecting a new clip to the new media input of the Action node to add it to the composite

When you do this, you should notice that the `Wall_Plate_111` clip's name appears in the Name column of the 3F and 3M rows of the Media list. Also, a surface corresponding to the new image should appear within the Action Schematic, with an Axis node automatically attached.

However, looking at the CFX Result pane of the viewport, you can see that the wall graphic is strangely translucent. That's because this graphic has no alpha channel, so connecting it to the Matte tab of the media input results in its luma channel being used as the matte. This is easily fixable.

If you instead have a clip with an improper matte (alpha channel) attached to it, you can also click the Matte Clip pop-up menu (currently set to Matte On), and choose Matte Off (see Figure 9.13).

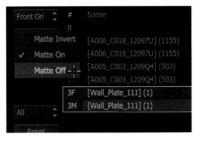

FIGURE 9.13 Turning off the Matte input to substitute a solid white matte for the unwanted luma channel matte

Now the wall is solid, but it obscures everything else, which is clearly not the desired effect. As an interesting aside, notice how, by default, lower media inputs have higher priority, appearing higher in the layered composite.

5. Click the Priority button to open the Priority list, then click image1 (currently at the top) to select it, and click the Push To Back button once to move the wall layer between the desk and mirror images. When you're finished, click the Priority button again to exit.

    Now the wall is where it should be, but it's a bit big relative to the scene, and the amount of visible detail in the image may be at odds with the scale of the rest of the scene.

6. Click the Wall_Plate_111 clip to open its parameters, then click the Resize button, and turn the Active button on. Enabling the built-in Resize parameters inside each clip node fits the Source resolution of the image into the currently specified Destination resolution, using the method selected in the Resizing group of controls.

    By default, Resizing is set to Centre/Crop, which crops the clip to fit into the current Destination resolution of 1920×1080 (which matches the resolution of both the project and the Action node). Incidentally, these controls are identical to those found in the Resize node; they're simply built into each clip node for convenience.

7. Choose Crop Edges from the Fit Method pop-up menu, then adjust the Position and Scale parameters to zoom into the wall image a bit, and slide it up and to the right so that the shadowed part of the wall butts up against the actual wall behind the woman, as shown in Figure 9.14. The settings are Position X -679, Position Y -145, and Scale 86.00.

FIGURE 9.14 Cropping and resizing the graphic to fit into the composite using the clip node's Resize controls

At this point, you can see the value of having two viewers: one showing you the output of the currently selected node and the other showing you the final effect. This lets you make adjustments to one node while seeing the final result within the context of the final effect.

Now for one final bit of housekeeping. As mentioned earlier, there are several operations that require each clip to have matching resolutions and bit depths, and a later exercise uses one of them. For this reason, it's a good idea to convert preemptively the bit depth of every graphic you import.

8. Click the RGB LUT button, and turn on the Active button. Since the Destination pop-up menu is set to 16 float by default, that's all you have to do.

At this point, the wall is nicely positioned and you're ready to proceed to the next step of this composite.

Adding a Garbage Matte to the Key

Unfortunately, the positioning of the wall now exposes some problems with your key. In particular, there's an unwanted intrusion at the top of the fake wall and some noise appearing at the edges of some corners. This can be addressed by improving the greenscreen key you made earlier using the nodes found in the MK Schematic.

1. Click the Action node to select it, and double-click the MK cell appearing on the 2F and 2M rows of the Media list (see Figure 9.15).

Another way of seeing one node while adjusting another is to use the Context option in the viewport. Right-click any node, choose Set As Context, and then set any pane of the viewport to Context 1 (Control+1).

As a warning, the RGB LUT settings are deceptive. Even though the Destination pop-up menu is set to 16 float, that doesn't mean the clip is set to 16 float; you have to turn the Active button on for this setting to take effect.

FIGURE 9.15 Double-click the MK cell to open the Master Keyer Schematic.

2. Choose 2-Up from the Viewport Layout pop-up menu; then click the empty right-hand pane, choose Result from the View pop-up menu (or press 4), and choose Fit from the Zoom pop-up menu. You should now have the MK Schematic on the left and a viewer showing the result on the right.

   You may have observed that there's a magenta cast over the image of the woman at the desk. By default, the Master Keyer (the MasterK node in the schematic) applies spill suppression to eliminate unwanted green fringing in the image. However, the lighting scheme has a lot of greenish yellow, and this suppression is being applied so indiscriminately that it's necessary to eliminate it. Fortunately, this is easy to do.

3. Add a Color Curves node to the schematic. Drag a link from the Colour Curves node's yellow output tab to the Result node's red input tab, overwriting the previous link (see Figure 9.16). Notice that since the Front image being output from the Master Keyer and the matte being created by the Master Keyer are separate links, you can eliminate the unwanted spill suppression by continuing to use the MasterK node's matte but applying it to the original image instead of the one output by the MasterK node.

FIGURE 9.16 Relinking the Front tab from the source image while still using the Matte tab from the MasterK node

Now it's time to take care of that unwanted bit of hallway at the top of the area reserved for the fake wall using the thoughtfully provided GMask node, which you used in the last chapter.

4. Click the GMask node to open its parameters, and then select the right-hand viewer pane to expose the object controls. Once you select the GMask, the viewer shows the actual matte as a grayscale image where white shows the opaque parts and black shows the transparent parts. You can see that in addition to the ceiling intrusion and fringing, there's probably a hole around the picture frame at camera left and some holes in the desk. It's amazing what you see when you take a look at the matte directly.

If the FX Nodes bin is open, it's necessary to double-click a node to open its parameters. Otherwise, single-clicking any node in the schematic will do the same thing.

5. To begin drawing, choose Draw Shape from the Tools menu (or press Shift+C), and then draw a shape that crops out the unwanted ceiling bit and fringing but doesn't intrude on the area around the woman's head and hand. Click the first control point you created to draw the shape, and then set the Colour slider to 0 to turn the GMask black, neatly masking all unwanted bits in the key. Since this is a locked shot, drawing the mask is all you need to do. There's no need to track or animate it.

It can help to zoom into what you're tracing while drawing a mask by Control+ Option+dragging in a pane of the viewport. You can do this even when you're in the middle of drawing a shape.

6. Now, to take care of the holes in the desk, create another mask by clicking the Add button, and this time draw a shape that includes the desk, running along the top edge, and surrounds all the parts of the wall that had unavoidable holes from the key. When you're finished, click the first control point you created to close the shape, and leave this one white, since you're masking in parts of the matte that you want to stay solid. The result should look something like Figure 9.17.

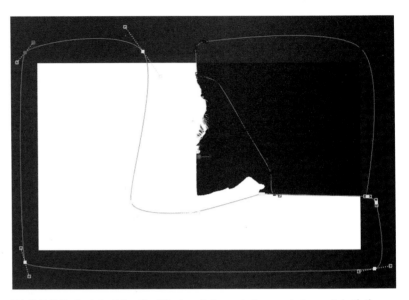

FIGURE 9.17 Using the GMask node to create two masks to repair both the transparent and solid areas of the matte

At this point, the matte is good, but, keeping in mind that you originally created a really fast, hard key just to have something for the rough cut, this is probably a good time to revisit what you did to see if it's possible to refine the key a bit more to retrieve more hair detail. After all, with the ability to use garbage masks to crop out hard-to-key areas, you can key with a lighter touch.

7. Select the MasterK node, then click the right-hand pane of the viewport, and press F4 to toggle to the matte. Zoom in on the woman's hair, and then hold the Option key down and drag with the pointer in the region around her hair until you see the Matte Overall, Matte E, and Range Highlights sliders. Adjust them to the left or right until you can see all of the fine fringing hair detail overlapping the greenscreen. Hold the Option key down again, drag until you see the Range B and Range D sliders, and adjust them to try to obtain more detail in the hair (see Figure 9.18). You'll know you're doing well when you can scrub through the early part of the shot where the woman turns her head and strands of hair don't seem to disappear. You'll likely see a lot more fringing in the tougher-to-key parts of the greenscreen material as a result, but that's okay because you'll be masking it out using the GMask later on.

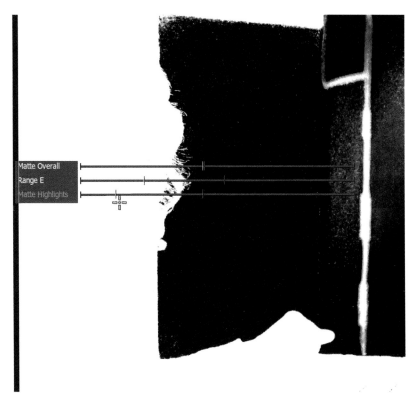

Matte Overall

Range E

Matte Highlights

FIGURE 9.18   Refining the Master Keyer matte to retrieve hair detail

8. Select the Matte Edge and, if necessary, click the right-hand pane of the viewport, and press F4 to toggle to the matte before you, then turn on the Blur button and set Width and Height to approximately 1.08, or just enough to knock the aliasing off the edge. If Erode is turned on from the previous exercise, turn it off, or minimize its effect until you feel like you've got good hair detail with a minimum of aliasing.

9. When you're finished, you may need to select the GMask node and readjust the overlapping garbage mattes to crop out the additional fringing and holes you created when adding back these details in her hair. While you work with the GMask, pay particular attention to the Auto Key button to make sure it's turned off. This button has a nasty habit of getting turned on when you're not expecting it, resulting in the automatic creation of keyframes whenever you

If you find you've accidentally created unwanted keyframes, click the Animation button to open the Keyframe editor, then move the positioner in the timeframe to a frame where your masks are as you want them, and with the proper channels selected in the list on the left, click the Keep button to keep that shape while deleting all other keyframes. Alternatively, you can click the Constant Shape button in the GMask controls to lock the keyframes to the shape at the frame of the positioner.

make an adjustment to a mask. When masking an unmoving subject, keyframes are not necessary.

10. When you're finished refining the MasterK and GMask node results, click the RETURN button to go back to the Media list.

This key is still pretty harsh, but it's okay for now. You'll have the chance later to revisit this composite and redo the keying operation from scratch once you learn more about how to work within the Modular Keyer Schematic.

Simple Color Correction to Match Layers

Now you have a nicer matte and a bright orange wall separating the woman from her evil doppelganger. However, the wall looks ridiculous in its current state; it clearly needs to be color-corrected in order to fit into the environment better and to blend in better with the additional hair detail you retrieved in the previous exercise. Fortunately, the Action node has built-in color-correction tools that you can use.

1. Select the Action node, and then open the Media list if necessary. Select row 3F, and double-click the cell in the CC column to enter the Color Correction editor. The default view of the viewer in the Color Correction editor is Result, which simply shows you the isolated wall. This is no use if you're trying to match the wall to its surroundings.

2. Choose Colour Correct Views ≻ Context:defaultcam from the View pop-up menu in the lower-left corner (see Figure 9.19). Now that you can see the overall composite, set the viewer to Log mode so that you can see the scene's true colors while you grade. You'll immediately notice that the wall turns a brilliant orange because the wall graphic isn't log encoded. That's OK, because you can address this with color correction.

FIGURE 9.19 Viewing the layer you're about to color correct in context

The color-correction controls are fairly standard Offset/Gamma/ Gain controls. A set of parameter sliders provides control over image contrast:

Offset Shifts the overall lightness of the image up and down, setting the black point, which is the darkest portion of the image.

Gain Adjusts the brightest part of the picture by setting the white point, stretching the lightness from the white to the black points to fit.

Gamma Redistributes the midtones to make the overall image lighter or darker.

Contrast Stretches or compresses the difference between the lightest and darkest parts of the picture around a central pivot point that's also adjustable.

3. Lower the RGB Contrast parameter to the point where the highlight on the wall isn't glowing horribly (around 33.00). Then lower the RGB Offset parameter until the dark part of the fake wall roughly matches the real wall it's meant to match (somewhere around −0.336).

   With the contrast of the image adjusted to match, a single color-balance control is used to adjust the color balance in the master, shadows, midtones, or highlights of the image, depending on which button you click.

   ▶ Master adjusts color throughout the tonal range of the image, from the darkest through the lightest parts of the image.

   ▶ The Shadows, Midtones, and Highlights controls allow for more targeted color adjustments within the darkest, middle, or lightest regions of the image, respectively.

4. With the Master button enabled, drag the color-balance control just a bit toward yellow to add some greenish/yellow to the fake wall that matches the highlights of the wall behind the woman (the color-balance numeric values are represented by Hue around 50 and Gain around 14.1), and then drop Saturation down to around 79. When you're finished, the settings should resemble those shown in Figure 9.20.

◀

Clicking the Master, Shadows, Midtones, or Highlights button to change which zone the color balance affects also changes which zone of the image the Gamma/Gain/Offset/ Contrast parameters adjust.

FIGURE 9.20   Color-correction settings used to match the fake wall to the real one

When the fake wall looks about right, you're finished. Click the RETURN button to go back to the CFX editor, and your composite in a pane of the viewport that's set to Log should look something like the one shown in Figure 9.21.

FIGURE 9.21   The color-corrected wall

Now you'll probably notice some green fringing in the woman's hair that wasn't visible before. Don't worry about it; it's something you'll correct later on.

Building the Door

Now that you have the woman keyed and have replaced the hole in the wall with a convincing-looking wall, it's time to start putting together the dimensional doorway. The doorway effect itself will be composed of several layers in order to create a more organic sort of effect. The elements you'll use are particle systems generated in a third-party application, layered carefully to create an animated result.

Cutting a Hole in the Wall

First, you'll create the basic door shape, with undulating edges created using a single animated movie file positioned to four different locations, using Axis nodes and some Action Schematic trickery.

1. Make some room in the ConnectFX Schematic, open the FX nodes bins, press C to isolate all nodes beginning with C, and drag a Coloured Frame node into the schematic. Then drag in an Action node, press Control+N to add an input, and connect the Coloured Frame node's yellow output to the media1 input's red Front tab, leaving the blue Matte tab disconnected.

2. Next, add a 2D Transform node, connecting the Coloured Frame's output to the 2D Transform node's red input tab and the 2D Transform node's yellow output tab to the blue Matte tab of the media1 input, as shown in Figure 9.22.

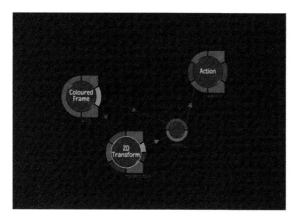

FIGURE 9.22 Using a 2D Transform node to create a simple rectangular matte to use with a Coloured Frame

3. Select the 2D Transform node to open its parameters, then turn off the Prop button underneath the Scale sliders, and use the Scale X (set to approximately 32.00) and Scale Y (set to approximately 75.00) parameters to resize the white shape to create a slightly wide doorway shape.

4. Drag the warpline_alpha clip from the Portal Graphics Elements bin of the Media Library into the ConnectFX Schematic, just below

the colored frame. Then select the Action node, press Control+N to create a second media2 input, and connect both its red and blue inputs to the `warpline_alpha` clip's output.

5. With the Action node selected in the ConnectFX Schematic, open the Action bin and double-click the Axis node in the bin three times to add three Axis nodes to the Action Schematic. Drag to move them to each side of the image2 (2) surface node, and then drag a link from the edge of each Axis node to the image2 (2) surface node to connect them, as shown in Figure 9.23.

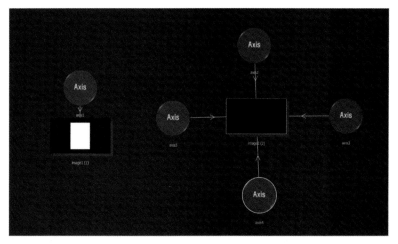

FIGURE 9.23 Creating three additional instances of the warpline_alpha animation to use as edges for the doorway

This graphic is an animated edge that you'll use to eat away at the edges of the white doorway that you've created.

6. The animated edge graphics emerge from nothing in the first frame, so drag the positioner in the timeline to about halfway through the shot in order to see the full graphic, and then double-click the top Axis node in the Action Schematic and set the Blend Mode pop-up menu to Subtract in order to see the `warpline_alpha` clip as a smoky, ghostlike animation running through the center of the white doorway graphic.

7. Set the proportionally locked Scale parameters to **47** so that the animated graphic is just a little bit wider than the doorway, and then drag the Y Position slider right (or drag it using the viewport layer widget) to move the graphic up to intersect the top edge of the rectangle (around 406). With the Blend mode set to Subtract, the graphic should appear to eat away at the edge of the "doorway."

8. One by one, select each of the three other Axis nodes you attached to the image2 surface, and adjust their Position X and Y, Rotation Z, and Scale parameters to scale and align each instance of the animated edge along each side of the rectangular doorway, until all four edges are being animated.

9. At this point, the edge of the rectangle may still look a bit hard despite the animated layers subtracting from it, so open the Media list, select row 1F, and adjust the built-in X Blur and Y Blur cells to 22 to feather the edges. This blurring should interact with the animated edges to create a nice, ghostly smokiness, as shown in Figure 9.24.

When changing the Blend mode of an image node (sometimes referred to as a *surface*) that's being instantiated multiple times by multiple Axis nodes that are connected to it, changing the Blend mode of the single Image node automatically changes them all.

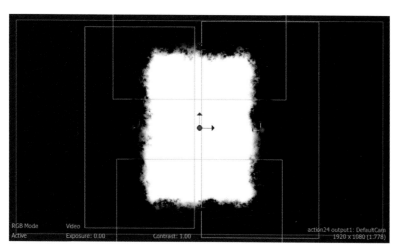

FIGURE 9.24 The doorway after layering the warpline_alpha graphic along the edges and using the Media list's blur function

Building a Dynamic Door Open

Now that you've created the ghostly doorway, it's time to create the effect of it opening, for which you'll use yet another prerendered particle animation. This time you'll use a layer that looks like an electrical hole burning open to create the illusion that the doorway is flaring out of nowhere. To make it look even more interesting, you'll create the effect of three pinholes opening up and merging to create the one doorway using three different instances of a single clip node.

1. Pan down in the ConnectFX Schematic to create more room, and drag the IonSpark_alpha clip into the schematic. Open the FX nodes bin, drag an Action node to the right of it, and press Control+N three times to create three media inputs. Finally, connect the Front and Matte tabs of each of the three media inputs to the yellow output tab of the IonSpark_alpha clip node, as shown in Figure 9.25.

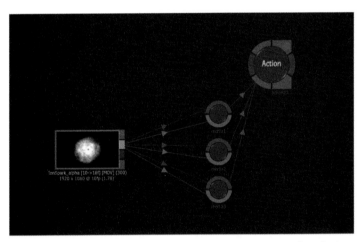

FIGURE 9.25 Creating three instances of the IonSpark_alpha layer with only one imported clip

Why connect the IonSpark_alpha three times? The answer is that each time you connect a clip node to another media input, you create another instance of that clip that can be composited alongside the others, a duplicate of sorts. The three media inputs then show up as three surfaces within the Action Schematic, each with its own Axis transform attached and ready to go. This is an important technique, because creating three instances of the IonSpark clip using multiple media inputs requires less computer memory than importing three IonSpark clip nodes. It's the efficient way to work.

2. Select each Axis node in turn (double-click if the Object editor doesn't appear), and use the Position X and Y or the onscreen controls in the output1:DefaultCam pane of the viewport to move the three duplicate `IonSpark_alpha` animations into a triangular arrangement, as shown in Figure 9.26. The dark center of each particle system should not overlap with any of the other layers.

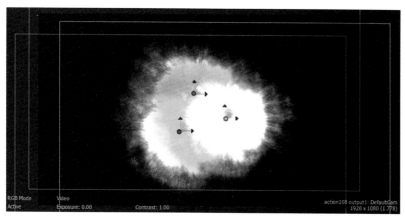

FIGURE 9.26 Arranging the three "burning holes" that will open up to form the doorway

With this arrangement, you'll animate each Axis node's Scale parameter to "open" each hole up into the door.

3. Select the first Axis node in the Action Schematic, and then move the positioner to frame 12:31:22+10, when the woman first turns towards the fake wall, and click Set Key to add a keyframe to this frame, freezing its size at 100 percent. Then drag the positioner back to frame 12:31:21+10, where the woman is looking straight ahead, turn on Auto Key, and set the Scale parameter to 0. If you scrub from one keyframe to the next, you should see the animated layer grow from nothing to full size.

4. Select the second Axis node, drag the positioner a few frames past the frame where the first hole is fully open, and click Set Key to create a keyframe to freeze the layer at 100 percent. If you don't see a Set Key button, open the Animation editor. Now drag the positioner to a few frames past when the first hole opens up, and set the Scale parameter to 0.

5. Select the third Axis node, and set another pair of keyframes that are slightly offset from the animation of the other two layers to animate Scale from 0 to 100. When you're finished, each of the three holes should begin growing at a different time, with their start frames offset from one another so that dragging the positioner through the start of the animation shows each hole at a different size, as shown in Figure 9.27. The timing and position of these holes do not have to be exact; they should just look good. When you're finished keyframing, be sure you *turn off the Auto Key button* to make sure that you don't accidentally create unwanted keyframes in other parts of this exercise.

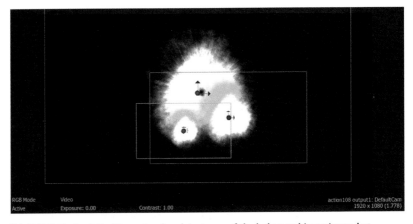

FIGURE 9.27 The scale of each instance of the hole graphics animated at different times to appear as if they're opening up

With this set up, it's time to put the "holes" and "doorway" images together to create the whole doorway effect.

6. Open the FX nodes bin, and drag a Comp node into the ConnectFX Schematic between the two Action composites you've just created. Connect the "doorway" Action node's yellow output tab to its red Front input tab, and then connect the yellow output tab of the "holes" Action node to the green Back input tab. The overall node structure should look like Figure 9.28.

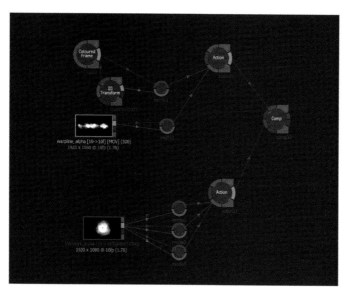

FIGURE 9.28 Putting the whole doorway effect together using a Logic Op node

7. Double-click the Comp node to open its parameters, and choose Multiply from the Blend Mode pop-up menu. The Comp node is like a simplified Blend & Comp node that combines only two images, but it has a longer list of blend modes from which to choose. Choosing Multiply preserves black wherever it appears in either layer, so that the black border around the door automatically crops the outer edge of the three holes graphics merged together. Now, if you scrub through the timeline, you should see the holes open up and then occupy the shape of the animated door, so that it's one unified effect (see Figure 9.29).

Why does the Multiply blend node preserve black? Because any pixel's color value multiplied by zero equals zero, no matter the order of the input layers. Blend modes are all about the math.

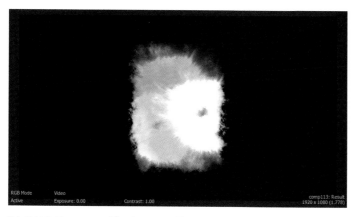

FIGURE 9.29 The doorway effect

Putting It All Together

Now you have a fake wall and a door. It's time to marry the two together to create the actual effect you're going for. In the process, you'll see how you can use two different images as the Front and Matte images of a media input for an Action node.

1. To actually use this graphic to cut a hole in the wall, drag a Negative node from the FX nodes bin into the ConnectFX Schematic, and connect its inputs to the Comp node's yellow output. This creates a suitable matte with a solid border surrounding an undulating region of translucence.

2. Link the Negative node's output to the media3 input's blue Matte tab. This works so long as both the Matte image and the Front image have the same resolution and bit depth. The node tree should now look like Figure 9.30.

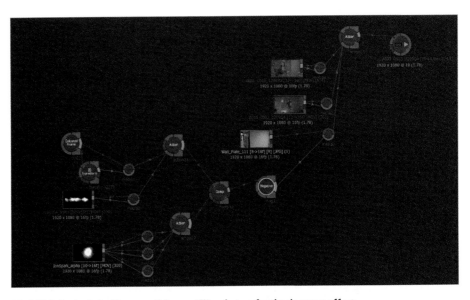

FIGURE 9.30 The overall ConnectFX node tree for the doorway effect

3. A hole appears in the wall but it's in the wrong place, and besides, the layer of the woman's duplicate holding the dart gun is still improperly reversed. Double-click the original Action node to open its Media list, and with the media3 input selected, set the Matte Clip pop-up to Matte On. You should now see the doorway cutting through the fake wall, although it's not quite positioned in the right place.

4. Select the 3F/3M rows in the Media list, then open the Action bin, and double-click the Source Matte node to add a surface and Axis specifically to adjust the incoming matte. You may need to Option+drag the top node of this new branch to another location to tidy up the Action Schematic.

5. Double-click the Axis node that's attached to the new branch, and adjust the Position X and Position Y parameters to move the doorway to a more suitable position on the wall to reveal the duplicate in the lab at frame 12:31:23+00 (291, 92 is a good coordinate).

6. Click the Axis node that's attached to the mirror plate of the standing woman, set Rotation Y to 180°, and adjust the Position X and Y parameters to fit the woman with the dart gun inside the "dimensional doorway." The result should look like Figure 9.31.

FIGURE 9.31 The CFX Result view of the finally positioned doorway cutting through the fake wall, toward the end of the shot, with the CFX Result viewport pane set to Log

Adding Plasma Shimmer

Well, that was certainly a process! However, you've now seen the full power of the Action node for assembling complex 2D composites. Now that you have such a nice effect, it's time to add just one more effect to put the doorway over the top — some animated crackling and sparking that eats away at the edges of the doorway. In the process, you'll start to see how accessing different image data at each step of the ConnectFX process tree lets you create additional effects using different aspects of layered images that you've already created.

1. Drag an Edge Detect node from the FX nodes bin to the ConnectFX Schematic, and link its Front input tab to the yellow output tab of the Comp node. The result should be that the Edge Detect node automatically creates an animated series of outlines tracing the crackly edges of detail from the doorway effect.

2. Select the first Action node, and press Control+N to add one more media input (labeled media4). Connect the Edge Detect node's yellow output to both the Front and Matte inputs of the media4 input.

3. Select the Action node, open the Priority list, and use it to push this new edge layer back so that it's between the woman at her desk and the doorway.

4. It's in the wrong position, so double-click the Axis node that's attached to the edge layer in the Action Schematic and use the Position X and Position Y sliders to move the edge layer to overlap the doorway. At this point, the Action Schematic is getting a bit crowded, so don't forget that you can Option+drag the top node in a branch to move the whole branch to another position in the schematic (see Figure 9.32).

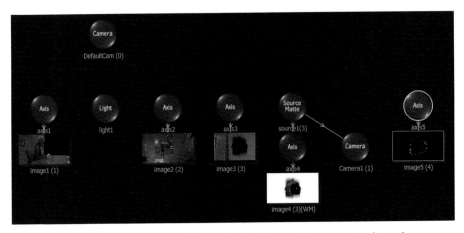

FIGURE 9.32 The main Action Schematic with all layers being composited together

5. With the Axis controls open, choose Add from the Blend Mode pop-up menu to create a hard, electric color interaction, and then raise the Transparency parameter slider to around **43 percent** to fade it down to be a little less intense.

6. The resulting "shimmering plasma" effect is a little sharp and harsh, so open the Media list and use the X Blur and Y Blur parameter cells of rows 4F and 4M to blur the edge layer by a value of 1, knocking the edge off of it a little. The end result should look more or less like Figure 9.33.

FIGURE 9.33 The final effect

Creating ConnectFX Clips

At this point, you've got a pretty sophisticated ConnectFX schematic going, but it's getting a little big. For the very last exercise of this chapter, you'll learn how to consolidate self-contained sections of a ConnectFX Schematic into a *CFX clip*, which is essentially a single clip that contains a ConnectFX Schematic inside itself.

Examining the overall ConnectFX Schematic, you should be able to see that the entire "doorway effect" portion of the tree, up to the Comp Node, is entirely self-contained. In other words, no part of this node tree is connected to any other part, except for the last Comp Node. This makes this section (shown highlighted in Figure 9.34) an ideal candidate for consolidation.

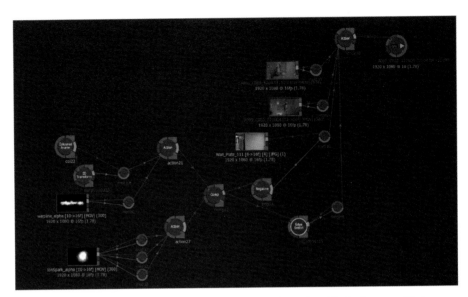

FIGURE 9.34 The current state of the ConnectFX schematic, with the doorway effect nodes selected

1. Right-click the Comp node, and choose Create CFX from the context menu. A new node is created, labeled Comp###[CFX]. This node contains both itself and every upstream node that's connected to the left of it.

2. To prove this, Shift+click the Comp node again to select it and all upstream nodes, and press the Delete key to eliminate them. Then connect the Comp###[CFX] node's yellow output tab to the red Front input tabs of the Negative and Edge Detect nodes, and select the original Action node to see the result. The node tree is significantly smaller, as shown in Figure 9.35, but the end result is the same.

   Once the node tree is consolidated, you can open the Timing view, select the ConnectFX clip you've created, and click the Render button to render that clip, caching its operations and speeding up your composite's performance. If you create a ConnectFX clip and then find that you need to modify the composite within it, that's easy to do.

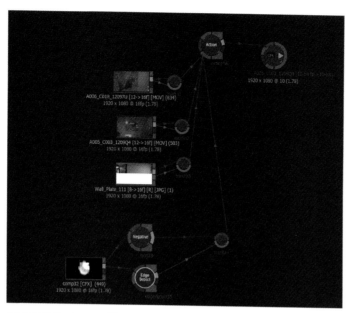

FIGURE 9.35   The newly consolidated node tree

3. Right-click the Comp## node you created, and choose Explode CFX from the context menu. The original node tree should reappear.

THE ESSENTIALS AND BEYOND

The lessons in this chapter demonstrate the flexibility that Action adds to the ConnectFX compositing experience. Now it's your turn to tinker with the composite you've created to make it even more interesting.

ADDITIONAL EXERCISES

▶ Adjust the transparency of the doorway using the Colour Correct node that comes before the Negative node.

▶ Add an Optics node between the mirror layer and the media1 input of the Action node. (Note: You'll need to add a Coloured Frame node and connect its output to the Optics node's blue Matte input for this to work.) Experiment and adjust its parameters to create a slightly purplish glow to what appears through the doorway. For added effect, animate the glow to be intense before the doorway opens and less intense as the doorway becomes fully open.

▶ Add a Deform node after the Optics node to create an undulating warping effect. Reduce the Amplitude parameter until the effect is subtler, and animate the Time Offset parameter to create a sense of motion.

CHAPTER 10

Working with Audio

In this chapter, you'll take a closer look at the process of refining your audio in the Autodesk® Smoke® environment. First you'll re-edit your production audio and add additional music and audio effects. Then you'll learn how to add audio effects from the timeline FX Ribbon. Finally, you'll use the Audio Desk to mix all of the audio tracks of your scene for a pleasing final result.

Topics in this chapter include the following:

▶ **Importing the opening scene**

▶ **Refining the production audio**

▶ **Using audio effects**

▶ **Adding music and sound effects**

▶ **Setting clip levels**

▶ **Mixing with the audio desk**

Importing the Opening Scene

First, you need to import the scene in which you'll be refining the audio. For the exercises in this chapter, you'll be pulling a more fully baked cake out of the oven, so to speak, because the imported clips will have the final effects to which you can time your sound design. All of the sound design in this chapter is adapted from the terrific work done on the audio of "The Place Where You Live," by Kelly Pieklo, when working at Splice Here in Minneapolis, who was generous enough to share the original source elements for use in the following exercises.

1. Open the Conform tab, click the Conform Task pop-up menu (with the gear icon), and choose Load New FCP XML/AAF/EDL from the context menu. The File Browser panel appears.

2. At the bottom of the Media Import dialog, a set of tabs lets you choose settings for the imported project. Click the EDL Import Options tab, and then click the Resolution From Project button to change it to Select Resolution, and check to make sure the settings are correct. The resolution should be set to 1920x1080, with Set To 16:9, 10-bit, and Progressive selected. When you're done, click Import.

3. Use the Bookmarks pop-up menu to navigate to the directory bookmarked in Chapter 2, which contains your downloaded book media; open the Scene EDLs folder in the sidebar, select the Open for Audio.edl file, and click the Import button.

4. This particular project uses separate media files for the video and audio used in each clip, so you'll need to change the way that media is matched to events in the EDL. Open the Match Criteria pop-up menu and choose File Name to turn this option off, while leaving the Source Timecode and Frame Rate options turned on.

5. Click the Set Search Location button to open the Set Directory browser, and use the Up button to reopen the top level folder that contains all of the downloaded media for this book. Click the Set button at the bottom right of this window; Autodesk Smoke is smart enough to check through each of the subfolders in order to find all of the media necessary to relink this project.

6. Click the pop-up arrow at the right of the Link Selected button, and choose Link Matched Sources from the pop-up menu (if this button is already set to Link Matched Sources, then you need only click it once). Every clip in the imported EDL should now be linked to the downloaded project media. Open the Timeline panel.

7. Drag the new Open_for_Audio sequence from the Conform Sequences Library into the Office Scene Library.

Refining the Production Audio

Before beginning any other audio work, you need to clean up the production tracks. In this scene, that means you need to eliminate unwanted background noise, clips with room ambience that doesn't match, yelled-out instructions from the director, and any other unwanted sound. In the process, you'll need to fill these holes in the soundtrack with *room tone*, which is the ambient sound of silence in a particular location.

1. Before you begin, click the Options pop-up menu, and choose Scrub Audio to enable audio playback when you're dragging the positioner around on the timeline. This can be useful when you're working on the audio of a project.

2. Play through the scene, and identify the clip audio that you need to replace.

   You should notice that the audio of the first, second, third, fifth, and eighth clips is either absent or completely wrong.

3. Hold the Command key down, and drag a selection box from any empty area of the timeline around the first three pairs of audio clips to select them. Then add to the selection by Command+clicking the audio of the fifth and last clips. Finally, make sure Link and Ripple are disabled, and press Delete to perform a lift edit to eliminate these clips.

   The audio of the fourth clip has the sound of the director saying "ding" as an audio cue to the actor.

4. Click the lock icon of track V1.1 to prevent changes to the video. Then use the JKL keys to move the positioner to a frame right before the ding, and press Control+Shift+V to add a cut to all tracks. Then use the Trim tool to roll the incoming half of the edit to the right to remove the ding. Notice that with Scrub Audio turned on, the Trim tool plays the audio as you drag edits around.

   The audio of the sixth clip has sections of lines from another take; the dialog should be eliminated, but the quiet moments of ambient room tone should be left in the timeline.

5. Use the Trim tool to roll the in point of each audio track associated with the sixth and seventh clips past the sound of the director saying the line "Thanks, Nina."

   You should now have a timeline with missing audio in parts and gaps in what production audio is left, as shown in Figure 10.1.

Holding down the Option key while scrubbing will also work if the Scrub Audio option is disabled. Also, holding down Command+Option while scrubbing will cause audio to scrub in a more "analog" style of playback, which can be more convenient for making out what sounds you're trying to listen for.

FIGURE 10.1 The timeline after eliminating unwanted audio

Now you need to fill those holes in the audio tracks. In some cases the sound recordist would have recorded a section of room tone, but in many cases you need to derive room tone from quiet sections of the regular production audio. First, you'll examine the audio from clip A0006_C024_1209GU to see if you can pull room tone out of it.

6. Press Option+2 to put the viewport into Source-Sequence viewer mode, and then right-click the last remaining audio clip in track A1 and choose Match ➤ Content from the context menu. This command opens a new copy of the original clip in the source viewer, placing this duplicate in the currently selected bin of the Media Library. Alternatively, you can choose Reveal ➤ Segment from the same context menu to find the original clip in the Media Library without opening it or duplicating it.

To examine the audio waveform of this clip more closely in order to see if there's a good section of ambient room tone, you'll use the green *source timeline* tab, as shown in Figure 10.2.

FIGURE 10.2 The source timeline tab always appears to the left of all the timeline tabs

The source timeline is something that you've so far ignored, but it's there to make it easy for you to scrub through a clip that's selected in the Media Browser. Within the context of doing audio work, the source timeline lets you examine the waveform of a source clip to help you make decisions about where to set in and out points.

7. Click the green timeline tab to the left to open the source timeline. If you like, you can click the timeline's right vertical scrollbar and

drag to the left to make the timeline tracks taller. Scrub through the audio tracks, and you'll discover that the sections of this track that you may have thought were quiet aren't really as quiet as you might have hoped. This won't work.

8. Open the Audio folder that you placed within the Office Scene library, and you'll see a clip named Office Scene Room Tone (the sound recordist came through after all). Select it to open it in the source timeline instead, play through it to find a quiet section free of microphone handling, and set in and out points.

     At this point, you've got a bit of a problem. The Office Scene Room Tone clip is a stereo clip, but if you click the Open_for_Audio sequence tab, you'll see that the audio tracks you want to edit to are mono tracks. Clicking the Office Scene Room Tone tab again, you should notice that the source-destination controls in the patch panel area cannot be connected; this is because stereo audio cannot be edited into mono tracks.

9. If necessary, click the stereo audio clip to select it; then open the Timeline Task menu (the gear), and choose Stereo ➤ Split Stereo Track. The source clip in this timeline is now split into two mono tracks, and the source-destination controls are enabled.

10. Click the Open For Audio timeline tab again, and notice that the source and destination controls in the patch panel area mirror the assignments made in the source timeline. Then press the Home key to move the positioner to the beginning of the timeline, and perform a series of overwrite edits to fill the empty area of tracks A1 and A2. Be careful not to overwrite any of the previously edited audio; you want to preserve the original sounds of the actor's movement.

11. To fill gaps that are narrower than the duration of the incoming segment of audio, press the Page Down key to move the focus of the positioner to track A1, move the positioner somewhere within the gap, and press X to set timeline in and out points to match the duration of the gap. Then clear the out point in the source viewer (select the source viewer and press Option+O), and perform an overwrite edit to fill the gap with the source clip.

12. With all of these gaps filled with room tone, Command+click each edit point between the audio clips on tracks A1 and A2, and choose Effects ➤ Audio Transitions ➤ Fade (or press CMD+T) to add an audio

You can also Command+drag a bounding box to select multiple clips and edit points in preparation for adding multiple transitions, as long as you don't also select the in point of the first clip in the Timeline.

fade to every audio edit at once, preventing unwanted clicks or pops. Please note that for this to work, no video item can be selected. When you're finished, the timeline should look like the one shown in Figure 10.3.

FIGURE 10.3 The timeline after editing room tone to fill the gaps and adding fades to each edit

With this accomplished, you've created a solid base upon which to build the rest of the sound design that you'll be adding to this scene — all without distractingly abnormal silences.

Using Audio Effects

At this point, the sole piece of dialog is the man's video message, but right now it sounds too perfect. In this next exercise, you'll learn how to apply and manipulate audio effects.

1. Select the first clip in track A3 of the man talking, and then press Control+Tab to open the floating FX Ribbon. Since you selected an audio clip, the FX Ribbon displays the Audio Effects tab, which presents a variety of audio effects for you to apply, as shown in Figure 10.4. Click the EQ button.

FIGURE 10.4 Summoning the floating FX Ribbon using Control+Tab

2. To work on the clip you want to EQ more intensively, Shift+click the speaker icon in the track header for audio track A3 to solo that track, then double-click the clip to which you added the EQ effect (*don't* double-click the EQ proxy) to open the EQ editor, which presents a series of handles inside a graph that you can use to boost or attenuate different ranges of audio frequencies. Although EQ can be effective for improving a speaker's presence or downplaying unwanted noise or sonic qualities of a recording, in this exercise you're going to use the EQ editor to *degrade* the man's voice to make it sound more like a speakerphone.

3. Click and hold the play button to access its pop-up menu, and choose Loop. Next, click and hold the play button a second time, and choose Selection. This procedure sets up the play button to loop the currently selected clip while you work.

4. Play the clip, and adjust the EQ handles in the graph while you preview the result. Try dragging the L and M2 handles *down* to attenuate the lower frequencies of his voice, and drag the M3 and M4 handles *up* to boost his higher frequencies. Note how these handles correspond to the frequency, dB, and Q parameters below. The overall result should be a tinny sound, but don't overdo it; it's important for the audience to be able to understand him clearly. One possible EQ setting is shown in Figure 10.5.

FIGURE 10.5 Adjusting EQ for a tinny "on the phone" sound

5. When you're finished with this adjustment, set the play button back to Normal and Once, and then click the EXIT button to return to the timeline.

6. Zoom the timeline vertically until you can see the EQ effects box on the clip you've just adjusted, and then drag it to the second clip in track A3 to copy it.

As you can see, applying audio effects using the FX Ribbon and the accompanying effect editors is very similar to applying video effects.

Adding Music and Sound Effects

Next, you'll cut in some additional ambience, effects, and music, in the process learning how to "spot" audio effects clips — match specific points of an audio effect to specific frames of the picture — and how to organize your tracks in Smoke.

1. Click the FX tab to hide the FX Ribbon, making more room for audio tracks.

2. Select the ATMOS 01 clip to open it in the source viewer, and set an in point one second into the clip (to leave some heads available for cross-fading) and out points to mark the first 43 seconds of the clip. This isolates a good section of general ambience, just before some more specific sound effects occur.

3. Option+click the Audio+ button to create a new stereo pair of tracks; then drag the source control to assign A1.L and A2.L to the new tracks 5–6, and edit the ATMOS 01 clip as many times into the new tracks as it takes to cover the entire scene. Use the Trim tool with Ripple turned off to resize the end of the last clip to conform to the last frame of video.

4. Select the edit point between the ATMOS 01 clips you just edited, and choose Effects ➤ Audio Transitions ➤ Fade to add an audio fade, as shown in Figure 10.6. This provides some "outside of the window" street ambience, which when mixed with the room tone will give more of a sense of place.

FIGURE 10.6 Adding stereo ambience to tracks A4.L and .R

5. Option+click the Audio+ button five times to create five new sets of stereo tracks, which you'll use for editing in some synced stereo sound effects and music.

6. With the viewport set to Src-Seq mode, select the PROD FX 01 clip, set an in point at the first frame of the clip, and then play through the source audio. It's a foley effect of the woman inhaling and exhaling that you want to sync to clip 02_Desk_FX.

7. In the timeline, set tracks A5.L and .R as the destination tracks; then move the positioner to the frame where the woman is about to exhale (12:30:28_03). In the source timeline, move the positioner to the frame where the sound of the exhale begins (01:00:47+05). To edit the audio clip into the timeline so that the frame at the source viewer positioner lines up with the timeline positioner, click the secondary edit pop-up menu, and choose Aligned Edit, as shown in Figure 10.7.

FIGURE 10.7
Using Aligned Edit to edit a source clip into the timeline so that the frame at the source positioner is aligned with the sequence positioner

The Aligned Edit command is useful for editing sound effects where you really want a particular frame to be synced with a specific frame of audio.

8. Set tracks A6.L and .R as the destination tracks, and then move the timeline positioner to the frame where the woman first touches the heads-up display (HUD), 12:30:22+09. Then select clip UI FX 01 to open it in the source viewer, and click the Overwrite Edit button to edit it into the sequence. This sound effect starts right at the beginning, so no in point needs to be set.

9. If you like, use your own judgment to edit UI FX 02 through UI FX 07 into the timeline to match the woman's physical interactions with the computer screen and the actions in the scene, such as the voice

conference chime ringing so that she "answers the phone," or you can proceed according to the following list.

On Tracks A6.L and .R:

▶ UI FX 01 at 12:30:22+09 and 12:30:34+05

▶ UI FX 04 at 12:30:23+13 and 12:30:36+08

▶ UI FX 06 at 12:30:49+15

On Tracks A7.L and .R:

▶ UI FX 03 at 12:30:32+17

▶ UI FX 05 at 12:30:49+05

10. Next, move the positioner in the timeline to the frame in the last clip where the "dimensional doorway" just starts to appear against the wall (around 12:30:55+21). Open the HUM FX clip into the source viewer, set an in point at the beginning of the clip, and move the source positioner to the part of the audio when the hum at the beginning starts to transform into something more extreme, around 00:00:10+15.

11. With the positioners so lined up, set tracks A8.L and A8.R as the destination tracks; then click the secondary edit pop-up menu, and choose Aligned Edit to edit that clip into the timeline to match the action of the sequence, with the quiet part of the hum sneaking up into the scene and the more dramatic part of the hum coinciding with the doorway actually opening.

12. Now, select the CUE01_FINAL clip to open it into the source viewer, and move the positioner to frame 01:00:30+13, at the very beginning of a dramatic bar of music. Then move the positioner in the timeline to the very beginning of the sequence, set tracks A9.L and .R as the destination tracks, and use the Aligned Edit command to edit the music cue into the timeline. Without setting an in point, the beginning of the incoming audio clip is cut off at the location of the positioner, which in this case is fine.

Now you have 16 tracks of audio adding ambience, sound effects, and music to the scene. Before moving on to a much-needed mix, it's worth taking some time to organize these tracks.

13. Click the header of track 3 in the timeline patch panel, and drag it down below tracks 5–6, so that all of the ambience tracks appear together. A tooltip lets you see where you'll be inserting the track (as shown in Figure 10.8); this actually moves the entire track, with all clips on it, to another position in the timeline.

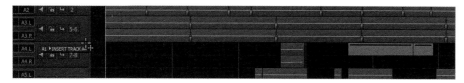

FIGURE   10.8   Dragging an entire track to reorganize your sound effects

At this point, you can see that you've been working in a fairly organized way. Using the destination track numbers, the ambience for the scene is now on tracks A1, A2, and A3.L and .R; the dialog appears in the newly moved track A4, VFX is in tracks A6.L and .R through A8.L and .R, and music appears in tracks A9.L and .R. This structure should resemble Figure 10.9.

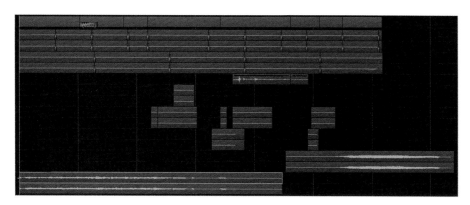

FIGURE   10.9   The edited audio cues for this scene

You can formalize your organization by naming each track, so you don't forget what is where.

14. Right-click the track A4 header in the timeline patch panel, and choose Rename Track. Enter **Dialog** into the Text Input window, and

click Enter. Nothing appears to have happened, but if you drag the border between the timeline patch panel and the video/audio tracks to the right, you can see that each track has a name, as shown in Figure 10.10.

FIGURE 10.10 Track names are revealed by dragging the timeline patch panel divider to the right.

15. Take some time to label the ambience, dialog, foley, SFX, and music tracks.

Setting Clip Levels

Now that you've edited together some nicely augmented sound for the scene, you're no doubt eager to start adjusting the levels of different clips to keep the different audio cues from train-wrecking into one another. In this next short exercise, you'll learn how to adjust the gain of individual clips.

1. Zoom into the CUE01 FINAL music clip in tracks A9.L and .R, and increase the track height so that it's easier to see the clip's waveform.

2. Open the timeline Options pop-up menu, and turn on Show Gain Animation if it's not on already. Move the pointer over the top track of CUE01 FINAL in the timeline, and notice how a black line with a square handle at the middle of it appears over the clip, as shown in Figure 10.11. This is an adjustable volume control just for that clip.

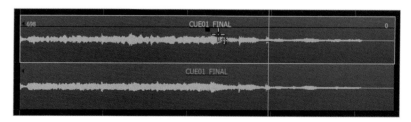

FIGURE 10.11 Individual clip Gain Animation audio controls

3. Drag the black square handle down to reduce (or attenuate) the volume of that clip to a point when the tooltip reads about -8.84 dB. While making this adjustment, you should also notice that the FX Ribbon has automatically opened up and a Gain parameter shows you the current gain of that clip. Whenever you adjust the Gain Animation control on a clip, a Gain FX box is automatically applied to that clip. If you find the Gain Animation control a bit finicky to work with, you can always use the Gain parameter in the FX Ribbon to make your adjustments.

4. Next, the PROD FX 01 audio of the woman sighing is a bit heavy-handed, so zoom into that clip in tracks A5.L and .R, and drag the Gain Animation control down to about -12.68, so that it doesn't sound quite so much like the microphone is right against her nose.

5. At this point, use your discretion and make individual adjustments to the various sound effects you've added for the woman's interactions with the HUD interface.

Mixing with the Audio Desk

Individual clip gain adjustments are really useful when quickly setting levels during an edit, but if you have an entire track full of clips that need adjusting, you can use the Audio Desk, which exposes a mixer interface that you can use to adjust the volume of an entire track. Track-level control is applied on top of clip-level control, so you have two levels of audio mixing that you can use together to mix the sound in a piece.

1. Press Option+1 to set the viewport to Player mode, and then choose Window ➤ Show Audio Desk from the menu bar, or click the Options pop-up underneath the Viewer and choose Show Audio Desk to open the track-based mixing controls, as shown in Figure 10.12. You'll want to choose Fit from the Zoom pop-up menu to shrink the viewer to the new size.

    At the left of the viewport are the vertical volume sliders, mute and solo controls, and buttons and pop-up menus for allowing the automatic keyframing of mixing adjustments and for showing which desk inputs are displayed when you have more audio tracks than you have room for track controls (up to eight can be displayed at one time).

Enabling Auto Key in the FX Ribbon before adjusting the levels via the Gain parameter or the clip gain handle lets you create animated changes in the levels that the black Gain Animation line will display.

FIGURE 10.12   The Audio Desk is a track-level mixer for your sequence.

At the right of the viewport are a set of High, Mid, and Low equalizer controls for each track. If you click the EQ Desk button, you can also reveal the Auxiliary Effects Desk, which has controls for Chorus, Delay, and Reverb that you can apply to selected tracks.

For this exercise, you'll be focusing on setting levels for the ambience of the room, since these tracks have more audio clips than you'll want to adjust one by one.

2. Click the square Gain Fader Lock button at the bottom of the audio meters in tracks 1 and 2. Even mono tracks are displayed in pairs, and this square button determines whether the two sliders act in unison. This button is automatically enabled for stereo track pairs, and it appears dark gray when enabled and light gray when disabled. These buttons can be seen in Figure 10.13.

FIGURE 10.13
The Gain Fader Lock
buttons, which lock the
volume controls of each
pair of faders together

Before you begin mixing, here's something you should notice. When you rearranged the audio tracks, the destination controls automatically renumbered themselves, but the actual track numbers did not. The faders in the Audio Desk refer to the track numbers, not the destination numbers. This means that track 3, which is the fifth track from the top in the timeline, still corresponds to fader 3 on the mixer. If you like, you can click and drag the mixer track number control to reassign audio tracks to different mixer channels.

3. You need to mix the ambience tracks, but it's difficult to evaluate them with the music playing, so click the Input Strip Display pop-up menu (which currently reads 1-8) and choose 9-16. Now you can click the Mute button for tracks 15 and 16 to disable the music temporarily while you work.

4. Choose 1-8 from the Input Strip pop-up menu, move the positioner to the beginning of the sequence, and then play the sequence. As it plays, drag the volume faders for tracks 5 and 6 down until the outside ambience sounds like it's really outside a window, somewhere around -4.8 dB.

5. Finally, fade tracks 1 and 2 down to lower the noise floor even further, to about -3 dB.

At this point, you should notice that the levels you've set affect every single clip on those tracks, so your ambience mixing is now done.

THE ESSENTIALS AND BEYOND

This chapter covered additional editorial commands useful for audio editing and refinement, as well as the basics of audio effects and mixing. Extra media is available, which you can use to design more fully the audio in this scene, providing you with ample excuses for additional sound sweetening, equalization, and mixing.

ADDITIONAL EXERCISES

▶ Create another set of stereo audio tracks into which to edit the provided fabric foley SFX (named FOL 01 through 10), and edit these cloth sounds to match the woman's movements, adding another layer of hyperrealism to the scene.

▶ Add the EQ effect to one of the cloth layers, and attenuate (reduce) the higher frequencies to give the cloth a more muffled sound. Once you achieve a good EQ setting, copy it to the other cloth sounds you edited into the sequence.

▶ Use either the clip level or track controls to reduce the cloth foley levels to a believable background volume.

CHAPTER 11

Color Correction

Smoke has two levels of color correction that you can apply. Using the tools in the timeline FX Ribbon, you can quickly apply primary and secondary color adjustments to clips right in the timeline using two different modes: the Colour Corrector or the Colour Warper. When applied, these adjustments can be applied to individual clips or to entire scenes using gap effects; when combined with custom masks drawn using timeline wipe effects, you can create sophisticated color corrections as you continue the process of finishing your program.

Topics in this chapter include the following:

▶ **Finishing log-encoded media**

▶ **Adding a color correction**

▶ **Setting up your environment**

▶ **Navigating a sequence while grading**

▶ **Using the Colour Corrector**

▶ **Shot matching using the Colour Warper**

▶ **Colour Warper primary adjustments**

▶ **Copying color corrections**

▶ **Colour Warper secondary adjustments**

▶ **Applying color corrections as gap effects**

▶ **Limiting a color correction using a wipe**

Importing the Hallway Scene

In this chapter, you'll explore the process of using the Autodesk® Smoke® timeline effects for doing color correction to adjust the color and contrast of clips in a program as you continue finishing it prior to final delivery. This chapter assumes some familiarity with color-correction terminology and procedures from other applications, and it uses a new sequence.

1. Choose the Hallway Scene library in the Media Library; then open the Conform tab, click the Conform Task pop-up menu (with the gear icon), and choose Load New FCP XML/AAF/EDL from the context menu. The File Browser panel appears.

2. At the bottom of the Media Import dialog, a set of tabs lets you choose settings for the imported project. Click the EDL Import Options tab, and then click the Resolution From Project button to change it to Select Resolution, and check to make sure the settings are correct. The resolution should be set to 1920x1080, with Set to 16:9, 16-bit fp, and Progressive selected.

3. Use the Bookmarks pop-up menu to navigate to the directory bookmarked in Chapter 2 that contains your downloaded book media, open the Scene EDLs directory, select the Hallway Scene .edl file, and click the Load button.

4. Click the Set Search Location button to open the Set Directory browser, and click the Up Directory button to navigate to your media. Click the Set button at the bottom right of this window.

5. If green checkboxes don't immediately appear in the status column for each of the media items in the Conform list, then open the Match Criteria pop-up menu and make sure that Source Timecode and Framerate are checked on, and File Name is unchecked (off).

6. Click the arrow at the right of the Link Selected button and choose Link Matched Sources from the pop-up menu. Every clip in the imported EDL should now be linked to the downloaded project media, except for the last clip on the timeline and the audio clips (see Figure 11.1), which still can't be found even though the matching clip is in fact part of your downloads.

FIGURE 11.1 The last clip doesn't relink automatically because of an inconsistency in the media.

 N O T E If you're having a problem with a clip in the timeline when trying to conform a sequence, you can get more information about that clip by pressing the (forward) slash key (/) and clicking that clip in the timeline. While slash+clicking a clip, a floating window appears showing you all manner of information about that clip that can be useful for troubleshooting.

7. Open the Match Criteria pop-up menu, and turn off Source Timecode. The clips should now display an exclamation point icon, indicating that there's a conflicting match that you need to resolve. If you right-click each of these exclamation point–flagged clips, you should be able to see the matching media appear in the Potential Matches bin of the Conform Media bin. Right-click each of the selected clips, and choose Link To for whatever name of clip is given. The audio clips may not relink properly, but for this lesson that's not important.

    When you're finished, each of the clips should show the linked icon that indicates each clip is matched. However, because this was such a thorny conform process, the last video clip in this sequence is not synced correctly.

8. Open the Timeline panel; then move the positioner to the in point of the last clip, turn Link on, choose the Slip tool, double-click the clip to show Trim View, and slip the clip so that the first frame of the clip is a few frames after the door starts opening in order to match the action of the previous clip in the timeline. Play through the edit, and slip the last clip as necessary for a smooth match-on-action cut.

As you can see, you never know when something is going to go wrong through a combination of media with differing characteristics. Fortunately, you can force a relink and do simple re-edits as necessary to resolve these types of problems. Now, using this sequence as your starting point, you'll learn how to use the color-correction features in Smoke to continue the process of finishing a program.

The scene you'll be working on in this chapter is a simple four-clip transition scene that takes the protagonist from one location to another, and it is designed to show off more of the environment in which the character of the physicist works. If you set the viewer to Log and play through the clip, you'll see that an elevator takes her through a subterranean basement with dismal lighting. While conceptually this is what the director was going for, the practical lighting shown in Figure 11.2 is a little *too* dismal for the final project.

F I G U R E 11.2 The original, ungraded look of the basement hallway scene

You'll begin by using timeline effects to apply color corrections to your clips to balance them for a more pleasing look.

Finishing Log-Encoded Media

Since the clips in this scene are log encoded, you have to make a decision about how you're going to output your project before you begin adjusting the color. If the goal is to output to film, or you're delivering a rendered sequence of graded effects clips destined for another project elsewhere, then you may need to deliver log-encoded files. In this case, you'd apply color-correction effects the same way you've been applying other effects — monitoring using either the Log mode of the viewer or by applying an appropriate 3D LUT (such as a film print emulation Look Up Table, or LUT), using the viewing settings found in the Options pop-up menu with a LUT selected from the LUT tab of the Preferences, and applying your corrections relative to the viewer's automatic adjustment. Since the viewer setting doesn't get rendered into the final output, this means that you can adjust your image relative to the way it will look after film printing while keeping the image data properly log encoded.

If you're outputting a broadcast video master for Rec.709 playback, however, you'll need to *normalize* the signal at the same time as you're grading it so that your output looks right for general viewing. This can be done in one of several ways. In post-production, normalizing a log-encoded image refers to the process of changing it from its original low-contrast, unprocessed state into a final image that's suitable for viewing.

Using Each Clip's Pre-Processing Options

One convenient way of normalizing log-encoded clips to give yourself a good starting point for a grade is to use the RGB LUT options found inside of each clip's Pre-Processing options.

1. Set the viewer to Video mode, press A to choose the Select tool, and select the first clip in the timeline (the woman leaving the elevator). Then double-click the Pre-Processing button in the FX Ribbon (after the Format Options button) to enter its editor.

2. Click the RGB LUT button, and turn on the Active button to its right to enable a LUT for that clip.

3. Choose Log To Lin to use the same color transformation with which you've been monitoring up until now, or Choose 3D LUT and then click the Import button to choose from the numerous LUTs that come with Smoke. For now, choose Log To Lin. Make sure the Destination setting is set to 16-bit Float.

   This transformation takes the low-contrast, low-saturation clip and turns it into what you've been looking at using the viewer settings — a more pleasing image that uses the full available range of the video signal. These settings permanently affect the image, however, and so you have reason to be concerned that the shadows are currently really dark and the highlights are being *clipped*. In other words, detail in the highlights is being discarded where it's brighter than the maximum image value that's allowed.

   Clipping is a particular problem because image data that's lost here won't be retrievable in later operations, so you'll need to readjust the default settings of the Log To Lin parameters if you want to preserve these parts of the signal.

◄

If you regularly work with Rec.709-encoded media, you can skip this entire section. However, an increasing number of digital cinema cameras allow for log-encoded capture in order to provide maximum image detail and latitude for grading, so this is valuable information.

4. Drag any of the Soft Clip parameters to the right (they're linked together via the Prop button at the right) until the image detail and color in the highlights of the wall outside the elevator return (around 214.000). As you make this adjustment, the curve to the right, as shown in Figure 11.3, shows you how your adjustment is affecting the image, as a soft roll-off at the top end that's designed to compress your highlights rather than pushing them outside the boundaries of what's allowable in the signal. Don't worry if this looks a bit dim; you'll be readjusting the image later to look the way you want it to.

FIGURE 11.3 Customizing the Log To Lin settings you're adjusting to normalize the image before grading

5. Now drag one of the Film Gamma sliders to the right to lighten the shadows a bit (a value of 1.000 is good). You don't want to overlighten the image, just keep the shadows from being too inky.

   When you're finished, you still have an image with higher contrast and saturation that you can use as a good starting point for the rest of your grade, but as you can see in Figure 11.4, you're preserving more highlight and shadow detail for use in subsequent operations via the custom settings you're applying.

6. Click the Exit button to return to the timeline. To apply this adjustment to each of the other clips in the timeline, drag the Pre-Processing effect from the ribbon, and drop it onto each of the next three video clips in the timeline to copy it.

You may have noticed that the Resize (RZ) effect has disappeared from the clips; this is a function of the 16-bit floating-point promotion that each of these clips has gotten as a result of the LUT you added. If you changed the LUT settings in the Pre-Processing editor back to 10-bit, these RZ effects would reappear because your sequence is set to 16-bit; but working in 16-bit float is convenient for grading, so it's fine to leave things as they are.

FIGURE 11.4 A normalized image with lower contrast that will be a good starting point for grading

Adjusting Each Clip Manually

Normalizing log-encoded clips using the Pre-Processing option of each clip is convenient, but not *necessary*. You can also choose, if you know what you're doing, to normalize log-encoded clips as part of the grade you're applying using the curve options found in the Colour Corrector and Colour Warper effects. The basic idea is to use a multipoint curve that expands the contrast using an s-shaped curve that's tailored to your particular imagery.

Applying a LUT Using CFX

You can also follow the very same procedure as normalizing, using the Pre-Processing options with CFX, by adding a LUT Editor node. The advantage of this method, especially if you're creating more complicated grades entirely within the ConnectFX environment, is that you can apply the normalizing operation either before or after your corrective adjustments. Adding a LUT after your grading adjustments makes it possible to retrieve image detail that the LUT might clip out; adding a grading adjustment after a LUT makes it possible to operate on the post-clipped image as a whole in the event that you want to clip out image detail to omit from your grade.

Another advantage of using the LUT Editor node in ConnectFX is that you can apply ConnectFX to a gap effect (covered later in this chapter) so that you can apply a single LUT correction to an entire range of clips on the timeline and change the LUT applied to every clip with one setting.

Adding Color Correction Effects and Working in the Timeline

The easiest adjustments to make to clip color and contrast can be made right from the timeline, using the Colour Correct or Colour Warper effects. This section describes how to apply the Colour Correct adjustment, and what Viewer options you can use to help you analyze and compare clips for adjustment.

1. Move the positioner to a frame of the first clip where the woman is just leaving the elevator; then press Command+Shift+A to deselect every other clip on the timeline, and click the FX ➤ Colour Correct button to add that effect. The FX Ribbon updates to show an abbreviated set of RGB Gamma, Gain, and Offset controls that you can use to control image contrast; Sat (saturation) and Hue controls that you can use to affect the global color of the image; and a pair of Gain and Hue controls you can use to make adjustments to the Balance, or color balance of the image (although these controls are a bit abstract to use in their numerical form).

   At this point, it's easy enough to start adjusting parameters to manipulate the image, but there's an addition tool you can expose to help you evaluate just what needs to be done in the image.

> ▶
>
> You can zoom into or out of any video scope graph by Shift+dragging within the scope area. You can pan around by Shift+Command +dragging.

2. Click the Options pop-up menu and choose Show Vectorscope. A vectorscope appears to the right of the image (shown in Figure 11.5 with the Scope - Colour 2D option selected), showing the 2D vectorscope analysis that's unique to Smoke. Colored dots appear that show the distribution of hue (as each point's angle around the scale) and saturation (via each point's distance from the center) appearing in the image, against a standard vectorscope graticule indicating the neutral desaturated center point of the graph, and boxes indicating the absolute angle of each primary and secondary hue (red, magenta, blue, cyan, green, yellow).

   There are two other vectorscope modes you can display: a monochrome vectorscope that shows a more conventional trace graph of the color analysis, and a Colour 3D vectorscope that shows the overall distribution of color and contrast within a three-dimensional RGB cube. The cube represents a space in which all color values fit via three coordinates: R, G, and B values are used to arrange the analyzed points of color similarly to X, Y, and Z coordinates.

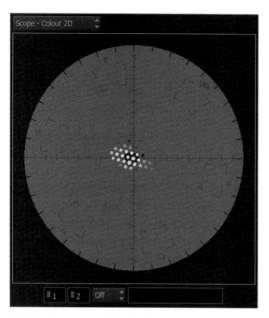

FIGURE 11.5 The Smoke vectorscope set to Colour 2D

3. Click the Scope pop-up menu above the scope view, and choose
   Waveforms ➤ Luminance to display a waveform analysis of
   luminance, which shows you the distribution of light and dark tones
   throughout the image on a scale of 0 (absolute black) to 100 (absolute
   white), as shown in Figure 11.6.

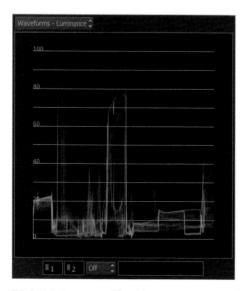

FIGURE 11.6 The video scope set to Waveforms - Luminance

With this analysis of contrast visible, it's now easy to see what kind of adjustment you can make to grade this image.

4. There's good highlight detail, but they could be brighter, so drag the Gain parameter to the right to raise it to around 112, lightening the brightest portion of the image while leaving the shadows dark. As you do this, you can see that the top of the waveform stretches upward, while the bottom remains where it was.

5. Next, the image seems a little murky and it's hard to make out details, so drag the Gamma parameter to the right to raise it to about 1.26. This redistributes the midtones visible in the middle of the Luminance (Luma) scope. The midtones will lighten, while the blackest shadows and brightest whites remain as they are. With these simple adjustments accomplished, the shot is definitely looking lighter (Figure 11.7).

FIGURE 11.7   The first clip with adjusted contrast

Comparing Adjustments in the Timeline

When color-correcting clips, one of the main goals to keep in mind is the need to make the color and contrast of different shots in a scene match one another, so that each clip looks consistent with the others.

1. Choose Tryptych from the View Mode pop-up, or press Option+3. This exposes a three-up display in the Viewer, and hides the video scopes. However, right now all three viewports show the same image, which isn't that useful.

2. Choose Prev | Cursor | Next from the Positioners pop-up menu underneath the right-most viewport, and the Tryptych view updates to show the previous clip (black right now because there is none), the current clip, and the next clip in the timeline. This makes it easy to compare clips while making adjustments so that you can adjust whatever color correction settings are required to make them match one another more plausibly.

3. Drag either the Colour Correct box in the FX Ribbon or the CC proxy (appearing on top of the first clip) onto the second clip in the timeline to copy your first adjustment. Move the positioner to the next clip, and see how the three adjacent clips compare in Tryptych view (see Figure 11.8).

In Prev | Cursor | Next mode, the previous and next clip positioners are locked into place. To freely position all three positioners to view specific frames of the previous and next clips, choose All Free.

FIGURE 11.8 The Tryptych viewer showing the three clips at and surrounding the positioner in the timeline

Now you can see the previous, current, and next clips side by side. You should also notice that the timeline shows three differently colored positioners; the previous clip positioner is green, the current clip is yellow, and the next clip is orange. This shows you which frames are being displayed in each viewer.

4. Select the second clip in the timeline. The middle image of the positioner looks a bit lighter then the left one, particularly if you look at the floor. To compensate for this, drag the Gamma control to the left to reduce Gamma until the brightness of the floor in each image looks more similar (a value around 1.150 should do the trick).

There are other adjustments we could make in the FX Ribbon, but more intricate grading can become cumbersome when using only parameter sliders. For more intricate work, it's time to begin using the Colour editors.

USING A BROADCAST MONITOR TO GRADE

For the majority of editing and compositing work presented in this book, it's not strictly necessary to work with an external broadcast display, although it helps to see what things will really look like to the final viewer. However, when doing color correction, having a display that matches the reference standard for broadcast viewing is essential.

With an AJA or Blackmagic I/O interface connected and the appropriate drivers installed, you can use the Broadcast Monitor tab of the Preferences to enable monitor output, sending the active viewport pane to the connected I/O interface for routing to professional video scopes and broadcast displays. Unfortunately, the Tryptych view cannot be sent out to video, so it's also a good idea to work with a computer display that can be calibrated to provide a more accurate image, for times when you need to do direct comparison on your computer's screen.

Working within the Colour Corrector and Warper Editors

Building upon the initial adjustments you made previously, it's time to start adding more detailed color adjustments using the controls found within the Colour Corrector editor.

1. Move the positioner to the first clip again, select it if necessary, and then do one of the following to open up the Colour Editor: double-click its Colour Correct button in the ribbon, or click the Editor button, or double-click the CC box on the clip in the timeline.

By default, the Colour Editor opens with the Viewer layout as the timeline. Because you were using the Tryptych Viewer before, the Tryptych Viewer is opened in the Colour Editor.

Like every other editor in Smoke, the Colour Corrector controls are arranged below the Viewport. However, there is one other viewing option that's unique to the Colour Corrector and Warper editors. If you like, you can also switch into an overlay mode in which the current clip occupies the full size of the screen, with the color controls superimposed over it.

2. Press Control+Escape to switch to Overlay mode. The Tryptych Viewer changes into a full-screen view of the current clip (see Figure 11.9). In this mode, whenever you click and drag to adjust a particular control, every control turns invisible for the duration of that adjustment, allowing you to see the entire image unhindered while you drag the mouse to make your adjustment. This mode isn't essential to making color corrections with Smoke, but in certain circumstances it can be quite helpful.

FIGURE 11.9 Color-correction controls in Overlay mode

You should be able to see that the histogram is currently weighted towards the right, since you lightened it quite a bit to make more detail visible. This has made the shadows a bit less dramatic, but there are more sophisticated tools available in the color editors that you can use to remedy this.

3. While in Overlay mode, click the Curves tab on top of the histogram to show the curve control, set by default to Luminance (via the Channel pop-up at the right). Those of you familiar with other applications, such as Adobe Photoshop or DaVinci Resolve, know that a luminance curve lets you make targeted adjustments to image contrast through careful placement of control points on the surface of the curve. However, curve manipulation in Smoke requires the use of the Tools pop-up.

4. Choose Add Points from the Tools pop-up menu (or press Shift+A), and then click the curve in two places to add two more control points; once in the middle of the two bottom and top control points that the curve starts out with, and once again between the middle and bottom control points. When you're done, the curve should look like it does in Figure 11.10.

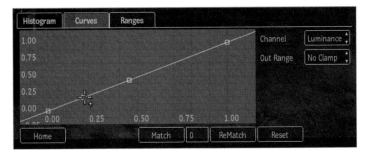

FIGURE 11.10 Adding two control points to the luminance curve

5. Next, choose Select from the Tools pop-up (or press Shift+M), and drag this last control point down slightly to make the bottom shadows of the image darker while leaving the lighter portions of the image alone. As you make this adjustment, the color controls all turn invisible, leaving a pair of coordinates to show you the results of your adjustment. For this exercise, somewhere close to (0.223, 0.164) should be good.

    As you can see, working in Overlay mode can make it easier to see what you're doing while making small adjustments on a single display. This mode is not necessarily as useful if you're grading while using an external broadcast display connected to an I/O interface, but it's still good to know about.

6. When you're finished, press Control+Escape to return to the regular presentation of the editor controls, as seen with the Tryptych Viewer.

Navigating a Sequence within the Colour Editors

Before continuing working on this scene, it will be helpful for you to know how to move from clip to clip from within the Colour Correct or Colour Warper editors. Before proceeding, it's important to understand that when you're inside one of the color editors, you can only move among clips that have the same effect applied to them corresponding to the editor you're within. If you want to work this way, this means that you need to apply the same color effect to all of the clips in the timeline that you want to make adjustments to.

1. Click the Exit button to return to the timeline.

2. Click the first clip in track V1.1, then Shift+click the last clip to select the entire range of clips in the timeline, and then click the FX button in the FX Ribbon and add the Colour Warper effect.

    By adding a Colour Warper effect to each of the clips in the timeline, you can use a pair of keyboard shortcuts to move from clip to clip within the Colour Editor, without needing to exit to use the timeline. This also works from within the Colour Correct editor with a range of clips that all have the Colour Correct effect. However, if you're within the Colour Warper editor, you can't move from a clip with the Colour Warper effect to one with the Colour Correct effect.

3. With the CW box in the FX Ribbon selected, double-click the first clip, or select the first clip and click the Edit button to reenter the Colour Editor. The Viewport should be set to Tryptych mode to reflect the Timeline Viewer setting, but you'll want to click the Options pop-up and check that the Positioners submenu is set to Prev | Cursor | Next.

4. Press Command+Option+down arrow to move to the next clip with a Colour Warper effect applied to it. Press Command+Option+up arrow to move to the previous clip in the timeline with a Colour Warper effect. Switching from clip to clip sets the controls of the Colour Warper to affect the new current clip (seen in the middle of the Tryptych view).

    It's also possible to play or scrub through the entire duration of the timeline from inside of the Colour Warper or Colour Correct editor, but there are two additional controls you need to set to enable this.

5. First, choose Timeline Range from the Options menu to the right of the transport controls. This changes the Timebar to display the current clip as a shaded region of the whole Timebar, which now represents the duration of the entire sequence (seen in Figure 11.11).

FIGURE 11.11 A shaded region of the timeline shows the position of the current clip you're color correcting.

6. Second, choose Primary Track from the Context pop-up menu at the bottom left corner of the color controls (or press Shift+F1) to enable the Color Editor viewport to show every clip within the current video track (and all clips below), as determined by the positioner's track selector. The default setting, Result, only allows the currently selected clip to be scrubbed by the positioner in the Timebar.

7. With these two settings chosen, you can now use the transport controls, spacebar, or JKL keys to play through the entire timeline, or you can drag the pointer within the Timebar to scrub through the entire sequence. This can make it easier to compare clips and see how they play together as you're making adjustments to balance the shots of each scene with one another.

8. For now, press F4 to set the Viewport to Result, and choose Segment Range from the Options pop-up, so that the scrubber shows only the current clip.

9. Use the Command+Option+up or down keys to move to the first clip in the sequence.

Understanding Video Scopes in the Colour Warper Editor

Video scopes in the Colour Warper work differently than they do in previous versions of Smoke, but unlike the Colour Corrector, which only has a histogram inside of its editor, the Colour Warper has both a vectorscope (which is hidden at the moment) and the histogram located in the control area. While the histogram is always visible, providing you with an always-on analysis of image tonality (or of the individual color channels), the vectorscope is hidden when the Viewport is set to display the Primary Track, so you want to make sure you're viewing the Result if you want to use it. In this section, you'll turn it on, and learn how to customize it.

1. Press Option+1 to set the Viewport to Player mode. You should be able to clearly see the vectorscope, which defaults to the 2D Scope presentation you saw in the timeline previously (see Figure 11.12).

FIGURE 11.12 The vectorscope in the Colour Warper editor

At the moment, the vectorscope is overlapping the image shown in the Viewport. You could shrink the size of the Viewport image to get it out of the way, but you can also resize and move the vectorscope.

2. Shift+drag with the pointer anywhere within the vectorscope to the left to shrink it, or to the right to make it larger. In this case, shrink it as small as it will go.

3. Option+drag with the pointer anywhere within the vectorscope to move it to the left, so it doesn't overlap the image.

4. To hide the vectorscope, click the Scope button, located at the bottom-left of the color balance controls. You can also click the Home button above to reset the vectorscope to its default size.

Adjusting Contrast with the Colour Warper

The Colour Correct effect is a very good tool for color adjustment, but there's a second color-correction effect you can use that is even more feature-rich: the Colour Warper. Where the Colour Correct effect provides all of the basics, the Colour Warper includes all of its features, and adds three separate color balance controls for Gamma, Gain, and Offset, as well as a set of *selective* controls for making targeted adjustments to color and contrast for specifically keyed ranges of the image (this will be shown in later sections of this chapter).

N O T E   As you work, it's a good idea to check that the Auto Key button at the right side of the editor control area is *turned off* if it happens to be turned on. For some mysterious reason, the Auto Key button likes to turn itself on when you're making color adjustments, but most of the time you probably don't want to animate your color corrections, so make sure this is turned off as you work.

> When making contrast and color adjustments, it's often helpful to see how your adjustment will affect the skin tone of any people in the scene.

1. Drag the positioner all the way to the end of the clip, and look at the histogram.

   Looking at the histogram, it's easy to see that this image isn't occupying the maximum possible tonal range; most of the histogram is in the shadows, and the highlights aren't stretching up as high as they could. This is an easy adjustment, but there are differences between how the Colour Correct and Colour Warper effects let you make contrast adjustments.

2. Drag the White slider to the left to raise the white point of the image, stretching out the highlights of the picture while leaving the shadows where they are, until the leftmost part of the histogram just touches the 1.00 line, which indicates maximum luma. As you make this adjustment, you can see a white histogram overlay stretch out, while a black histogram underneath shows the original contrast analysis of the image for reference (see Figure 11.13).

   By now you've probably noticed that there's no Gamma parameter between the Black and White point parameters that let you stretch the black and white points relative to one another. That's because, in the Colour Warper, gamma is adjusted via the Gamma curve that appears over the histogram by default.

FIGURE 11.13 Adjusting the White parameter of the image using the histogram for reference

3. Drag the middle control point up to lighten the midtones of the image so that the woman is easier to see. As the curve bends upward and the image lightens, the middle values of the histogram stretch farther to the right, pushing the top highlights over 1.00. As you can see, the Gamma curve and White adjustments are interactive with one another, so drag the White slider to the left until the leftmost part of the histogram is touching the 1.00 line in the graph again.

   Using these controls, you've expanded image contrast to occupy the full available range of the video signal so that the highlights are as bright as they can possibly be and the shadows are as dark as they can possibly be. You don't always want to maximize contrast in this way, but it makes sense for this image because there are clipped light fixtures directly in view to define maximum white, and the low-key lighting scheme implies that the shadows should be quite dark, so a 0 percent black point makes sense.

4. Press Option+3 to set the Viewport to Tryptych mode (be sure that the Positioners submenu of the Option menu is set to Prev | Cursor | Next). You can easily see that the current and next clip in the sequence don't match.

5. Press Command+Option+down arrow to move to the next clip, and then use the White slider and the Gamma curve to create a matching adjustment (seen in Figure 11.14).

FIGURE 11.14 Matching the contrast of two neighboring clips

At this point, you've created a subtle, but useful match between the image lightness of the two main angles of this part of the scene. Before we continue, it's probably a good idea to save your work.

Color Balancing with the Colour Warper

The Colour Warper provides similar color-balancing controls to those you used in Chapter 9 to match the fake wall to the shot of the actor. However, instead of having only one color balance control (or color wheel) with overlapping handles for the Lift, Gamma, and Gain adjustments, the Colour Warper gives you three separate Shadows, Midtones, and Highlights color balance controls (see Figure 11.15).

FIGURE 11.15 The three color balance controls in the Colour Warper

Whenever you're color-correcting a scene, it's a good idea to scrub through the entire sequence of clips to see if there's one that does a good job of setting the tone you want. Up until now, we've been focused on the first two shots in this program as you've learned how to make simple adjustments, but now that you're moving on to color balancing, it's time to switch strategies and begin working on the last clip in the sequence, which will give you a better starting point for the color of the rest of the clips in this scene. With that done, you'll learn how to more easily match the other clips in this sequence to the last one.

1. Press Option+1 to set the Viewport back to Player mode, so the vectorscope is more easily visible. Then, press Command+Option+down arrow twice until the laboratory clip is visible (it's a lot warmer then the hallway shot).

2. Scrub forward to a frame where the woman is stepping through the pool of light on the floor, and take a look at the vectorscope to compare its analysis to the image you see in the Viewport (see Figure 11.16).

FIGURE 11.16 A vectorscope analysis of the range of hues and saturation in the image

The Colour 2D representation isn't necessarily as precise an analysis of hue and saturation distributions as the more traditional monochrome view that's available in the timeline, but it's a lot easier to read, and the outer boundaries of saturation, which you need to keep track of for quality control purposes, are accurate.

Here are some things that you can learn to spot within the vectorscope graph:

▶ There are lots of saturated reds and oranges extending far from the center of the vectorscope due to the spinning police light on the wall, her red hair, and her skin tone.

▶ There's a bit of not very saturated blue in the frame, close to the center point of the graph, coming from her blue shirt.

▶ There's an unexpected amount of fairly saturated greenish yellow appearing throughout the scene.

The yellow/green tinge comes from the fluorescent practical lighting being used in the scene and also from bounce light coming from the huge greenscreen that happens to be behind the camera. While the lab should look industrial, this is a bit much and should be corrected.

When using the Shadows, Midtones, and Highlights color balance controls, it's good to familiarize yourself with which regions of image lightness each of the color balance control ranges will affect so that you can most effectively neutralize the color you don't want. As the names imply, Highlights affect the brightest parts of the image most, and the darkest least; Shadows affect the darkest parts of the image most and the brightest least; and Midtones affect the middle values most, and the brightest and darkest least.

In this case, knowing that the yellow/green in the image is coming from greenscreen spill, a quick glance at the picture confirms that most of the unwanted color falls not in the highlights but in the dim highlights and bright shadows of the image, so the Midtones color balance control should take care of this.

3. Click the Midtones button, and then drag within the color balance control (the color wheel) toward the complementary, or opposite, color of the one you're trying to eliminate. You want to get rid of the yellow, so drag anywhere within the middle of this control towards blue. As you make this adjustment, you should see the colored portion of the vectorscope graph realign closer to the neutral center of the scope where all neutral blacks, grays, and whites in the image appear. Meanwhile, a black graph shows the original distribution of color in the scene. Additionally, as you make this adjustment, the histogram graph switches to Warp mode, and a set of three curves colored red, green, and blue show a graphical analysis of how you're rebalancing the color of the scene (see Figure 11.17). Note that as soon as you release the Midtones control, the "virtual trackball" goes back to its centered position, so that the histogram's color curves are your main indication of exactly what the color balance controls are doing to the image.

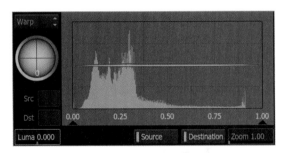

FIGURE 11.17 Adjusting the Midtones color balance control to neutralize the yellow spill in the image

4. At this point, the image looks a lot better, but there's some coloration in the highlights that looks a bit odd because of the greenish cast coming from the fluorescent lights. To fix this, drag the Highlights color balance control just a little bit toward a blue/magenta mix to

make the white just a little bit whiter. If this adjustment causes a bit too much magenta to creep into the midtones, go ahead and drag the Midtones control down toward cyan, just a bit, until you're happy with the relative neutrality of the image. Notice as you work that the Highlights control sticks to a position, showing you the angle and intensity of the adjustment.

5. Now the image looks fairly natural, but the colors throughout the image appear lackluster. To remedy this, drag the saturation slider right, just a bit, to increase the intensity of colors to give some pop back to the woman's red hair and the red lighting in the shot, but not so much as to send the reds in the vectorscope beyond the boundary of the R target. This also puts a bit of coloration back into the light. That's okay because you don't want to drain all the interesting variation out of the lighting completely — you just don't want things to look ugly.

6. Lastly, the color adjustments have made the shadows look a bit washed out, so drag the Black slider to the left a bit until the left edge of the largest portion of the vectorscope graph just touches 0.00 in the scale.

The final result, when compared to the original, should have a lot cleaner range of color and more "pop" then the original, as seen in Figure 11.18.

If at any point you don't like your color balance adjustment and want to start over, you can click the Balance button to reset just the color adjustment for the selected tonal range.

If at any point you find that you want to reset an individual parameter value without resetting everything else, you can right-click a parameter and choose Reset Channel (Current Value) from the context menu.

Before

After

FIGURE 11.18 Before and after the Colour Warper adjustments made in this exercise

Shot Matching Using the Colour Warper

In this next exercise, you'll learn how to use the Colour Warper to perform automatic color matching as you match the look of the hallway to that of the lab set. The Colour Warper's auto color matching function does its match based on the output of any effects that are applied to the clip you're matching to, which is why it was important to grade the last clip in the sequence first in the last exercise.

1. The automatic color matching function in Smoke requires you to apply the color match from within the target clip, which is the clip you want to copy another clip's look to. Press Command+Option+up arrow twice to move to the wide-angle shot of the woman walking through the hallway toward the camera.

2. For this procedure to work, you need to be able to simultaneously see the target clip, as well as the source clip that you're copying the look from. Press Option+3 to set the Viewport to Triptych mode. Then, choose All Free from the Positioners submenu of the Options pop-up menu. Next, Choose Timeline Range from the Options pop-up. Finally, choose Context ➤ Primary Track from the View mode pop-up.

3. With all of this set up, you can click the rightmost panel of the Viewport to select that third image, and then drag the positioner to the last shot.

FIGURE 11.19 The Triptych display used for shot matching

4. For your first adjustment, click the middle pane of the Viewport, then drag the positioner in the middle pane to a point where the woman walks into the light, and notice that the overall image is fairly desaturated. Increase saturation to about 1.5. This exaggerates the color cast being created by the lighting fixtures in the hallway.

   To match the general lighting scheme in the hallway to that of the lab set, you'll use the Match controls.

5. Click the Select button, and you'll be prompted to "Select an area to be modified." Do this by dragging a bounding box to sample a large section of the highlight underneath the fixture on the wall (see Figure 11.20). The blue "light" of the Select button should turn on after you do this.

6. Next, click the Select button again, and when prompted to "Select an area to match to," drag a bounding box to sample an analogous long section of wall highlight falling off from the lighting fixture in the last clip, also shown in Figure 11.20.

FIGURE 11.20 Sampling a highlight in the image you want to adjust (a) and then sampling an analogous highlight in the image to which you want to match the image (b)

Immediately after you sample the second image, the Highlights color balance and white point of the clip you're adjusting are automatically modified to create a match. The Colour Warper is smart enough to know that when you sample an area in the highlights of the image, it should adjust the Highlights controls of the color effect to create the best match.

7. Now follow the same procedure to match the lower part of the door at the left of the frame in the current clip to the part of the same door where the red hand truck meets the floor of the lab clip to which you're trying to match, as shown in Figure 11.21. This time, the black point and Shadows control will be automatically adjusted to create a relatively close match.

FIGURE 11.21 Sampling a shadow on the door in the image you're adjusting (a) and then sampling an analogous shadow in the same door within the image to which you're matching it (b)

At this point, you've made the hallway clip look quite a bit closer to the lab, especially when compared with the first clip in the scene that's still visible at left (see Figure 11.22).

FIGURE 11.22 The hallway clip after automatic matching to the lab clip

Now it's time to finish the match by making a few manual adjustments. Ironically, the automatic matching controls have done such a good job that now the same color cast that you needed to eliminate from the lab shot has reappeared, to a lesser extent, in the hallway shot. Fortunately, this is an easy fix.

8. Drag the Midtones color balance control toward blue/magenta (see Figure 11.23) until the greenish/yellow cast diminishes.

FIGURE 11.23 Manually getting the green out of the midtones

9. If you look at the histogram at the middle of the control area, you'll see that all of the automatic adjustments are making the shadows of the destination image that's been adjusted (in white) lighter than the original source image (in black), which was deliberately lit to have a moody silhouette of the physicist as she walks up the hallway. Choose Gamma from the Trackball Option pop-up menu to display the curve controls.

10. The original gamma adjustment you made is still there, but it now needs to be altered. Drag the middle control point down a bit to make the midtones darker. Next, choose Add Points from the Edit Mode pop-up menu (Shift+A), and then click to place a control point in the middle of the bottom half of the curve, as shown in Figure 11.24. Next, choose Select (Shift+M), and drag this new control point down a bit to darken the shadows, until you feel that the shadows of the hallway clip convincingly match those of the lab set.

You can compare the before and after state of a clip by pressing F1 to switch the View mode pop-up to Colour Warper Input ➤ Front, and then pressing F4 to switch back to the Result.

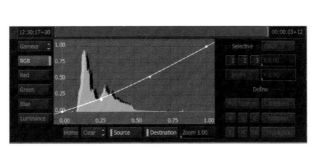

FIGURE 11.24 Adding control points and then adjusting them to darken the shadows and lighten the midtones

Keep in mind that these are two separate environments with differences in lighting that are obvious to the audience. Thus it's not necessary that the two clips match *exactly*; they just need to be in the same ballpark so that it's not jarring as the character moves from one location to the next, which can be seen in Figure 11.25.

Original

Final

FIGURE 11.25   The final adjustment to achieve a plausible match between the hallway and the lab, versus the original shot

Copying Color Corrections

Now that you've matched the hallway shot to the lab, you can take a shortcut by applying the very same correction to the other hallway clips. However, to do this, you need to go back to the timeline.

1. Click the Exit button to return to the timeline.

2. If necessary, expand the height of the timeline tracks so you can see the CW proxy boxes applied to each clip.

3. Drag the CW proxy box from the second clip onto the first (see Figure 11.26), and you'll see the copied correction as soon as you drop it. Copying timeline effects to other clips with the same effect always overwrites the previous effect in the target clip.

FIGURE 11.26 Copying a color-correction effect from the second clip to the first by dragging the effect box in the timeline

4. Drag the CC box from the second clip onto the third as well, and then play or scrub through the entire sequence to see that the entire scene is now balanced.

Qualification in the Colour Warper to Make Secondary Adjustments

Now that the scene is balanced, it's time to do some more detailed work to hone the look of this piece. This next exercise will show you how to create secondary corrections to adjust specifically colored areas of the image using the Colour Warper. In Smoke, *secondary corrections* are also called *selectives*. The selective controls use the Diamond Keyer, which is also available in other Autodesk products, to do advanced keying in order to isolate a region of the image for specialized adjustment using the Color Warper's color and contrast controls.

1. Move the positioner to the first clip, and double-click its CC box to enter the Colour Editor. Press Option+1 to put the Viewport into Player mode, which makes it easier to evaluate the image.

   While the rest of the hallway is now balanced to match the scene, the elevator lighting was yellow and dingy to begin with, and remains so in this grade. You can fix this with a secondary correction by using the selectives.

FIGURE 11.27 The first hallway shot has too much yellow in the elevator.

2. Choose Sel 1 (selective 1) from the Work On pop-up menu that's to the left of the Shadows, Midtones, and Highlights controls. The image becomes grayscale in preparation for you to sample a range of colors to isolate.

3. Click Pick Custom (located with the other selective controls to the right of the histogram), and then use the sample cursor to click and drag a single diagonal sample from one edge of the overhead light in the elevator to the other. The yellowish color that you've isolated becomes saturated to show what you've done, while the rest of the image that will remain unaffected remains desaturated.

4. Choose Matte from the View pop-up menu (underneath the Work On menu) to see the matte you've created. Your results will vary depending on what exact part of the image you sampled, but in any event the black area of the matte shows the part you're trying to isolate, while the white part of the image shows the part that you want to exclude from the correction. If black or gray is bleeding over the woman and the floor, as shown in Figure 11.28, this means that those parts of the image will also be somewhat included in the operation.

When sampling this image, avoid dragging the sample cursor across the frame of the lighting in the ceiling of the elevator, or you'll create an initial matte that's too coarse for this lesson. Sample only the yellowish, translucent, plexiglass light covering.

FIGURE 11.28 The desaturated and matte views of the selective isolation you're creating

5. Using the Luma controls located below the more colorful Diamond Keyer control, drag the Low Softness parameter slider (the leftmost of the four parameter sliders seen in Figure 11.29) to the right to raise it until you've eliminated all of the floor and most of the woman from the matte. Don't worry about the portions of the matte that fall on part of the woman's face and the wall; you're isolating a region of light, and the matte is simply showing you where there's strong lighting spill that will be included in the adjustment. This is actually a good thing when you're grading.

FIGURE 11.29 The Luma Softness and Tolerance parameters for adjusting the region of the image being isolated

6. Choose Result from the View menu to go back to looking at the full-color image, but leave the Work On pop-up set to Sel 1. This lets you see the color adjustment you're about to make, while limiting it to

only the region of the picture you isolated using the Sel 1 controls. With this done, adjust the Highlights color balance control toward blue to neutralize a bit of the yellow from the lighting.

Using selectives, you can make corrections to problem areas of the picture without changing what's good about the current adjustment. However, selectives can also be used creatively.

7. Press Command+Option+down arrow twice to move to the close-up of the woman just before she enters the door to the lab, and play through it. The environment of the hallway matches, and the dark doorway is nicely foreboding, but the woman's face is a bit dark, disappearing into the door during a moment when it would be good to see the pensive expression on her face. You can use a selective to brighten her face to be more visible.

8. Choose Sel 1 from the Work On pop-up menu, and then click Pick Custom and drag along the skin on the woman's face, avoiding her hair and clothes. When you're finished, choose Matte from the View pop-up menu to see how good the isolation is (see Figure 11.30). Your results will vary depending on exactly which pixels you sampled.

FIGURE 11.30 The initial matte created by sampling the woman's face

This is a good start, and might actually be okay if all you were going to do was a saturation adjustment or minor color balance operation. However, when doing any sort of contrast adjustment in a grade, you really want a solid matte with good isolation, otherwise you could introduce unsightly noise into the picture. For this image, you'll get the best results using the Diamond Keyer control (see Figure 11.31). There are two shapes superimposed over a flattened RGB cube shape: a gray inner Tolerance shape and a black outer Softness shape. By dragging each shape's control point handles, you can redefine the range of color and saturation that's used to create the key.

Like other controls and viewers in Smoke, you can Control+Command+ drag to pan and Control+Option+ drag to zoom to get a better view of the parts of the control you want to manipulate.

FIGURE 11.31 The Diamond Keyer control

9. Drag the handles of the inner and outer shapes to refine the matte, including as much of the woman's face and neck and excluding as much of the background as you can. Then, drag the Softness and Tolerance parameter sliders of the Luma control below to fine-tune the key even more. As you work, it's fine if some of her hair is included in the operation. You'll be shrinking the outer Softness shape, and you will eventually need to zoom and pan into the control to see what you're doing (see Figure 11.32).

   If you've managed to isolate the face, but you're still having trouble with spots behind her neck and on her chest, or with too much of her hair being included in the matte, there's another tool that you can use to refine this matte.

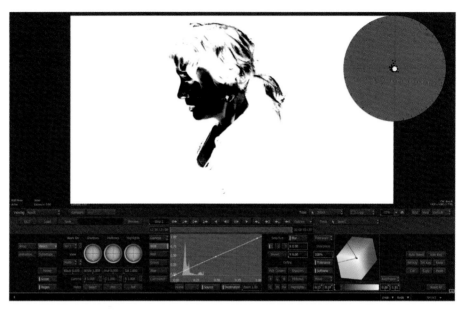

FIGURE 11.32 Fine-tuning the Diamond Keyer controls to isolate the woman's face

10. Click the Plot button, next to the other match controls underneath the color balance controls, and click or click+drag on the woman's neck, hair, or any other feature of the image you're having trouble identifying within the Diamond Keyer controls, and a black dot shows you where that value is so that you can either include it in or exclude it from the matte. A red line shows the plot sample on the Luma slider control.

11. When you're satisfied that you've isolated as much as you can using the Diamond Keyer control, adjust the Luma Softness parameter sliders below to exclude as much hair as you can. Don't overadjust so that the matte becomes crunchy; stop at the point where there's a gentle gray falloff between the parts of her hair that are included in and excluded from the matte, something like what is shown in Figure 11.33.

12. Now that you have a good key, choose Result from the View menu; then go to the Gamma curve and drag the one middle control point

FIGURE 11.33 One possible skin-tone matte

up to lighten the woman's face and hair highlights just enough to make her pop out from the background. With this adjustment, her skin might look a bit yellow, so drag the Midtones color balance control a bit towards reddish-magenta to make the image look something like that in Figure 11.34. To get a before and after look at your selective adjustment, you can simply turn the 1 button off and on in the selective controls.

FIGURE 11.34 Before and after a selective color adjustment to lighten the woman's face and hair highlights, exaggerated for print

13. Click Exit to return to the timeline, and notice how there are a set of three identical selective buttons labeled 1, 2, and 3. Toggle button 1 off and on to see how you can turn selectives off and on after you've applied them.

Applying Color Corrections as Gap Effects

So far, you've applied corrections and adjustments on an individual, per-clip basis. However, there's a way of easily applying all manner of adjustments to multiple clips in a scene, using gap effects. *Gap effects* describe the ability in Smoke to apply effects to selected gaps in the timeline, creating what is often called an *adjustment layer* in other applications. When you superimpose a gap effect over other clips in the timeline, all clips appearing underneath have the gap effect applied to them. There are many reasons to do this, and we'll explore these in the following series of exercises.

Applying One Look to a Whole Scene

A great reason to use gap effects when color correcting is when you want to apply a single "look" or style adjustment to a whole series of clips all at once. In this exercise, you'll see how to do this.

1. Press Option+1 to set the Viewer to Player mode. Then, move the positioner to the first clip in the timeline, and select that clip. Then click the Track+ button to create another video track.

2. With the focus of the positioner on track V1.2 and the clip on track V1.1 selected, press Shift+V to select a piece of gap on track V1.2 that's the same length as the clip underneath, as shown in Figure 11.35.

FIGURE 11.35 Creating a cut — a selected piece of gap in the timeline — in preparation for applying an effect to it

3. Click FX ➤ Colour Warp to add the Colour Warper effect to the selected gap, and it turns into a clip. Select this clip, and the name "Gap" appears over it.

4. Right-click the Gap clip, choose Rename from the context menu, enter **Hallway Grade** in the text-entry dialog, and click or press Return. The gap effect now has a name identifying what it does.

5. Double-click the Hallway Grade gap effect to open the Colour Editor. Now that you have a basic grade going for the hallway scene, you want to add a bit of style. In particular, you'd like to play off the abundance of fluorescent lighting in the scene to give a more distinctly greenish tone to the overall scene and, in the process, make the entire lab complex seem unsettling. However, you just want to add a tinge of green — you don't want to wash the entire picture in green. To do this, you'll use a secondary correction.

6. Choose Sel 1 from the Work On pop-up menu, and then choose Matte from the View menu. At the moment, a black field covers the image, indicating that the entire image is currently selected for adjustment since you've not yet picked a range of color or lightness upon which to work.

7. Find the group of buttons labeled Define, to the right of the histogram, and click the Midtones button. This creates an automatically defined Luma key that excludes both the brightest highlights and the deepest shadows, as shown in Figure 11.36.

FIGURE 11.36 Creating a luma key matte of just the midtones of the image

8. If you like, you can adjust the Low and High Softness Field parameters to include more of the shadows and highlights, but make sure that you exclude the darkest and lightest parts of the image if you want to avoid creating an overall tint.

9. To make the adjustment, choose Result from the View pop-up menu and then drag the Midtones color balance control toward an olive green. Figure 11.37 is exaggerated for effect, but it shows one possible adjustment.

FIGURE 11.37 Limiting a green adjustment to the image using the matte created with selective 1

10. Click the Exit button to go back to the timeline, choose the Trim tool from the Editorial Mode pop-up menu (or press R), and make sure Ripple is disabled. Then select the out point of the Hallway Grade clip, move the positioner to the end of the sequence, and press the E key to perform an *extend edit*, which resizes the clip so that the selected edit point in the timeline is moved to the location of the positioner, as shown in Figure 11.38.

FIGURE 11.38 Doing an extend edit to resize the Hallway Grade clip to the entire length of the sequence

If you move the positioner through the sequence, you can now see that the green midtones tint is being applied throughout the entire sequence. If you want to make a change, all you need to do is open the Hallway Grade clip's Colour Correct effect and alter its settings. Furthermore, if you need to apply custom adjustments to one clip and not another, you can treat a gap effect clip like any other clip, keyframing the effect or cutting it into multiple pieces, each with its own settings.

11. Finally, drag the Hallway Grade clip from the timeline to the Hallway Scene library in the Media Library, and then drag it back into track V1.2 where it came from. As you can see, you can save gap effects into the Media Library for future use, dragging them back to the timeline whenever you like.

Limiting a Color Correction Using a GMask

In this next exercise, you'll see how you can use a timeline GMask effect to limit a color correction with a shape in a gap effect clip.

1. Move the positioner to the last clip in the sequence. The lab set is nicely lit, but you'd like it to be a more cave-like environment, with a sense of the light falling off at the edges of the frame. Time to add a vignette!

2. Select the last clip in track V1.1; then click Track+ to create another video track, and press Shift+V to select a piece of gap to match the duration of the selected clip.

3. Add a Colour Correct effect to the gap, and then drag the Gamma parameter slider in the FX Ribbon to the left to lower the gamma to somewhere around 0.52. This darkens the entire image, but what you want to do is limit the darkening effect to the outer edge of the frame. To do that, you'll need to add a GMask.

4. With the gap effect still selected, click FX ➤ GMask to add a GMask effect to the gap.

5. Click the Colour Corrector effect in the FX Ribbon again and click the Use Mask button all the way to the right to turn it on, which sets this clip to use the GMask effect to limit the correction, as opposed to creating transparency for compositing. Finally, double-click the GM box or GMask button in the FX Ribbon to enter the GMask editor.

The GMask timeline effect works exactly the same as the GMask node you used in Chapter 8. The only difference is that you have to set up the image seen in the Viewport a little differently than you do when using CFX.

6. Right now, the Viewport shows only white. To see the image you want to work on, you need to select Context ≻ Primary Track from the View pop-up menu at the bottom left of the GMask editor controls. Now, as long as the positioner focus was on the top video track, the whole image should appear.

7. Click the Add button that's to the right of the control area (labeled Object) to add a geometry layer. Then, use the draw tools to create a simple oval surrounding the center of the image. Drag the Offset parameter slider to the left to feather the oval outwards as seen in Figure 11.39, and you're finished (for now).

> When drawing a mask, you can hold the Shift key down and drag to draw a freeform shape with control points automatically applied to conform to what you draw.

FIGURE 11.39 Creating a GMask to vignette the frame

8. Click Exit to go back to the timeline.

Back in the timeline, you should see — nothing! The GMask you applied is having no effect, because the GMask effect is occurring after the Colour Correct effect, and it turns out that their positions need to be reversed for the Colour Correct effect to inherit the GMask you want to use to limit it. Fortunately, this is easy to fix.

9. Click and drag the GMask box in the FX Ribbon to a position in front of the CC box. Immediately, the Colour Correct effect becomes limited by the mask. However, the current effect is the opposite of what you need, with darkening happening at the center of the vignette rather than the edge.

10. Using the GMask controls appearing on the bottom row of the FX Ribbon, click Outside to invert the mask. The result is a nice, feathered edge, as shown in Figure 11.40.

F I G U R E   1 1 . 4 0   Creating an oval using the timeline wipe effect to limit a color correction

This is an incredibly versatile technique, because you can limit Colour Correct or Colour Warper adjustments using any mask you can draw. And you can even apply this gap effect to an entire range of clips.

THE ESSENTIALS AND BEYOND

As you can see, combining color-correction timeline effects, gap effects, and timeline wipes to create custom mattes lets you apply primary and secondary corrections in many different ways.

(Continues)

THE ESSENTIALS AND BEYOND *(Continued)*

ADDITIONAL EXERCISES

▶ Delete the Hallway Grade gap effect, and create a new one with a completely different look, as if the hallway were well lit, with neutral highlights and desaturated color overall.

▶ Add a new gap effect to the first clip, use a selective in the Colour Warper to isolate the blue jacket on the coat rack of the elevator, and increase its saturation all by itself.

▶ Add a new gap effect to the second clip, and use color correction, along with a GMask, to create a feathered shadow on the floor of the hallway along the bottom of the frame to give the shot more depth.

CHAPTER 12

Adding Titles

You know that you're getting finished with a program when you start adding titles to it. The Autodesk® Smoke® platform has a complete set of titling tools that let you add everything from an interstitial title page, to a lower third, to a scrolling credit sequence for the end of a movie.

Topics in this chapter include the following:

▶ **Adding text effects on the timeline**

▶ **Saving and reusing styles**

▶ **Arranging and styling text**

Adding Text Effects on the Timeline

In this first exercise, you'll apply the Text effect on the timeline as a gap effect in order to create a simple lower-third title.

1. If necessary, open the Hallway Scene sequence you created in Chapter 11, and press Option+1 to put the viewport into Player mode.

2. Select the first clip in track V1.1, and then press Shift+V to select a gap of the same length in track V1.3.

3. Click the FX ➤ Text button in the FX Ribbon to create a Text gap effect, and double-click it to open the Text editor. Set the Zoom pop-up menu to Fit.

4. Click the New Layer button to create a new text layer at the top of the screen. Text is entered within layers, and you can create as many layers as you like to organize different pieces of text. Next to the New Layer button are additional buttons for setting layer priority (which layer is in front), selecting layers, deleting layers, and grouping layers (these buttons are shown in Figure 12.1).

While you can also apply text effects directly to media clips in the timeline, by applying them to gap effects on a separate track, you can easily turn all titles off when you need to output a textless version of the program.

FIGURE 12.1 Text layer-creation and management buttons

5. Type **U of M High Energy Physics Lab**, press Return, and type **Two years later...** on the next line. By default, the text is left justified and uses the Discreet font that accompanies the Autodesk Smoke installation. However, you'll probably want to customize this for your particular program.

6. Click quickly four times within the text layer box to select all of the text inside, and then click the Font field that currently reads "Discreet" to enter the font browser. Then choose Auto from the Font Type pop-up menu that's underneath the browser columns and to the left of the Font Preview area. Otherwise, you won't see any other fonts as you browse.

7. Click System Fonts in the Subdirectories column of the browser. At first, the browser is empty, so open the Font Type pop-up menu underneath the file browser and choose "Auto." Now the Files column will show a long list of every font installed on your computer. This can be difficult to navigate, however, so click the Library View button at the upper-left corner of the screen to switch the browser to a thumbnail preview of each font. Initially, you won't see anything but empty outlines; so click the Generate Proxy button to build a set of font proxies that you can see.

8. Scroll down the list, and click the `Futura.ttc` proxy to select it, and then click the Load button to load that font into the current text layer. The selected text should now be restyled.

9. To make this a lower-third title, you'll need to reposition the text layer, so make sure that the Axis button is currently selected and use the Y parameter slider (within the Axis control group) to move the text down (see Figure 12.2). In order to see the title and action-safe borders of the screen while you work, click the Grid button; then choose Action & Title from the Safe pop-up menu, and click the Grid button again to hide these controls. Position the text at the bottom-left corner of the inner green title-safe box.

FIGURE 12.2 The Axis controls, set to alter the entire layer

10. At this point, the text looks a bit boring, so triple-click the text "Two years later…" to select it, and change the Font Size parameter to 37. Now it's a bit close to the line of text above it, so change the Leading parameter so that the text box once again sits right on top of the inner green title-safe box.

11. You might have noticed that the "U of M" text has a bit too much space between the three sets of characters. Adjust the kerning by placing the text cursor to the right of "U" and adjusting the Kern parameter until it reads -10.

12. A faster way to work is to select the line of text you want to kern, choose Rekern from the Text Mode pop-up menu (or press Option+K), then use the left- and right-arrow keys to position the text cursor (in this case, to the right of "of"), and use the up- and down-arrow keys to adjust the Kern parameter until it reads -7. If you're typographically inclined, go ahead and kern the rest of the title as you see fit. As you can see, any selected text within a text layer can be individually styled and adjusted.

    You may have noticed that there are numerous styling options appearing as a stack of buttons that let you turn on the Fill, Underline, Outline, Back, Shadow, and Blur options for text (see Figure 12.3).

    It would be convenient to add a Back (background) color behind the lower-third text that you've just created, but if you want to customize this background beyond the default size of the text, it can be easier to apply it as a second text layer.

The Text Mode pop-up menu, near the lower-left corner, lets you choose an editing tool to use within the view-port. If at any point you find you cannot edit or select text, choose Edit from this menu.

The Kern parameter updates to show the individual kern setting applied to whichever character the text cursor is placed on.

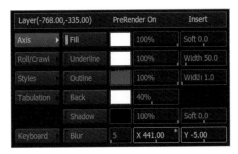

FIGURE 12.3 Text options can be turned on and off via buttons with accompanying options

13. Click the New Layer button again to create a second layer. This time, don't type anything, but instead turn on the Back button in order to enable the colored background option. Click the Layer Axis button (which currently reads Top/Left) to set it to Centre, and then adjust either of the Scale parameters to make the bar stretch all the way from the left to the right of the screen.

14. Next, adjust the Y parameter to move the white bar down until it's centered between the two lines of text, turn the Prop (proportional) button off, and raise the Scale Y parameter until the white box is slightly taller than the text itself.

15. Drag the percentage parameter slider to the right of the Back button to the left to increase the transparency of the background. Then, to change its color, click the Back color swatch button to open the color picker; then click the Pick button and sample some of the green from the wall, and click OK. The end result should look something like Figure 12.4.

16. Finally, click the text-ordering pop-up menu (underneath the New Layer button), and choose Bottom to move the green background bar behind the white text.

If you're creating titles for broadcast, you won't want to use the default maximum white value, since that can cause quality-control errors. Instead, alter the Fill color to create 95 percent white.

17. Click the EXIT button to return to the timeline. It's time to refine the title's timing. Press R to choose the Trim tool, select the end point of the gap effect clip, move the positioner to the halfway point of the first clip in track V1.1 of the timeline, and then press E to make an extend edit, resizing the gap effect clip so that the selected output moves to the frame of the positioner.

18. Right-click the end of the clip and choose Add Dissolve from the context menu to fade the title away.

FIGURE 12.4 The lower-third title that you've created

Saving and Reusing Titles

Now that you have a fully built title, you may want to use a version of it again. There are several ways that you can save titles and styles for recycling later.

1. Create a new library in the Media Library and name it **Titles**.

2. Press Option+Shift and drag the gap title effect you created into the Titles library. This saves the effect into the library without removing it from the timeline.

3. Select the title clip you moved into the library, wait a moment, and then click the name to select it for renaming, type **Lower Third**, and press Return. Now you can edit the Lower Third clip into any sequence where you want a lower-third title.

    Now it's time to create an end credit style for individual title cards.

4. Right-click the Titles library in the Media Library, choose New Sequence, change the name to **End Credits**, and click Create.

5. Right-click the Titles library, navigate to the Downloaded Smoke Media folder you created, open the Audio folder, select CUE07_ FINAL, and click Import.

6. Open the End Credits sequence you created, and drag CUE07_FINAL in its entirety into tracks A1.L and A1.R (by default a stereo pair of tracks). You'll use this music cue to time the end credits.

7. Zoom out of the timeline a bit, and play through from the beginning of the audio track, stopping at the first guitar chord (10:00:04+12).

8. Edit the Lower Third clip you saved into track V1.1 so that it cuts in at that frame. Remove the fade-out, and use the Trim tool to extend the duration so that the clip ends just before the first frame of the next bar of music; the waveform should make the correct position clear (10:00:09+16). The result should look like Figure 12.5. You're using this gap effect as your starting point for the title that you really want to create.

FIGURE 12.5 Timing a title to the second bar of music

9. Double-click the gap effect that you just edited to open the Text editor, and then click Delete All to eliminate all text layers.

10. Click the New Layer button to create a new text layer; then click the Layer Axis button to change the transform point to the center of the layer, choose Centre from the Paragraph Justification pop-up menu, and, if necessary, set Kern to 0. The font settings are remembered from the last text layer you created, which is sometimes good and sometimes not so good; you need to keep an eye on your text settings whenever you want to create a new layer.

11. Type **Directed by** as the only text in this layer.

12. Double-click the text in this layer; then click the Fill color control, use the Colour Picker controls to select a pale eggshell blue color, previewing the result in the viewport, and click OK.

13. Drag the Y-Axis parameter slider to the left to move the current text layer until it appears a little bit above the center of the screen.

14. Click New Layer to create a second text layer; then change the Font Size parameter to **50**, type **Egon Spengler**, and reposition it vertically to appear below the first text layer at the center point, which is a Y coordinate of 0. If necessary, use the arrow buttons next to the New Layer button to choose the first layer and reposition it to fit more pleasingly.

15. Double-click the "Egon Spengler" text, use the Fill color control to choose a slightly more vivid color of blue, and click OK. The result should look something like Figure 12.6.

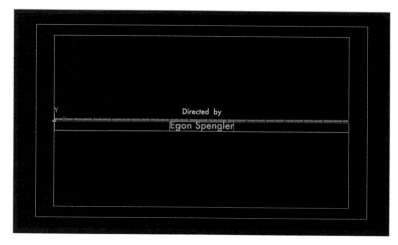

F I G U R E　1 2 . 6　The first title card

Now that you have two differently styled text layers, it might be a good idea to save the style you've applied to each layer for future use.

16. Click the Styles button to reveal the controls for saving and applying style presets.

17. To save an individual style, select a text layer, click the Define Style button (underneath the grid of nine style buttons), and then click the numbered style button to which you want to apply it. That button updates to show the saved style, along with information about the size and font used (the keyboard shortcut for applying that style appears as well).

18. To reset that style button, click and hold the Define Style button (which is actually the Style Option button), choose Clear Style, and click the button to which you just saved a style to clear it.

19. To save all current styles in use, click and hold the Style Option button and choose AutoStyle. Each of the two styles you've used is automatically saved.

20. Click the EXIT button to return to the timeline.

Arranging and Styling Text

In this next exercise, you'll learn how to use more of the features of the Text editor to style title cards in different ways.

1. Select the title clip, press ⌘+C to copy it, then move the positioner to snap to the end of it (press Shift if the Snap button is turned off to turn snapping on temporarily), and press ⌘+V three times to paste three more copies of the title clip.

2. Open the second title, and change the two text layers to **Written by** and **Dana Barrett**. If you find that you are unable to edit text, either click the Text Mode pop-up menu and choose Edit, or press the Escape key, which toggles you between editing text and moving text within the Text editor. Click EXIT when you're finished.

3. Open the third title, and change the first text layer to **Starring**. For this title card, you need to have two names side by side (stipulated in the contract, don't you know).

4. Select the second text layer, delete the name, and then click the Tabulation button. The Tabulation controls let you add multiple columns to text layers via tabs with individual justification.

5. Choose Left from the Paragraph Justification pop-up menu so that the second text layer is left justified overall.

6. Click the Add button (in the Tab group shown in Figure 12.7) twice to add two tabs.

FIGURE 12.7
The Tabulation controls

The tab widgets you added to the top ruler of the second text layer can be dragged, or manipulated, via the Position parameter to approximately equidistant positions from the center of the screen, or you could calculate the exact placement mathematically. Fortunately, you don't have to do any of this, because every parameter in Smoke has a built-in calculator.

7. You know that the overall width of text layer 2 is 1535 because of the Paragraph Width parameter, so select the first tab in the layer ruler, click the Position parameter of the Tabulation controls, and use the calculator to enter **1535/4**. This places the first tab at exactly one-fourth of the total width of the layer, or 384.

8. Now select the second tab you created, click the Position parameter, and use the calculator to enter **384*3** to place it three-fourths of the total width of the layer.

9. Select each tab marker, and choose Centre from the Justification control in the Tabulation controls (*not* the Paragraph controls). Notice that the direction of the tab marker changes to indicate its justification. Now any text added at these tabs will be center justified, so you can use these tabs as if they were columns.

10. Press the Tab key, type **Peter Venkman**, then press the Tab key again, and type **Janine Meinitz**. When you're finished, the title card should resemble Figure 12.8.

FIGURE 12.8 Horizontally arranged titles using tabulation

> Once you've created a set of tabs, each new line of text you add to a text layer inherits the same tabs, so you can create long columns of text on as many rows as you need.

11. Click the EXIT button to return to the timeline, and open the fourth title clip.

    For this last example, you need to create an "Introducing" title card with two actors' names, one over the other, separated by "and."

12. Replace the text on the first text layer with **Introducing**, and replace the text on the second layer with **Raymond Standtz**.

13. This layer isn't styled correctly, so select all of the text on this third layer, click the Styles button, and click Style 1, which should correspond to the paler text color.

14. Click the Axis button, then click New Layer, type **and**, and then use the Y-Axis parameter to move this layer below the first name in the credits.

15. Click New Layer again, and type **Louis Tully**. Again, this text isn't styled correctly for names, so select the text, click Styles, and then click the Style 2 button. Now click Axis, and use the Y-Axis parameter to move this layer to the bottom so that each line of text is correctly spaced vertically.

    When you're happy with the vertical spacing, you'll no doubt notice that the entire set of titles appears a bit low. There's an easy way to fix this so that you don't end up moving each layer separately.

16. Click the Select All button, and then use the Y-Axis parameter to move all of the layers up by the same amount. The end result should resemble Figure 12.9.

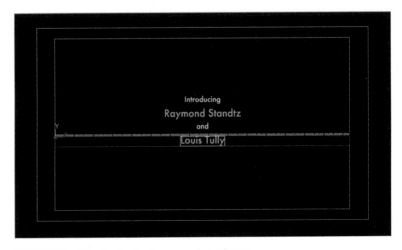

FIGURE 12.9 Vertically arranged text layers

OTHER WAYS OF WORKING WITH TEXT

The Text effect, applied either as a gap effect or directly to a clip (which can be useful for subtitles that you want to travel along with a clip during re-edits), is but one way of working with text. In addition, a Text node is available from within ConnectFX, which you can use for compositing text in 2D, extruding text in 3D using Action, or as a matte for creating text-shaped adjustments via other combinations of nodes. Furthermore, Smoke gives you the ability to import Photoshop files with rasterized text from within the Action node bin by double-clicking the Import node and selecting Photoshop as the Import Type.

THE ESSENTIALS AND BEYOND

The exercises in this chapter only scratch the surface of the capabilities of text effects. These techniques lay the foundation for all other effects, however, and it's worth spending some time making sure that you're comfortable with the essentials that go into creating the ubiquitous title card.

ADDITIONAL EXERCISES

▶ Create two additional styles of lower thirds, using different fonts, arrangements, and background layers.

▶ Build a new set of end credit cards, using different fonts and colors.

▶ Use the keyframing controls to animate the Axis controls of the text layers to create slow zoom-ins for each of the alternate title cards.

CHAPTER 13

Exporting from Smoke

Once you've finished everything you can inside the Autodesk® Smoke platform, it's time to export your project. Smoke supports a variety of export types, depending on what you need to give to whom. You can export individual clips as image sequences or audio files, or you can export an entire sequence as a movie file or as an AAF export, in order to have your audio worked on more comprehensively at an audio facility.

Topics in this chapter include the following:

▶ **Preparing to export**

▶ **Exporting your project**

▶ **Exporting an EDL or AAF file**

▶ **Exporting a movie**

▶ **Exporting a file sequence**

▶ **Exporting audio**

▶ **Archiving your project**

Preparing to Export

Before you export anything, it's important to know that Smoke exports clips and sequences in their *entirety* only. If you set in and out points for a clip or sequence, they will be ignored, and the entire clip or sequence will still be exported.

If you want to export part of a clip, or a portion of a sequence, you need to create a new *export sequence* expressly for the purpose of exporting and then edit only the portion of the clip or sequence you want to export into it. You can then use the Export command on the export sequence to output what you need.

Additionally, many clients request bars and tone, slates, sections of black, countdown, and other leader elements that need to be edited into the timeline prior to the program start. Smoke has commands for creating color bars, audio tone, and color source clips (which can be set to black) in the File ➤ New menu. In conjunction with timeline text effects, you can create whatever kind of leader you need for tape output, and you can add 2-pop audio sync cues at the head and tail of a sequence timeline prior to exporting AAF for sound work.

Exporting Your Project

Exporting a clip or sequence can be incredibly easy if you use one of the supplied presets that come with Smoke. Alternatively, it can be more complicated if you take advantage of each preset's extensively customizable features.

In essence, to export either a clip or a sequence, you'll follow these steps:

1. Right-click the clip or sequence you want to export in the Media Library, and choose Export (⌘+E). For this exercise, export the Visitation scene that you created in Chapter 5.

2. When the Media Export window appears, choose a volume and directory to save the resulting export to by using the file browser at the top. Once you choose a location to export to, the Export options become available, as shown in Figure 13.1.

FIGURE 13.1 The basic Export options

3. Choose what type of output you want from the Export pop-up menu. The options include the following:

Sequence Publish This option is used to export an AAF or EDL of the selection.

Movie This option is used to export an MXF, QuickTime, or H.264 movie file.

File Sequence This option is used to export an image sequence in one of the supported file types, which include DPX, OpenEXR, Tiff, and JPEG.

Audio File This option is used to export an audio file in one of the supported file types, which include AIFF, MP3, and WAVE.

For this exercise, choose Movie.

4. Choose one of the available formats from the Format Preset pop-up menu. Which formats are available depends on the Export type you selected in step 3. For this exercise, choose Final Cut Pro (ProRes 422 HQ).

5. Enter a name of your choosing in the Filename field, and click the Export button.

It can be as simple as that. However, if you need more specific output, the Show Advanced Options button exposes additional settings from which you can choose. These settings are described in more detail in the following sections.

Exporting an EDL or AAF File

Typically, Smoke is used to finish a program, so the final output is usually a movie file or image sequence with accompanying audio file. However, in the event that you need to transfer a project to another editing environment, or export multiple audio tracks via AAF for more sophisticated sound design and mixing elsewhere, you can choose Sequence Publish from the Export pop-up menu, which exposes the following options (among others):

AAF For Avid Pro Tools   This option lets you export your audio tracks in a way that can be imported into Pro Tools.

EDL Publish   This option lets you export your sequence as a single video track and multiple audio tracks using a CMX 3600 EDL format that's unique to Smoke.

Simple Publish   This option exports the video and audio media of a program, either as individual clips or flattened tracks.

In the Advanced Options for each of these format presets, you are presented with options to export the selected sequence with video and/or audio tracks enabled or disabled. You also have the option of separately enabling or disabling the export of video media and audio media.

A *Pattern field* lets you define how the output files should be named, using both plain text and bracketed *tokens*, which automatically insert various text strings into the filename. The available tokens can be added via a pop-up menu to the right of the Pattern field.

If you're electing to export video or audio media, separate Video Options and Audio Options tabs are available that let you define the media format and

◄

Keep in mind that even though an export may appear to be complete, Smoke may need to continue processing exported media in the background, so you may need to wait longer than you think for your exported media to become available. In these cases, exporting is done in the background using Backburner, which enables you to continue working as the export proceeds. To check on the status of your render, you can click the small button at the bottom-left corner of the Smoke UI (two upward-pointing arrows) to view the Status Display, which shows all of the background jobs being processed.

customize media parameters such as compression format, resolution, bit depth, and sampling, depending on your needs.

Exporting a Movie

When you choose Movie from the Export pop-up menu, the Advanced Options change to reflect the fact that you're outputting a single file. The Movie Options tab lets you choose the format, compression type, and profile. You also have the option to include or exclude audio.

The YUV Headroom button lets you choose whether you export the video data as full range (when turned off) or video range (when turned on). Full-range data is typical for RGB-encoded media destined for digital cinema viewing, VFX work, or other RGB-oriented workflows. Video range data is more typical for Y'CbCr (often referred to as YUV) encoded media destined for broadcast. If in doubt, be sure to check ahead to see what is required for delivery.

Additionally, you can turn on a Use LUT button in order to apply a 1D LUT or 3D LUT with which to process the exported output. This can be useful for quickly normalizing log-encoded media or for applying a film-simulation or other image-processing LUT operation for a variety of utilitarian and creative workflows.

As with other export formats, a Pattern field lets you define how the name of the media being output will be written.

Finally, a series of Resolution options lets you define the frame size, bit depth, and scan mode (interlaced or progressive) of the output. If you're changing the resolution on output, other parameters let you adjust how the change in frame size should be handled (via letterboxing or zooming and cropping).

Again, separate Video Options and Audio Options tabs are available that let you define the media format and customize media parameters such as compression format, resolution, bit depth, and sampling, depending on your needs.

Exporting a File Sequence

When you choose File Sequence from the Export pop-up menu, the Advanced Options are limited to Video options, and the available Video Format options include still-image formats only. You also have the option to process the output using 1D LUTs or 3D LUTs.

There are more options for file naming, including how many digits to use for frame padding (remember that image sequences are identified by a frame number included with the filename) and whether or not to use the timecode of the exported media to generate the frame number.

Exporting Audio

As you would expect, choosing Audio File from the Export pop-up menu limits the Advanced Options to the audio format you want to use, separate compression settings if any are available for the format you've selected, and bit depth and sampling rate for the audio output.

A Mixdown pop-up menu lets you choose whether to export the audio tracks as is or to mix the available tracks down to mono, stereo, or 4-track audio files.

The Pattern field lets you define a simple name for the exported audio media.

Archiving Your Project

While Smoke 2015 has no facility for exporting project files as used by other postproduction applications, this functionality is covered by the Archives functionality in the MediaHub.

When you archive a project or sequence, you essentially write the project data and media to one or more self-contained *archive* files. These files contain everything necessary for restoring that project or sequence in its entirety, including all clips and effects.

Archiving a Project or Sequence

You can archive an entire project or a set of one or more sequences. You can also archive a collection of clips, but that may be a bit redundant since there are many other ways of storing and exchanging collections of media files all by themselves.

Be aware that Smoke archives everything as uncompressed DPX files, regardless of your Preferred Format setting. This results in the creation of files that are larger than your original compressed sources, so your archive may be significantly larger than your original project or sequence.

Before you begin the process of archiving a project or media, there are a few ways you can help keep your archives lean and usable:

> ▶ Remove unused media and sequences from the Media Library of a project, and unused clips from tracks of a sequence, prior to creating an archive. For example, if you have clips in lower video tracks that are hidden from view by clips on higher tracks during playback, those can be removed to save space.

▶ Use clear naming conventions for media and sequences to make it easy to browse the contents of an archive in cases when you only want to partially restore the contents.

▶ Use the Consolidate Media command on effects clips within a sequence that you're going to archive if you want to save the end result and not the original effect; media with smaller handles will be archived as a result.

Once you've done this simple housecleaning, the process of creating and writing to an archive is as follows:

1. Open the MediaHub, and click the Archives button at the top of the file browser.

2. Use the file browser controls to open a volume to which you want to write the archive, and then click the New Archive button.

3. In the New Archive Creation dialog (see Figure 13.2), enter a name and a comment (optional), and choose a file size to which you want to limit archive files. If you're ultimately storing the archives on optical or LTO media, or if you're uploading archives to a cloud-based service, you may want to limit the maximum size of an archive; this means that larger projects will be automatically segmented into multiple archive files. Don't worry; this is perfectly fine and multiple archive files are easily restored. Also, if you choose a large maximum size but don't write that much media to it, the resulting archive will only be as large as the actual media that's archived.

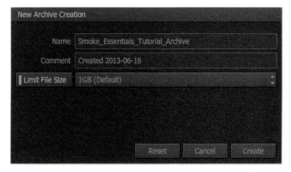

FIGURE 13.2 Available options when creating a new archive

4. Click Create.

5. The archive list appears, currently empty, waiting for you to put something into the archive, and you have two options:

    a. To archive the entire project, including all of the contents of the Media Library, click the Archive Project button at the bottom. This is all you need to do; Smoke will begin writing the archive. This can take a long time and create an enormous archive, so don't do this now.

    b. To archive only specific files or sequences, drag them from the Media Library into the archive list. For this exercise, drag the End Credits sequence you created in Chapter 12 into the archive list.

6. After dragging one or more clips or sequences into the archive list, the available buttons underneath change to Archive and Clear Pending. But before you begin, click the Archive Options tab.

7. You can choose from the following options, as shown in Figure 13.3:

    Linked Archive Options   These options let you choose how the file path to the archived media is set once the archive is restored. Use Archived Path is convenient if you'll be restoring the archive to the same volume from which it came. Convert To Local Path is preferable if you'll be restoring the archive to a completely different volume.

    Archive Verification   This option lets you choose whether to verify the archive you're creating automatically after it's written. Disabling this saves you time but at the expense of the peace of mind of knowing that the archive you've written is stored safely to whichever volume you've specified.

    Media Options   You can choose to Cache Media On Archive or not. When this option is active, all sources, if they were linked files and not cached, will be cached for a self-contained archive. Two additional options are under the Cache Media On Archive button when active. You can choose to archive any rendered frames or exclude them. Excluding the rendered frames is a good way to lessen the size of your archive, as you can always re-render these frames later. If you choose to not activate the Cache Media On

Archive button, then your options in the menu will change to these four choices:

Include Renders and Cache: This will archive any existing clips with their cache and all renders. Any uncached sources will just save the linked path to the file.

Exclude Renders: This will archive all cached media and linked media but exclude all rendered frames.

Exclude Source Media Cache: This will exclude all source cache files but still retain all rendered frames. Your media will be referenced as a linked file.

Exclude Renders and Cache: This will ignore all renders and cached frames; all sources will be saved with just links to the file. This will be the smallest archive size when complete; it's essentially a metadata archive.

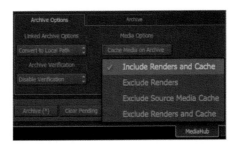

FIGURE 13.3 The archival options, with Cache Media On Archive inactive (top) and active (bottom).

8. Once you've selected the appropriate options, click the Archive button and the archive will begin writing. In this case, the archive should write pretty quickly.

9. When the archive is finished, click the Close Archive button. The archive list closes, leaving only the file browser, which should show your archive on whatever volume you chose.

Restoring an Archive

Restoring the contents of archives to the currently open Smoke project is simple. An added bonus is that you don't have to restore the complete contents of an archive; you can elect to restore only those clips and sequences that you need, leaving the rest alone.

1. Open the MediaHub, and click the Archives button at the top of the file browser.

2. Use the file browser controls to open the volume that contains your archive.

3. Double-click the archive you want to restore. The archive list appears, showing the contents of that archive. If it's a segmented archive, you may be asked to identify the location of the other segments. Locate them when prompted.

4. When a folder appears within the archive list containing the contents of the archive, drag the clips or sequences you want to restore to a location in the Media Library. For this exercise, drag the End Credits sequence you archived into any library of the Media Library. The sequence appears grayed out.

5. Click the Restore button. After some time, the grayed-out items in the Media Library become solid, and the restoration is complete. The project and media have been copied to the same volume that's used by the current project.

◄

If you change your mind while restoring an archive, simply click your mouse to interrupt the operation, and click Confirm when asked if you want to abort.

THE ESSENTIALS AND BEYOND

This chapter covered, in broad strokes, all of the options that exist for exporting projects and media. The methods are flexible, and there are a lot of options, so it's a good idea to become familiar with how to set up different sorts of exports.

ADDITIONAL EXERCISES

▶ Export the sequence you created in Chapter 10, "Working with Audio," using the AAF for Avid Pro Tools preset.

(Continues)

THE ESSENTIALS AND BEYOND *(Continued)*

▶ Export only a portion of a single clip by editing it into a new sequence and then exporting that sequence as a DPX file sequence.

▶ Export the sequence you created in Chapter 5, "Editing Dialog and Advanced Trimming," using the EDL Publish preset. This time, however, use the Advanced Options to disable audio and video media export—you just want the EDL.

Answers to Additional Exercises

Chapter 1

▶ Autodesk trainer Grant Kay created the Autodesk® Smoke® Learning Channel on YouTube. It is a free collection of training videos covering all aspects of Smoke functionality. It's a fantastic searchable resource for learning more about specific features, and it does a good job of highlighting keyboard shortcuts and hidden features of Smoke.

▶ The General Discussion section of the Smoke AREA Discussion Forums provides a discussion list for questions, tips, and techniques that are shared by the Smoke user community.

▶ The online Smoke User Guide is a searchable collection of hierarchical help articles covering the entirety of Smoke functionality. Click the Search button at the top of the table of contents to access a search interface to find what you're seeking, or click the small plus button to the left of the topic in which you're interested to reveal more information.

Chapter 2

▶ To create a new project file on the same volume as the currently selected project, you need to choose File ➤ Project and User Settings. Then click the New button, and the Create New Project window appears. Here you can enter a name, config template, and bit depth for the new projects. Enter any name you like, choose the config template named 1920x1080@23976psf.cfg, set the bit depth to 10-bit, and click Create. Please note that if you want to create a new project on a different volume, you need to quit Smoke and restart it to choose from the volume's pop-up menu.

▶ When importing the Lab Scene and Opening Scene EDLs in order to practice the conform process, you need only follow steps 1 through 12 to obtain a successful result. However, once you've imported the first EDL, the conform list will be full, preventing you from following the instructions in step 3. Instead, you'll need to open the Conform Gear pop-up menu to choose Load New EDL.

Chapter 3

▶ Given the way that this chapter walked you through the process of organizing your media, the Default Library becomes empty and is no longer needed. There's nothing special about the Default Library, and it can be harmlessly deleted if you don't need it. However, if you ever add anything to the Media Library without selecting an existing library first, a Default Library will be created to contain the new item.

▶ It's common practice for editors to review available footage in order to get better acquainted with all of the performances accessible to them. As you play your clips, you can press the M key to add markers to the timebar underneath the viewer, noting significant moments in the media. Once you've added several markers to a source clip, you can use ➤-up-arrow and ➤-down-arrow keys to jump the timebar's positioner from one marker to the next.

▶ In Full Width mode, you can see more of the columns of information that reveal details about each clip. Clicking in the header of the Bit Depth column will sort all of the clips in the Media Library by their bit depth, making it easier to spot which clips happen to be 12-bit rather than 10-bit. Incidentally, you can right-click any column header to open a context menu that lets you show and hide different combinations of Media Library columns, and you can drag columns to the left and right to rearrange them.

Chapter 4

▶ When rippling the outgoing and/or incoming sides of the edit between clips 3 and 4, it helps to turn Snapping off and zoom into the timeline. Also, if you turn off Focus On Trim in the Options pop-up menu, you can play through the clip and stop when the positioner reaches a frame to which you want to ripple part of an edit in order to use the positioner's location as a sort of temporary marker. You'll want to turn it back on when you start rolling edits in order to experiment with different trim positions.

▶ To create more intercutting in order to add a bit more energy to the scene, you can cut away to the wide shot toward the door from the frame where the woman picks up the black case on the desk to where she sits down about to open it (20:57:40+12 to 20:57:45+12), and then you can cut away to this shot again from when she plucks the capacitor out of the electrical panel to when she turns from grabbing a new capacitor out of the case on the desk (20:58:00+13 to 20:58:03+11). As you make these edits, be sure to match the woman's action in one shot with the same continuous action in the next. Furthermore, see if you can pick up the pace by cutting forward a few frames at these edits.

Chapter 5

▶ Of the three times "sit down" is said at the beginning of this scene, the last one is the easiest to eliminate, since the second character's mouth is *just about* turned away from the camera, and it's a wide shot, making it even less obvious that her mouth is moving. Turn off the Link button, put the positioner right before the third instance of "sit down," move the focus to track A1, and then press Control+V to add an edit to the audio clip. (Remember that you can press the Page Up and Page Down keys to move the focus up and down.) Do the same to the audio clip on track A2. Then turn off Ripple, and resize both audio clips to create a hole where the "sit down" dialog was. This opens an audible gap in the room tone, so move the positioner just past the sound of the door closing (source timecode of 11:40:09+14) and add edits to audio tracks A1 and A2; then move the positioner just forward to the end of that small section of silence (to 11:40:10+03) and insert another set of edits. Copy this small section of "room tone," create two additional mono audio tracks (A3 and A4), and paste the room tone twice into these new tracks by changing the focus of the positioner to track A3.

▶ For the second and third additional exercises, you can refer to the final edit of this scene in the full movie of "The Place Where You Live" (available online) to see how the author cut this scene. However, feel free to deviate from this edit if you find a way you like better.

Chapter 6

▶   The process of shortening each clip in this already-edited sequence is a perfect excuse to use the Trim tool with Ripple turned on, but make sure that you turn on the Link button so that the audio and video don't go out of sync while you're working. Additionally, don't forget that you can double-click any edit point to open the Trim view, within which you can ripple the outgoing and incoming portions of that edit or roll the edit point itself.

▶   Setting the Strobe parameter to a number greater than one makes playback look like it's subtly stuttering.

Another fun effect is to set the Timewarp quick menu to Frame Interpolation, and the Frame Interpolation pop-up to Trails; setting a number of Pre frames creates a ghostly motion trail in advance of real-time motion in the frame, while setting a number of Post frames creates a ghostly motion trail frame that follows real-time motion in the frame. Combining this with slow-motion or fast-motion percentages can create a number of eerie and interesting effects.

▶   Don't forget that the way to change a dissolve to a dip-to-color dissolve is to click the To/From Colour button among the dissolve's controls in the FX Ribbon. Also, when experimenting with different color settings, keep in mind you that can use the Pick button in the color picker to choose any color from either the image or the Smoke interface itself.

Chapter 7

▶   A quick shortcut to take when starting this is to zoom up the vertical height of the tracks until you can see the Action effects box (labeled AC) on the first video screen clip and drag it to the second video screen clip to copy the Action effect, using it as a starting point. Then double-click the AC box to open the Action editor. If you scrub the positioner in the timebar, you'll notice that you've also copied the tracked Position X and Position Y data, so you'll need to eliminate the tracking without losing the starting position that you have now. Right-click each of the Position X and Position Y parameters, and choose Reset Channel (Current Value) from the context menu to eliminate the tracked keyframes while keeping the current position of the window. Then you can simply customize the Position X, Position Y, Rotation Y, and Scale parameters until the man's image is reversed and appears correctly positioned relative to the reverse shot of the woman. If you want to use the Stabilizer to match the slight motion in the shot, you can track the desk surface, but don't forget to use the Axis tab parameters to return the Position X and Y of the floating window to where it's supposed to be located.

▶ While a simple dissolve may seem like the easy choice to introduce and dismiss the video screen, you should try different wipes instead for a more designed appearance.

▶ To put a copy of the woman's hand in front of the floating window, create a third video track, and then turn off the Link button and copy the clip in track V1.1. Next, move the positioner to snap to the beginning of the clip you copied, move the focus of the positioner to track V1.3, and paste the video clip so that it lines up with the matching clip on track V1.1. Select the new clip on top, add an Action effect to it, and open the Action editor. Open the Media tab and double-click the K (keyer) cell corresponding to the video clip's 1F and 1M item in the list, and follow the instructions you used previously to make a primary sample of the wall in the background. Choose Matte from the pop-up at the lower-left corner, and then use the Sampling Patch 1 through 3 options to sample parts of the woman's hand, setting each patch button's corresponding Patch Box pop-up menu to White so that those samples add to the white held-out area rather than to the transparent black region. Next, choose Matte from the Sampling pop-up menu, and click different parts of the matte to make her hand and forearm as white as possible and the background wall as dark as possible. (With a solid white arm, you won't escape some gray fringing in the wall.) Once you're satisfied that you have the best tradeoff of white hand to slightly grayish wall, set the MasterK node's Result Output pop-up back to Front CC, click the Matte Edge node to open its controls, and set the Width to 1.00 to make the gray on the wall disappear. Next, turn on Blur, and set the Width and Height to 2.00. Finally, set the image back to Result using the lower-left pop-up menu, and you'll notice that her hand looks strangely gray. This is because the MasterK node is outputting a spill suppressed version of the image to the final Result node. To defeat this, connect the Front clip node's yellow output tab to the red Front input tab of the Result node. Go back to the Timeline, and turn on the Comp effect on at the right of the FX Ribbon. This enables compositing, and you should now see that her hand appears in front of the video image. Return to the timeline, and save yourself some rendering by trimming the beginning and end of the clip on track V1.3 to match the appearance and disappearance of the woman's hand.

Chapter 8

▶ As you try to create a matching contact-lens effect in the other eye, here are some tips to help you work more quickly. Don't import another EyeInterface layer; instead, pull another link out of the yellow output tab of the EyeInterface node and connect it to another MUX node. Using multiple MUX nodes connected to one clip rather than multiple clips saves you processing time (read: rendering time), and it is a more efficient way to work for projects using the same media multiple times. Also, see which nodes you can duplicate by copying and pasting from what you've already done in order to save yourself some effort. Finally, disconnect the video clip of the woman's eyes from the middle red Front input tab of the Blend & Comp node, and reconnect it to the green Back input tab. Then, the second animated contact-lens branch of the node tree to the now unused Front2 and Matte2 input tabs of the Blend & Comp node.

Chapter 9

▶ Since the Colour Correct node is adjusting the values of a branch of the image that's being used as a matte, if you reduce the RGB Gain parameter in the Master controls, you'll dim the image that defines transparency and make the doorway more opaque. To see what you're doing while making this adjustment, you can right-click the Action node and choose Set As Context. Then select the viewer in the viewport that you're using to look at the image, and choose Context 1 from the View pop-up menu. Now when you click the Colour Correct node to view its controls, you're still viewing the result of the Action node where you can see the exact effect your adjustment is having. When you want to see the current node in the viewport again, select the appropriate viewer and press F4.

▶ The Optics node creates a glow effect, with inner and outer levels of glow represented by two color controls. The simplest way of using the Optics node is to connect the Front, Back, and Matte input tabs to the mirror clip's yellow output tab. The Matte input will take the mirror clip's luma channel, which will be used as a luma matte to dictate where to put the most glow (the highlights) and where to put the least glow (the shadows). If you like, you can modify the Matte input by inserting a Colour Correct node between the mirror clip and the Matte input tab and then lowering the Master Gamma parameter to restrict the glow only to the highlights of the image. The default settings of the Optics node are far too intense, so you'll want to lower Size to about 4% and Intensity to about 2%. Then, experiment with choosing different intensities of a purplish color for the Interior and Exterior glow colors. When choosing a color using the RGB sliders of the Colour Picker dialog, keep in mind that the sliders themselves are showing you a preview of what color you'll be choosing if you move the slider in that direction.

▶ While the Deform node has a lot of parameters, you don't need to adjust that many to get what you need. The Crumple option in the Deform Type pop-up menu gives the best effect for this shot, resulting in an irregular series of interacting waves. Setting the Amplitude to 2.00 yields a nice level of deformation that's noticeable, yet it doesn't deform the image too unflatteringly. To animate the deformation, move the positioner to the very first frame of the timebar and turn on Auto Key. Then drag the Time Offset parameter slider to set a keyframe. Next, move the positioner to the very last frame of the timebar, and increase the Time Offset parameter. The higher a number you choose for the second keyframe, the faster the image will undulate. When you're finished, be sure to turn off the Auto Key button.

Chapter 10

▶ The foley sound effects (clips FOL 01 through 10) are also good opportunities to use the Aligned Edit command to line up a good cue point in the cloth source audio with an action in the video, using the source positioner to find a good audio sync spot and the record positioner to find a good video sync frame.

▶ Once you've created a good cloth EQ setting (lowering the M4 and H controls just a bit are a good start), you can copy it to the other clips in the timeline by expanding the height of the track until you can see the audio effects box. Then you can drag the EQ box to other cloth audio clips to copy that setting.

▶ Typically, the sound of cloth rustling is very quiet. You'll notice if the cloth sound isn't there, but it shouldn't be in the forefront of your mix. Lowering the mix to somewhere around -8 dB should work. Once you've set the clip gain for one of these cloth effects, you can copy the gain setting to others by dragging the GN effects box to other FABRIC FOL clips.

Chapter 11

▶ When creating a new gap effect, keep in mind that when you click anywhere within an empty track, you automatically select a gap equal in duration to the entire sequence, to which you can easily apply any effect from the FX Ribbon. When desaturating the image, another good tip is to remember that you can selectively desaturate the shadows, midtones, and highlights of an image by selecting one of these tonal ranges in the Colour Corrector editor and then adjusting the Saturation parameter.

▶ When doing a secondary correction on just one subject within the image, you need to use one of the Colour Warper's selectives. You choose a selective to adjust from the Work On pop-up menu, and you define a selective's matte using the selective controls to the right of the histogram in the middle of the Colour Warper editor. To define a custom color as a selective, click the Pick Custom button and drag on the feature you want to isolate. When adjusting the resulting selective, you can choose Matte or Sel from the View pop-up menu to the left of the color wheel's controls in order to see how your selective is isolated against the background. Matte shows a high-contrast image of just the matte, whereas Sel shows the selected area in color and the unselected area in grayscale. While in Matte or Sel viewing mode, you can adjust the color cube controls to refine the selection, zooming in to see the controls better by Control+Option-dragging and panning around by Control+Command-dragging. Choose Result from the View pop-up menu when you want to see the adjustment you made to the resulting selective.

▶ Add both color correction and GMask effects to a gap effect above the second clip. First, edit the color correction and lower the Master RGB Gamma parameter to darken the image by about the amount you want to darken the floor. By doing this first, you can see the masks effect in the second step. Next, open the GMask editor, and start by clicking the Add button, and then clicking to draw a four-point shape that isolates the floor. Then either use the Offset control to feather the shape inward so that the light-to-shadow falloff appears natural or choose Advanced Gradient and adjust the outer and inner shape control points individually to create the kind of shadow falloff you want, ideally more feathered at the top than at the bottom.

Chapter 12

▶ The easiest way to create different styles of existing titles is to duplicate what you've already made and edit the Paragraph and Font styling parameters. Remember that you need to set the Text Mode pop-up menu to Edit in order to edit the text or set it to Move to drag the text-editing box around within the frame.

▶ To animate text most simply, use the Axis controls with Layer enabled. To zoom into a piece of text, use the Scale parameters with Prop (proportional) turned on. Move the positioner to the beginning of the timebar; then right-click both of the Scale parameters and choose Set Keyframe from the context menu. Then move the positioner to the end of the timebar, add keyframes to both Scale parameters in the same way, and this time adjust either of the Scale parameters to increase the size of the titles to the end state. If you want to finesse this movement, you can enter the Animation editor by clicking the Animation button at the left edge of the Text editor. To see the keyframes you've created automatically, click the Filter tab at the right of the Keyframe editor, turn on the Animated button, set the Animated Expansion pop-up menu to Exp & Col, and set the Auto Frame pop-up menu to All. Now you can see the keyframes you've created along with their Bezier handles with which you can adjust the ease of their motion.

Chapter 13

▶ Right-clicking a sequence in the Media Library and choosing Export from the context menu accomplishes all exports. Remember that you have to select a destination from the Local Devices browser before the export options become enabled. You choose the type of export from the Export pop-up, in this case Sequence Publish, and then you can choose from the available presets from the Format Preset pop-up, in this case one of two AAF for Avid Pro Tools presets.

▶ To set up export of only a section of a sequence, you must first copy and paste that section into a separate sequence. Export always exports the entire sequence that is selected.

▶ To access the Advanced Options, you need to turn on the Show Advanced Options button. To export an EDL without also exporting accompanying media, you can choose Export ≻ Sequence Publish and Format Preset ≻ EDL Publish (8-bit DPX and WAVE); then turn on Show Advanced Options and turn off both the Export Video Media and Export Audio Media buttons. Do not mistakenly turn off the Include Video and Include Audio buttons that are to the right of the Format pop-up menu, because that will disable video and audio events from being written to the EDL, producing nothing.

Index